Including Families of Children with Special Needs

Neal-Schuman purchases fund advocacy, awareness, and accreditation programs for library professionals worldwide.

Including Families of Children with Special Needs

A How-To-Do-It Manual for Librarians®

REVISED EDITION

Revised by Carrie Scott Banks

Sandra Feinberg, Barbara Jordan,
Kathleen Deerr, and Michelle Langa

An imprint of the American Library Association

Chicago   2014

Printed in the United States of America
18 17 16 15 14   5 4 3 2 1

Extensive effort has gone into ensuring the reliability of the information in this book; however, the publisher makes no warranty, express or implied, with respect to the material contained herein.

ISBNs: 978-1-55570-791-0 (paper); 978-1-55570-894-8 (PDF); 978-1-55570-895-5 (ePub); 978-1-55570-896-2 (Kindle).

Library of Congress Cataloging-in-Publication Data
Feinberg, Sandra, 1946–
  Including families of children with special needs : a how-to-do-it manual for librarians. — Revised edition / Sandra Feinberg, Barbara Jordan, Kathleen Deerr, and Michelle Langa; revised by Carrie Scott Banks.
     pages   cm
  Revised edition of: Including families of children with special needs / Sandra Feinberg . . . [et al.]. ©1999.
  Includes bibliographical references and index.
  ISBN 978-1-55570-791-0 (alk. paper)
  1. Libraries and children with disabilities—United States. 2. Libraries and families—United States. 3. Libraries and preschool children—United States. I. Jordan, Barbara A. II. Deerr, Kathleen. III. Langa, Michelle A. IV. Banks, Carrie Scott. V. Including families of children with special needs. VI. Title.
  Z711.92.H3F45 2014
  027.6'630973—dc23   2013019765

♾ This paper meets the requirements of ANSI/NISO Z39.48-1992 (Permanence of Paper).

This book is dedicated to our families: Richie, Jake, and Teddy; Fred, Courtney, and Eric; Al, A. J., and David; Frank and Zach; and Katie and Paul, who did without us so much of the time during the creation of this work. Thanks for your support, understanding, and good humor.

It is also dedicated to Reggie and his mother, Sharon.—C. B.

Contents

Preface

When Anthony and his mother first came into the library, I didn't have a clue how to communicate with them. They were both profoundly Deaf and did not speak, although both could read lips a bit. After some back and forth with a pen and some scrap paper, I was able to help them find the book Anthony needed for school. When they left, I was both relieved and embarrassed: relieved because they had gotten what they came for and embarrassed because it had been such a difficult process.

Realizing that Anthony would be back to return the book, and facing a long boring week of jury duty, I borrowed a book on American Sign Language (ASL). When they did come back, I shocked Mrs. C. by signing "OK" in response to a question and asking her name. That was all it took. They became regulars at my library and brought the rest of the Deaf community with them. Six months later, when I had learned a small but targeted ASL vocabulary, I found out the C. family had been to three other branches in our system before they got to my library. They kept coming back to ours because I had learned those first four signs. One year later, we hosted the National Theater of the Deaf and crammed over 100 people into the small, storefront library. Two years after that, I became the librarian in charge of The Child's Place for Children with Special Needs at the Brooklyn Public Library.

The C. family's visit was not my first insight into the limits of my library school education. In my previous neighborhood library, I was appalled that a 10-year-old with an intellectual disability had been told that he could not get a library card because he could not write his name. Parents asked me if I knew any good books for children with Down syndrome. I did not. Did I know any other parents of a child with Cri du chat syndrome? As it happened, I did—but not because it had been part of my formal training for librarianship.

It had, however, been part of my personal background. People with disabilities have always been a part of my life. My best friend in elementary school had cystic fibrosis. I had volunteered to tutor a child with a learning disability and interned at an inpatient pediatric psychiatric facility and as a special education teacher's aide. One more piece of the puzzle fell into place when I was in high school; after years of being told by teachers that I was sloppy, lazy, unmotivated, and not living up to my potential, I was diagnosed with dyslexia and dysgraphia. For me, disability has always been natural.

In the first children's room I worked in, I met a child who used a wheelchair and could not get into the library. One of the pages and I developed a system: I would speak with the patron outside the library, and the page would find the books and bring them out. It was an imperfect system. Later, at my next library, a father of a child with AIDS asked me to read to his son in the hospital. The hospital would not let me. It was with the hope of addressing situations like these and helping other librarians avoid the mistakes I made that I came to revise *Including Families of Children with Special Needs*. I bring to it my own beliefs that disability is natural, inclusion is a civil right, and Universal Design is the tool to get the job done.

Those of us working in public libraries, school library media centers, and hospital libraries are most concerned with serving children and youth with disabilities and their families because they are in our communities. In the 2008–2009 school year, 13 percent of public school students aged 6 to 21 years received special education services nationally. This translates into 6.5 million children in the United States (Institute of Education Sciences, 2011). In any given community, approximately one child out of every six will get speech therapy, go to counseling, go to the resource room, attend classes exclusively with other children with disabilities, be taught by a teacher in a hospital, or receive some other service that allows him or her to learn. Hundreds of thousands more require special accommodations, such as a quiet place to take a test or an electronic note taker. Note that the Institute of Education Sciences (2011) count did not include those children under the age of five who have a disability. Each child with a disability has a family that is also affected.

This revised edition of *Including Families of Children with Special Needs* is a step-by-step guide to serving those children and youth with disabilities as well as the brothers, sisters, parents, grandparents, and other people involved in their lives. By integrating the methods of educators, medical and psychological therapists, social workers, librarians, and parents we can enable children with disabilities and their families to make full use of the library's resources. In the end, you will come away with an understanding of the needs of children and youth with disabilities and of those of their families and with the knowledge to meet those needs in the library. This book will give you an overview of what frameworks, tools, and materials are needed to successfully welcome children with disabilities into your library.

Part 1, "Understanding Inclusion," lays the groundwork. We will look at the philosophy of inclusion and how it benefits children with and without disabilities, their families, and our libraries, as well as the legal requirement to serve all children. Next we look at the research in child development and supporting families. This section concludes by presenting the framework for developing inclusive library services: Multiple Intelligences theory and Universal Design.

Part 2, "Getting Your Library Ready," helps you examine where you are now. It covers assessing your library's current ability to serve youth with disabilities and their families and the needs of this community. The next step is staff training, and we provide an overview and specific tools. Involving the community in these processes follows. Finally, we present specific guidelines and ideas for designing fully inclusive services and programs.

In Part 3, "Developing Collections and Services," we move to specifics. How might inclusion work in your library? How can you make your library barrier free? What equipment do you need? How does Assistive Technology work? Where can you find the books you need? How and where do you find reliable electronic resources?

Much has changed since the first edition was published in 1999. The basic disability rights laws have been renewed and updated. We have solid research to support the benefits of inclusion. Multiple Intelligences theory has become part of mainstream educational practice. Universal Design has moved from the field of architecture to education. We are recognizing the unique needs of siblings of people with disabilities. More libraries have had success with model inclusive services. There are more children with autism, and they are much more visible. Computer technology has become integral to the work of all libraries, and Assistive and Adaptive Technology has substantially improved. This revised edition addresses all of these issues.

This revised edition is considerably wider in scope than the original, which was limited to preschool children and their families. The current work includes school-age children and teens as well and covers an expanded range of disabilities. Previously, the focus was on children with developmental disabilities, but this revised edition addresses the needs of children with all types of disabilities. This edition also covers the needs of Spanish-speaking children with disabilities and their families, looking at cultural competency as well as Spanish-language resources.

As librarians we tend to know a little about a lot of things and a lot about very few things, but we need to know enough to get the job done and, more important, enough to look for what we do not know. It is my hope that this revised edition of *Including Families of Children with Special Needs* will be enough to get you started in providing services to children and youth with disabilities and their families and that you will continue to learn more throughout your career.

The last time I saw Anthony was when I visited his high school. He was doing well and thinking about going to college or becoming a carpenter. He still loved to read. It did not take much to turn Anthony, his sister Cleopatra, and their parents into regular library patrons. Once they felt welcome, you could not keep them away. This is the crux of the matter. Ramps, Adaptive Technology, and Braille books lay only the physical basis for including children with disabilities and their families in the library. Ultimately, it is the attitude of the staff, the seamlessness of the services, and the welcoming environment that will keep them coming back.

Reference

Institute of Education Sciences. 2011. "Children and Youth with Disabilities." National Center for Education Statistics. http://nces.ed.gov/programs/coe/indicator_cwd.asp.

Acknowledgments

For the 2012 Edition

The revised edition of this book owes a debt of gratitude to the Brooklyn Public Library and staff of The Child's Place for Children with Special Needs who have continued to support inclusive library services in the 17 years since the New York State Developmental Disabilities Planning Council's Library-Based Parent Resource Center Initiative began. Lisa Chow of the Brooklyn Public Library and Patrick Timony of the Access Services Department of the DC Public Library were instrumental in helping me parse Assistive and Adaptive Technology for Chapter 10. This chapter also relies heavily on the knowledge of the staff at TechWorks (New York City), in particular Liz Voluz and Maribeth Flynn, and the SHARE Library (Samuel Hausman Activities Resource and Education Center on the United Cerebral Palsy campus, Brooklyn, NY) and its librarian Fran Levinson. The contribution of Nicholas Higgins, the Correctional Services Librarian at the New York Public Library, to the discussion of incarcerated parents was essential. The section on sensory storytimes rests on the solid foundation of Barbara Klipper's deep understanding of and enthusiasm for them. My understanding of the role of school librarians owes much to Irene Henderson, the librarian at PS 396 in Brooklyn. Finally, it was Marti Goddard, the manager of Access Services at the San Francisco Public Library, and Sarah Hamrick, Director of Library Public Services at Gallaudet University, who opened up the world of the Association of Specialized and Cooperative Library Agencies to me and connected me with other librarians serving people with disabilities.

For the 1999 Edition

Thanks are extended to Lorianne Hoenninger of the Association for Children with Learning and Developmental Disabilities, Julie Klauber of the Suffolk Cooperative Library System, and Colleen Moseman of the Long Island Toy Lending Center for Children with Disabilities for sharing their resources and expertise.

Recognition is also extended to those involved in the Partners for Inclusion Project (Suffolk County, NY, 1993–1995), which provided the basis for so much of the work represented in this book. Among those in the project are the staff of the Middle County Public Library

(Centereach, NY), especially Lois Eannel, Mary Schumacher, Ellen Friedman, Doreen Holmes, and Carolyn Liljequist; the staff of the Mastic-Moriches-Shirley Community Library (Shirley, NY), especially Rachel Catan and Eileen Curtin; project coordinator Noreen Buckhout and Ellen Paige Horst; Steve Held, Christine Clarke, Tom McMath, Barbara Morgan-Salvador, Amy Toole, and Amira Simha-Alpern of Just Kids Early Childhood Learning Center (Middle Island, NY); Ellen Woodward, Joan Smart, Tina Malone, and Patricia Davison of Starting Early, Developmental Disabilities Institute (Selden, NY); Janice Orland and Barbara Ross of the Bureau of Services for Children with Disabilities, Suffolk County Department of Health Services, as well as the many Early Intervention service providers who participated at various stages of the project; and to the New York State Department of Health, Bureau of Child and Adolescent Health, particularly Donna Noyes, Wendy Shaw, and Dan Frering. Their collaborative efforts resulted in positive change and enhancement of library-based services to the families and children with special needs who reside in these communities.

We are especially grateful for Margaret Sampson for her personal and professional contributions to our understanding of the parents' perspective and the friendship, support, and encouragement of all of our efforts on behalf of families. A special thanks is extended to the families and children with special needs who live in the Middle Country and Mastics-Moriches-Shirley communities for their willingness to share their experiences and to work with us to educate ourselves and our communities regarding the issues they face on a daily basis. Without their participation, this book would not have been written.

Contributors

Special recognition is given to the following professionals for contributing their expertise and authorship:

Chapter 11

    Rachel Catan, Mastics-Moriches-Shirely Community Library

    Lois Eannel, Middle Country Public Library

    Virginia Reed Maloney and Susan J. Oliver, National Lekotek Center

Chapter 12
   Anna Lobosco, New York State Developmental
      Disabilities Planning Council

Their knowledge and commitment to services for families and children with disabilities are exemplary and greatly appreciated by the families and professionals with whom they work. Our manuscript is more valuable because of their willingness to share their expertise.

1

PART 1
Understanding Inclusion

What's Inclusion All About?

This is the first time my daughters have attended a program together.

—*Father of two daughters, one with a developmental disability,*
at a music program at the Brooklyn Public Library

Take a moment to observe children in the library. They watch each other as often as they look at books. They talk to other children or adults in the children's areas and interact with staff in a storytime program. They form attachments and make new friends. Children are, by nature, social beings. They need to play with and observe peers. Being part of a group is almost as important as eating or sleeping. Simply put, children want to be included with other children. For children with disabilities, this need is often unfulfilled.

Children with disabilities are often segregated from their typically developing peers because of their "special needs." In many situations, they are denied the opportunity to grow and learn from friends and peers in their neighborhood, schools, and other community settings. When they become adults, having been educated in segregated special education classrooms or residential schools, these children can lack the basic social skills for interaction with peers without disabilities. They and their families may continue to be isolated within their communities.

This kind of segregation and isolation is detrimental not only for families and children but also for society as a whole. An inclusionary philosophy recognizes that children have more things in common than not: all children need some form of accommodation. Keeping children with disabilities apart from their typically developing peers creates bigger problems later in life and does not take advantage of the

One History of Inclusion

1918 Soldiers Rehabilitation Act enshrines the concept of job training for veterans with disabilities.

1935 The League for the Physically Handicapped stages sit-ins at Works Progress Administration (WPA) offices demanding jobs for people with disabilities; several thousand are created.

1954 *Brown v. Topeka Board of Education et al.* defeats the principal of "separate but equal" in education when it comes to race.

1961 The American National Standards Institute publishes the first standards for architectural accessibility. This is the culmination of a movement begun by veterans in the 1950s.

1962 Edward Roberts, a polio survivor with quadriplegia, sues to gain admission to the University of California.

1963 President Kennedy calls for the deinstitutionalization of people with mental retardation and mental illness.

1971 *Pennsylvania Association for Retarded Citizens v. Pennsylvania* establishes that educational segregation is unconstitutional.

1973 Rehabilitation Act requires reasonable accommodations for people with disabilities in employment, education, and telecommunications by entities that receive federal funding.

1974 The last of the laws, known as "ugly laws," allowing for the arrest of people for simply looking different or

wonderful openness of young children to new experiences and their nonjudgmental attitude toward differences. Inclusion and opportunities for typical social experiences during childhood are critical for the healthy development of all children and of society.

Definition and Benefits of Inclusion

Inclusion, as a philosophy and a national movement, reflects the efforts of parents, professionals, and people with disabilities to reverse the isolation experienced by those with disabilities. What is the meaning of inclusion? In humanitarian terms, inclusion is a welcoming, a celebration of diverse abilities, and a profound respect for the contributions all children can make. It is a belief that more diverse communities are richer, better, and more productive places in which to live. Inclusive communities can create a future with a better life for everyone.

In the legal sense, inclusion is a term that advocates that children, regardless of their diverse abilities, have the right to participate in typical community settings where children without disabilities are found and will benefit from that participation. It supports families of children with special needs and their efforts to join in community life, have access to unbiased information, and participate fully in the decisions surrounding the education of their child. Inclusion encourages the child with a disability to participate in playground activities, child care settings, nursery schools and public schools, and activities at the local library.

Inclusion, as a national movement, encompasses the humanitarian and the legal perspectives. Inclusion creates communities that "are filled with individuals who are different from one another. But their shared participation in a given community connects them to one another" (Snow, 2001: 392). Indeed, the most compelling expression of inclusion is the fulfillment of a child's desire to have a friend and be accepted and valued as an individual. For families of children with special needs, this is a priority.

The concept of inclusion is integral to providing library services. An individual's prerogative to participate in activities and have access to resources is a basic tenet of library service. The American Library Association's (1996) Library Bill of Rights opens: "Book and other library resources should be provided for the interest, information, and enlightenment of all people of the community the library serves." Inclusion expands on this principle by encouraging librarians to welcome diversity within the library environment and to design services based on individual needs. As with any group of library patrons, children with disabilities and their families may or may not want to be included in all library programs. The principle of inclusion means that librarians will make it possible for any child, with or without a disability, to participate in library service.

Inclusion benefits not only families and children with disabilities but also the other participants in an inclusive activity and the staff that make it happen. The library vignettes in the following sections, collected during parent focus groups (*Early Childhood Quality Review Initiative for Public Libraries*, 1995), through individual interviews with parents (Langa, 1996), through Carrie Banks's experience in inclusive library settings, and through research, help paint a picture of how inclusion works and what it looks like in the library.

Benefits for Children with Disabilities and Their Families

Motivation to Gain or Practice a Skill

A child with a disability benefits from playing with peers without disabilities, because the interaction often motivates the child with a disability to gain or practice needed skills. In addition, the opportunity for the development of inappropriate behavior derived from social exclusion can be reduced or eliminated.

One little boy and his mother attended the library's early childhood program from the time he was six weeks old. The boy had gross motor skill delays and needed to practice climbing steps with his physical therapist. He did not have any accessible steps on which to practice where he lived. Because of their regular involvement in library programs, the mother knew the library's Early Childhood Room had a loft area with steps. It was the perfect opportunity to encourage this skill in a natural way. The mother asked the library staff if the physical therapist could accompany the family to the library's workshop or meet at the library to practice step climbing, much in the way typically developing children do. A time was selected that did not conflict with other library service, and the therapist sometimes participated while

demonstrating a disability in public, is repealed in Chicago, Illinois. / *Halderman v. Pennhurst* establishes the right to community-based services for people with developmental disabilities.

1975 Head Start is established, with the provision that 10 percent of the seats must go to children with disabilities.

1976 Linda Bove, a Deaf actor, signs a long-term contract with the Children's Television Network.

1983 Americans Disabled for Accessible Public Transit (ADAPT) stages protest at the American Public Transportation Association conference demanding equal access to public transportation.

1988 Federal Fair Housing Act is amended to include, among other things, provisions prohibiting discrimination against people with disabilities. This is the first time disability rights are addressed in broader civil rights legislation.

1990 Americans with Disabilities Act takes effect, providing for equal rights for people with disabilities.

1999 The Supreme Court rules that individuals with disabilities must be offered services in the most integrated setting in *Olmstead v. L.C. and E.W.* / Ryan Taylor, a nine-year-old in Oklahoma, wins his lawsuit and the right to play soccer with his walker.

2007 New York State designates the third week of October as Disability History Week.

the workshop was going on to help the child in his natural environment. The mother further related that her son missed a ranch exhibit previously on display in the library. He looked for it repeatedly. She was so pleased that he had made attachments and connections based on his library experience—an important step for him!

At the Brooklyn Public Library's The Child's Place for Children with Special Needs, a child on the autism spectrum first demonstrated mastery of a skill he had been working on for years during a garden program at which he was a regular. One day he and his mother were late, and the librarian took a few minutes to reread a book just for him. When she asked him to point out the purple flower, he did. His mother was skeptical when told this story, because his teachers had been working on this skill in class since pre-K. So, the librarian asked him to point to the red flowers and he did. In this natural environment, it quickly became clear that he reliably knew his colors, just like the other kids. His mother was very proud. After attending programs supported by the Building Bridges Project in Upstate New York, parents reported that their children with disabilities became more independent in the library (Wemett, 2007: 16–17).

Increased Choices and Options

A child with a disability has access to a greater range of choices and increased opportunities to develop language, social, and problem-solving skills, when using the wide array of library programs, collection, and services. For example, a mother of a child who was hard of hearing approached the children's library wondering if the library would provide a sign language interpreter so that her child could attend storytime. The interpreter was provided, and the child was able to attend storytime. She was introduced to a variety of books and fingerplays and interacted with the other children in the program, many of whom wanted to learn this special new way of talking too! The mother and child continued to participate in library programs and learning activities, working with the librarian to design these programs and activities so that they were accessible to her child.

Through a collaborative program between the library and a local Early Intervention provider, an Early Intervention teacher became familiar with the library's services and asked if she could bring some children to storytime to enhance their language and social interaction skills. She and the librarian decided on the most appropriate program and, after attending storytime, these children brought their families back to select books and to use the library on their own.

Opportunities for Friendship

Friends are essential to our lives. They "open the door to social and emotional growth, they help smooth the rocky road of life, and they let us know we are valued" (Snow, 2001: 424). Not long after the Brooklyn Public Library started its internship program for teens with and without disabilities, two volunteers, one with a disability and one without, who often worked together, became friends outside of the library. One day the mother of the teen with the developmental disability called the librarian to chat about her daughter. Her daughter was spending too much time on the phone and neglecting her chores because she was at the mall with her friend. The mother was thrilled to be dealing with these typical teenage problems that she thought her daughter would never have. The price of friendship was one this mother was happy to pay. The Building Bridges program validated this result, noting that inclusive programs "promoted socialization between typical peers and the youth with disabilities" (Wemett, 2007: 17).

Source of Acceptance and Support

For children with disabilities and their families, the library can be a vital source of acceptance and support in the care of their children. It can also be an access point for balanced information and resources. Strong collections, a welcoming environment, and knowledgeable, open staff can open our doors to these potential patrons.

During a parent/child workshop, the children's librarian noticed that one child did not seem to be verbalizing at all (Feinberg and Deerr, 1995). The librarian spoke with the mother about the child's language development, and the mother expressed a great deal of anxiety over the child's lack of speech. During the workshop series, a visiting speech therapist approached the mother at the request of the librarian. She gave a pack of information to the mother and told her about a center where she could take her child for testing. The mother did so, and it was found that the child was experiencing a delay in language development. The mother was able to enroll the child in a special program. She came back to the librarian to express her thanks and seek out further information and resources. She also shared the difficulty her husband was having accepting the problem. The librarian gathered the information the mother needed about the child's speech delay and also located parenting books on raising a child with special needs, known as exceptional parenting, that specifically discussed the acceptance issue. The mother was pleased to be able to pass these books on to her husband.

The mother of a child with a serious physical disability shared this story: She remembered having a casual conversation with a children's librarian regarding her child's equipment needs. Several weeks later, the librarian mailed her the catalog of an agency that deals with Assistive Technology for children. The parent stated that this extra effort was totally unexpected and reinforced her feeling that the library and staff really had accepted her child and were genuinely concerned about his needs.

Paula Holmes, a library trustee and the mother of two children with disabilities, put it this way:

> When librarians interact with a child who has a disability they are modeling behavior for every patron in the library as well as building trust with that child and that family. . . . In building trust with a child, librarians help the child become an advocate for himself. They reassure the parents that they are not alone in this journey. (Holmes, 2007: 24)

Benefits for Children without Disabilities and Their Families

Acceptance of and Pride in Diversity

When inclusion is the library's norm, children without disabilities learn at a young age to appreciate and accept the diverse abilities of all children. One mother described her child's wonderful imaginary play that reenacted her visits to the library. Her daughter played library at home, arranging books to be checked out. She organized activities with herself as teacher/librarian and her dolls as attendees. The children read for friends, parents, and toys in attendance. She even read to her dolls using sign language.

The Brooklyn Public Library's The Child's Place includes the Picture Exchange Communication System (PECS), primarily used with people on the autism spectrum, in its program. One day, the use of this system with a child led to a broader discussion of the different languages spoken in that city in a single day. When a child asked about the system, the librarian responded that that was how Dominick talked. She then asked everyone there which of them spoke another language at home. Over half of the children raised their hands. When the librarian told them that she had grown up speaking German at home and also knew sign language, a lively discussion ensued with each child demonstrating his or her language with pride. Everyone went home knowing a new word in a new language that day. Dominick's new word was "amigo," which was printed on his PEC board below the picture and English word for "friend."

Better Understanding of People with Disabilities

Families of children without disabilities gain a greater understanding of disabilities, and they also develop a sense of pride in their children's natural ability to accept and appreciate differences in others. A parent focus group participant related that her child had learned to "behave and interact with others" and had also learned that "all children are not the same as her" after attending a library program that included children with disabilities. The parent expressed pride in her child's acceptance of differences and was pleased that this opportunity was offered at the library. It has often been documented that children without disabilities develop empathy, positive attitudes toward people with disabilities, and improved social skills when they participate in inclusive school and recreation activities (Powers, Singer, and Sowers, 1996: 349).

Benefits of Inclusion for Libraries and Librarians

Impetus to Reexamine Library Practice

What works for children with disabilities and their families, works well for others as well. This is a basic tenet of Universal Design, which is covered in Chapter 6. Learning to identify ways and design programs to include children with disabilities encourages us to examine rules, procedures, policies, facilities, programs, collections, and services. Any resulting improvements often benefit all patrons.

A library received a grant to develop a circulating toy collection for children with special needs, birth through age three. The children's librarians responsible for building the collection were excited about providing this new service. Toys arrived daily and were processed and made ready for circulation. A brochure was designed and a colorful notebook assembled. Just before the availability of the collection was announced to the public, the librarians thought about the child and parent checking the toy out at the circulation desk. How would other children feel? Wouldn't a child who wasn't qualified for the program want to check out such an attractive item? In fact, wouldn't the child with special needs stand out as "special" or "different"? The librarian approached the director and presented her dilemma, asking if it would be possible to purchase toys from the regular budget and allow all children to check out toys. The director agreed. Inclusion, in this instance, instigated the development of a new and exciting collection for all of the children in the community. Likewise, an FM system purchased to make library programs accessible to people who are hard of hearing can be used for simultaneous interpretation into another language, increasing the potential audience for the program.

Expansion of User and Support Base

Inclusion offers the opportunity for libraries to widen their circle of users and supporters while satisfying the needs of children with disabilities and their families. When one library conducted parent focus groups, some of the most active participants were parents of children with disabilities. They made suggestions such as streamlining registration procedures, relocating the library's suggestion boxes to elicit regular customer feedback, and conducting support groups for parents. These focus group parents became part of the library's regular user base and continue to interact with staff and administration on improvement of services. They brag to others outside of the library district about how supportive the library has been. They are staunch library supporters and can be counted on to vote in the library's annual budget adoption and trustee election.

This type of support is particularly important in times of tight budgets. It can encourage agencies to work together rather than compete for shrinking funds. At a meeting of Brooklyn Developmental Disability service providers during the height of the Great Recession in

2012, a speaker made an offhand remark to the effect that her agency did not spend money frivolously like the library. As a groundswell of murmured objection grew in the audience of over 80 people representing at least 45 local service provision agencies, the chair of the meeting, which was already running late, interrupted the speaker and announced that disrespect toward the library was not tolerated in this group because the library is "our friend."

Expanding our patron base also expands our fundraising opportunities. Governmental agencies that fund disability issues become potential funders. Private foundations with interests in accessibility, inclusion, and specific disabilities welcome applications from libraries pursuing these goals. One library's collection of books on autism spectrum disorder was funded by the Autism Society of America. Another used money from the state's Developmental Disability Council to purchase hi-lo books for teens with developmental disabilities that were used by a much broader audience, including English-language learners and new adult readers.

Opportunities for Staff Development

Through experiences with children with disabilities and their families, library staff have an opportunity to increase their competencies and skills. One library, after reaching out to families and children with special needs, was overwhelmed at the response it received. The support staff expressed anxiety over how some of these children behaved in the library, and there was resistance that needed to be overcome. The head of the department realized that her staff needed skills to interact appropriately with these families and children and to integrate them into the library environment. She contacted staff from the developmental disabilities school with which she was working. They provided a social worker who met with the library staff to sensitize them on issues surrounding families and children with disabilities. They discussed specific problems and designed practical solutions. This type of training is crucial to making libraries a welcoming place. As one disability rights advocate told Carrie Banks, "It's all about attitude. Nothing else matters."

Welcoming families and children with disabilities into our libraries and designing inclusive services is not a fad. All children select resources and activities to participate in at the public library based on individual interests. Children with disabilities need and have a right to these same choices. The reality is that children with disabilities are either proactively included or they are in practice excluded. It is incumbent upon us to develop a greater understanding of various types of disabilities and be sensitive to the needs of youth and their families. We can take the lead in ensuring that children with disabilities are welcomed and served and effect the change needed to create a truly inclusive library culture.

Resources

Crossley, Katheryn. 2000. "Inclusion: A New Addition to Remedy a History of Inadequate Conditions and Terms." *Journal of Law and Policy* 4: 239–259. http://law.wustl.edu/journal/4/Crossley.pdf.

Jarombek, Kathy, and Anne Leon. 2010. "Leadership at Its Best: Library Managers Spearhead Successful Special Needs Programming." *Children and Libraries* 8, no. 2: 54–57.

Perrault, Anne Marie. 2011. "Rethinking School Libraries: Beyond Access to Empowerment." *Knowledge Quest* 39, no. 3: 6–7.

References

American Library Association. 1996. "Library Bill of Rights." American Library Association. http://www.ala.org/ala/issuesadvocacy/intfreedom/librarybill/index.cfm.

Early Childhood Quality Review Initiative for Public Libraries. 1995. Centereach, NY: Middle County Public Library.

Feinberg, Sandra, and Kathleen Deerr. 1995. *Running a Parent/Child Workshop: A How-To-Do-It Manual for Librarians.* New York: Neal-Schuman.

Holmes, Paula. 2007. "A Parent's View: How Libraries Can Open the Door to the 20 Percent." *Children and Libraries* 5, no. 3: 24.

Langa, Michelle. 1996. *Notes from 1994 Parent Interviews.* Centereach, NY: Middle County Public Library.

Powers, Laurie E., George H. S. Singer, and Jo-Ann Sowers. 1996. *On the Road to Autonomy: Promoting Self-Competence in Children and Youth with Disabilities.* Baltimore: Paul H. Brookes.

Snow, Kathie. 2001. *Disability Is Natural: Creating New Lives for Children and Their Families!* Woodland Park, CO: Braveheart Press.

Wemett, Lisa C. 2007. "The Building Bridges Project: Library Services to Youth with Disabilities." *Children and Libraries* 5, no. 3: 15–20.

What Does the Law Say?

2

[A]ssure that all children with disabilities have available to them . . . a free appropriate education. . . .
[A]ssure that the rights of children with disabilities and their parents . . . are protected.

—*IDEA–I*

The Congress finds that . . . physical or mental disabilities in no way diminish a person's right to fully participate in all aspects of society.

—*ADA*

In addition to a philosophical basis for providing services for children with disabilities there is a legal reason, which is set forth in three federal laws: the Individuals with Disabilities Education Act (IDEA), the Americans with Disabilities Act (ADA), and the Rehabilitation Act of 1973. These laws are designed to promote independence and increase productivity for all members of society, eliminate discrimination based on disability or perceived disability, and ensure that all children enter school ready to learn and receive a free, appropriate education.

It is not only laws, however, that drive inclusion of children with disabilities in the library setting. The spirit of these laws is central to the fundamentals of good library service and to the ethics of our profession. Familiarity with the basic legal requirements and guidelines increases the librarian's understanding and knowledge of inclusion and should encourage more informed and appropriate implementation of inclusive practice. How the law informs the practices of Early Intervention (EI), preschool special education providers, and public schools directly affects how librarians can work collaboratively with their community partners to welcome children with special needs and their families into the library.

Individuals with Disabilities Education Improvement Act of 2004 (IDEA-I)

Definition

IDEA–I is the federal law that ensures that all children up to the age of 21 receive a free and appropriate education in the least restrictive setting, regardless of their disability. Federal courts have extended the upper age to 23 in cases where the local educational authorities were deemed negligent in providing needed services. When first enacted in 1975 as the Education for All Handicapped Children Act (Public Law 94–142), this law established legal categories for children with disabilities that impacted their ability to learn and focused on children ages three and older. It entitles students to evaluation and, after evaluation, to the supports they are found eligible for, including special education services, transition services, Assistive Technology, and related services that are codified in an Individualized Education Program (IEP). In 1986, Congress amended the law to include children three years of age and younger, and it was renamed the Individuals with Disabilities Education Act (IDEA). This amendment was reauthorized in 1994 as "Part C." IDEA was again reauthorized in 2004 as the Individuals with Disabilities Education Improvement Act (IDEA–I) (NYSED: Special Education, 2011).

Part C defines infants and toddlers with disabilities as children under the age of three who need EI services because they are experiencing developmental delays in one or more of the following areas: cognitive development, physical development, language and speech development, psychosocial development, and self-help skills. The definition also includes children who have a diagnosed physical or mental condition that has a high probability of resulting in a developmental delay, such as Down syndrome.

Under Part C, EI services must be developmentally appropriate, provided under public supervision, and have no costs to families except where state statutes establish a payment system based on a sliding scale fee or allow for health insurance reimbursement and consequent parental co-payment. These services can include family training, counseling, special instruction, speech therapy, hearing education services, occupational therapy, physical therapy, psychological services, medical services for diagnostic or evaluation purposes, social work services, vision services, transportation, and Assistive Technology devices and services. Evaluation is considered one of the Part C services. Part C is optional for the states, and the vast majority have opted in.

The EI services a child receives must be described in an Individualized Family Service Plan (IFSP), which is a legally binding document, and delivered in a natural environment. This natural environment can be the child's home or a community setting in which children without disabilities typically participate, such as day care, family day care, a park, or a library. For some children, however, the natural environment can be a center-based program or even a hospital or rehabilitation center if their needs warrant it. Inclusion embraces these children and their families, making the library an accessible and welcoming environment and encouraging families and young children to make use of library facilities and resources.

Under Part B of IDEA the focus shifts from the family to the child ages three to five. Instead of an IFSP, an IEP is developed. Services are provided in the Least Restrictive Environment (LRE) rather than a natural environment. A continuum of services is outlined in the law from least to most restrictive: General Education with Related Services, General Education with Special Education Teacher Support, Collaborative Team Teaching/Integrated Co-teaching, Special Class Services, Day and Residential Placement, and Home/Hospital Instruction. The actual placement depends on the needs of the child. A public library that offers programs for preschoolers can serve as a least restrictive setting, helping to fulfill the requirements of the law.

Students between the ages of 5 and 21 receiving special education services also have an IEP and are also required to receive special education services in the LRE. These children, covered under of IDEA–I, are entitled to a Free Appropriate Public Education (FAPE). The public library has a role to play here too. It can, for example, be the LRE for a student to receive "home instruction" from an itinerant special education teacher, a more restrictive placement on the continuum of services.

Key Concepts in Special Education

Free Appropriate Public Education (FAPE)

National Dissemination Center for Children with Disabilities (NICHCY)
http://nichcy.org/schoolage/qa-series-on-idea/qa1#fape
NICHCY provides a clear definition of FAPE.

Least Restrictive Environment (LRE)

PACER Center Fact Sheet
http://www.pacer.org/parent/php/php-c7.pdf
PACER Center offers a parent friendly look at the requirement for the Least Restrictive Environment.

Response to Intervention (RTI)

National Association of School Psychologists (NASP)
http://www.nasponline.org/resources/handouts/revisedPDFs/rtiprimer.pdf
NASP's primer for parents is a concise outline of RTI.

Individuals with Disabilities Education Act

For more information about IDEA Parts B and C go to:

- http://idea.ed.gov/: This is the official IDEA site from the U.S. Department of Education.
- http://nichcy.org/laws/idea: This is an independent look at IDEA from the National Dissemination Center for Children with Disabilities (NICHCY).
- http://www.fape.org/: This comprehensive, up-to-date website from the PACER Center covers issues relating to IDEA.

With Part B services and students aged five and up, the school library media center now comes into play. Children receiving special education services are entitled to the same access to the school library media center as general education students. Any modification of curriculum or material must carry over to the school library media center. If a child is entitled to large-print or Braille books, the school library media center must make them available. Students requiring Adaptive Technology or sign language interpretation are entitled to have access to it in the school library. School library media specialists may be part of the IEP team and may be entitled to see the IEP if it has ramifications for library service.

Entitled Services under IDEA-I

IDEA–I establishes the right of each child under age five who is suspected of having a disability that affects his or her ability to learn to have access to certain services. These services include referral, service coordination for Parts B and C, a multidisciplinary evaluation, an IFSP or IEP, and due process safeguards. Librarians who want to take the initiative can collaborate with EI and preschool special education providers in the implementation of the mandated services. We can also collaborate with school systems to ensure that older students receiving special education services have the same access to library services as their general education peers.

Child Find

Under IDEA–I, states are required to locate, identify, and evaluate all children with disabilities from birth to age 21. Many states have implemented Child Find projects to achieve this objective. Usually focused on finding the youngest children, these projects are run by the lead agencies under Parts B and C of IDEA.

The Child Find programs offer a unique opportunity for partnerships with librarians. Child Find staff can train the library staff on basic child development, Child Find's objectives, and proper referrals. The library can allow Child Find staff to conduct outreach in the library and distribute information about EI and special education services. These partnerships are mutually beneficial; however, the real beneficiaries are children with disabilities in the community and their families.

Referral

Toddlers and preschoolers suspected of having a developmental disability are entitled to a referral to the lead agency established within each state. Infants in states that have opted into Part C have the same right to referral. The referral is the child's entry point into the EI and preschool special education systems. Depending on the state, referrals can be made by a parent, day care providers, pediatricians, nurses, and other selected early childhood professionals. Children five and older may be referred by a parent, the Committee on Preschool Special Education, a teacher or other school professional, a doctor, a judicial officer, or a designated person in a public agency. Students between the ages of 18 and 21 may refer themselves. Parents must consent to the evaluation unless their parental rights have been suspended by legal proceedings. Starting with the referral process and extending through the evaluation, determination of eligibility, and receiving of special education services, children have the right to confidentiality. Librarians must honor this right, as we do for all our patrons.

It is important for librarians to be aware of the referral process and understand how they can help to identify children who may be qualified for services. We can:

- familiarize ourselves with our state's EI and special education system's referral process;
- contact local EI providers and their service coordinators for networking and information purposes;
- provide information on disabilities and the referral processes for parents, day care providers, early childhood professionals, and academic support professionals such as tutors;
- understand developmental milestones and, if a potential delay is recognized in the library setting, learn how to approach parents and caregivers in a supportive manner;
- enhance communication skills in the provision of information and referral to parents; and
- make library resources available to parents and educators.

Librarians can also help with the referral process in unexpected ways. It is still sometimes the case that a child's first group experience is a library program. A parent or caregiver may gain a frame of reference for developmentally appropriate behavior for the first time. Comparisons among children may lead a parent or a librarian to suspect a delay. Being familiar with the EI and preschool special education referral system can help us to support parents in a non-threatening way. For example, one librarian opened a conversation about a two-and-a-half-year-old who didn't talk by saying, "She's so observant." The mother responded by stating that although the child was very observant, she did not talk. The librarian replied by acknowledging that she had noticed that and asking the mother what she thought. This conversation eventually led to a referral to an EI portal in their community. Another librarian allowed a speech evaluation to take place in the library when other venues were not possible and time was of the essence. When a child is struggling in school, we can suggest speaking with the appropriate special education official. The more comfortable we are with the process and the more we approach it as routine, the less unusual, and therefore less stigmatizing, it will seem to families.

Service Coordination

Under Part C, each family is entitled to service coordination to avoid duplication and fragmentation of EI services. The service coordinator should also help ensure that the child is getting the services mandated in the IFSP and other benefits he or she may be entitled to, such as Supplemental Security Income (SSI). Usually, a service coordinator is assigned by the lead agency or its designee shortly after a referral is made. Service coordination has been a critical component of Part C. The service coordinator is responsible for:

- obtaining information regarding the child and family, which includes the child's health history and developmental status;
- obtaining permission to release medical and other records pertaining to the child's suspected delay;
- informing the family of the program and the family's rights under the state law;
- explaining the protections offered by state law regarding the family's health insurance;
- assisting the family in understanding and arranging for screening or multidisciplinary evaluation of the child;
- helping the family obtain answers to any questions it may have about the evaluation process and results;

- exploring with families of eligible children their options for services;
- explaining the IFSP and the family's primary role in developing and implementing that plan; and
- explaining due process rights to the family.

It sometimes happens that a family may be unhappy with its service coordinator. The family has the right to change coordinators.

Under Part B, service coordination for preschoolers is handled by a member of the multidisciplinary team working with the child. Consistent with the change in focus from family to child, service coordination under Part B exists to ensure that provided services are unduplicated, comprehensive, and dedicated to improving the child's academic performance as outlined in his or her IEP. Service coordination is not provided for school-age children. However, the child may be eligible for service coordination as a Medicaid waiver service.

For librarians, what is important about service coordination is the recognition that parents, service coordinators, and members of the multidisciplinary team need to be informed about and comfortable with libraries and all of the resources they can offer, because library services are potential components of any child's IFSP or IEP. Inter-agency relationships and librarian/parent/professional partnerships provide the mechanism for sharing information about library service with all the parties involved. Through these partnerships, families become aware of which library services are appropriate and available for their child, and these services and programs can be incorporated into the child's individual plans.

Likewise, librarians become more aware of the resources available to them. We can learn which agencies have particular expertise and tap effective parent advocates to teach advocacy skills to other parents. Why not invite a service coordinator to give a talk about EI and special education services at the library? Or gather a panel of social workers, parents, and other professionals to discuss new ideas in the autism field.

Multidisciplinary Evaluation

Children, under Part B and Part C, are entitled to a multidisciplinary evaluation to assess their unique strengths and needs in five areas of development: cognition (learning), speech and language (communication), fine and gross motor (walking and

Potential Outcomes from an Early Intervention Evaluation

When a referral is made to the Early Intervention Program, a service coordinator is assigned and an evaluation arranged. The evaluation can result in the following findings:

- The child is found ineligible for services at that time.
- The child is found currently ineligible for services but at risk for developing a delay or more profound delay. In this case, in some states, the family may receive preventative services, particularly if the referral was the result of part of a child abuse report.
- The child is found eligible for services.

movement), social-emotional (relating to others), and adaptive development (self-help). This evaluation must identify activities and services that build on the child's strengths to meet his identified needs. Only properly trained and licensed individuals are allowed to conduct the evaluation. Evaluations are administered as indicated in all areas related to the child's suspected disability. Children of all ages are entitled to Assistive Technology evaluations. In addition, when the child's behavior is an issue, she has the right to a functional behavioral assessment. If parents disagree with the evaluation, they have the right to an independent evaluation at no cost to the family.

Individualized Family Service Plan (IFSP) under Part C

As part of this evaluation, the child's family directs an assessment of its own resources, priorities, and concerns to determine the ability to meet the developmental needs of the infant or toddler. Once the child is determined to be eligible, an IFSP is developed. This service plan:

- addresses the child's eligibility, abilities, and areas of need;
- lists the family's resources, priorities for the child, and concerns about the child's development;
- describes the expected goals for the child, how these goals are to be achieved, and time lines to determine the child's progress toward these goals;
- contains a description of what EI services are needed and the frequency and duration of these services;
- addresses how these services will be delivered in a natural environment where children without disabilities participate; and
- provides specific details regarding the family's expected outcomes for the child and how the evaluation team intends to achieve these outcomes.

Because the family and child's needs change over time, the IFSP is designed to be a fluid document that can be revised at any time. The parent has the right to choose which service, if any, the child will receive. The IFSP must be reviewed every three months in order to determine if it still best meets the needs of the child and family.

Individualized Education Program (IEP) under Part B

When a child above the age of three is found eligible for special education services, an IEP is developed by a committee designated by the child's school district. The committee must include the parents, among others. The IEP is a legal document that guides those providers who are working with the child to improve the areas relative to his or her academic performance. Short-term objectives toward meeting long-term goals are included. Under IDEA–I, IEPs, which were previously reviewed annually, may now be multiyear.

When a child turns three, she must receive a classification in order to receive special education services. For a preschooler, the classification is "preschooler with a disability" or "preschool disabled." For a school-age child it will be one of the following:

- Autism
- Deaf-blindness
- Deafness
- Developmental delay
- Emotional disturbance
- Hearing impairment
- Intellectual disability
- Multiple disabilities
- Orthopedic impairment
- Other health impairment
- Specific learning disability
- Speech or language impairment
- Traumatic brain injury
- Visual impairment including blindness

This classification is a significant change from EI and a troubling factor for many parents who do not want their child labeled. Librarians can help parents research the topic and weigh their fear of the effects of a label against the consequences of not getting the services for which their child is eligible and may need. Different parents may reasonably come to different conclusions about the relative merits and drawbacks of labels. It is important that we continue to offer support to the parent regardless of our own feelings in order to continue to be a resource for the family.

IEPs for children ages three to five differ significantly from those developed for children six to twenty-one. For a preschooler with a disability, if more than one service is provided to a child, a service coordinator, usually the child's special education teacher, is designated. There is no such provision for older students. Three-to-five-year-olds are deemed eligible for services only if there is a significant delay, usually as defined by the local educational authority. For five-to-twenty-one-year-olds, a Response to Intervention (RTI) model may be used to determine eligibility for services. That is to say, a child may receive special education services, particularly for a learning disability, if the child is experiencing a delay and responds to a specific, scientific, research-based intervention. Provision is made for older children who are at risk for needing special education services to receive Early Intervening Services (EIS). These services are meant to address issues early on and to prevent the need for special education services. Finally, Part B requires a plan for the successful transition of a child to adult life. Typically the areas addressed include employment, housing, and social networks. This planning must begin by age 16 and usually encompasses multiple agencies.

While federal law establishes the basic framework for the education of children with disabilities, its implementation at the local level varies considerably. Librarians must be familiar with local policies and procedures in order to assist parents. We can best serve individuals with disabilities and their families by establishing and maintaining relationships with the various agencies involved.

Librarians can play an important role in developing and implementing these plans. The family may request that the evaluation itself or one of the specific services needed by the child take place in a neutral setting or natural environment, one where the child is comfortable. Why not the public library? Maybe attendance at the library's storytime could be written into the child's IFSP or IEP to support language and social skills development. Public libraries could be a significant part of EIS. For example, library programs that emphasize any of the early literacy skills could be useful to kindergarteners. A child could receive mandated tutoring services or home instruction in the library. Transition-age students can explore vocational interests by volunteering at the library. Or a knowledgeable librarian can suggest alternative venues. Libraries can partner with local education agencies to host screening programs or Child Find workshops.

Six Early Literacy Skills

- Oral language and vocabulary: knowing the names of things and concepts
- Phonological awareness: hearing the smaller sounds that make up words
- Letter knowledge: knowing the alphabet, letter names and letter sounds
- Background knowledge: story grammar and contextual knowledge that allows children to understand what they are reading
- Print conventions: the structure of books and text

(Adapted from the Association for Library Service to Children and the Public Library Association's Every Child Ready to Read program.)

This type of coordination will occur only with a concerted and ongoing effort on the part of librarians and an agreement with the relevant agencies. Whether the library wants to commit to this extensive a role is an individual decision. We can further support families by focusing on development of professional skills and knowledge. We can join the family and interdisciplinary team in offering great options for inclusion and education within our communities just by making available traditional library programs and services designed to meet their needs.

School library media specialists have a better defined, and sometimes mandated, role. If a child requires Accessible Instructional Material such as books in Braille or audio format, they must be available through the school library media center. Behavior management plans developed for classroom use must be used throughout the school, including in the library. School library media specialists may be part of the team that develops the IEP and the curriculum modifications.

In addition to the formal role, the school library media center is often used informally as a quiet place for someone to calm down. It can also be a designated alternative testing site and is a great place for students with disabilities to volunteer.

Due Process

Eligible children are entitled to certain legal protections under IDEA–I, known as due process rights. Parents have the right to examine all records pertaining to the assessment, screening, and eligibility determination of their child prior to educational planning meetings. They have the right to collaborate on writing the IFSP or IEP and to examine it at any time. Changes in services cannot be made without their written consent and usually must be discussed at a properly convened educational planning meeting, unless the parent waives this right. Parents have the right to appeal decisions they disagree with and the right to the timely resolution of complaints. In the interim, the child has the right to pendency—to continue to receive the services currently being provided in the same setting. Finally, parents have the right to written notices and summaries of documents in their native language and to simultaneous interpretation into their native language at any and all meetings. Students have the right to participate in the process, including attending IEP meetings. After age 18, the students must be included in the IEP meetings unless someone is acting as legal guardian for them.

The appeal process is another area where libraries have an important role to play. Some local education authorities are reluctant to make information on special education services available to parents, particularly in languages other than English. Libraries can seek out this information and make it available to families. The Internet can be a good source of information, particularly in languages such as Spanish.

Americans with Disabilities Act of 1990 (ADA)

The ADA is the federal civil rights legislation that guarantees equal protection to people with disabilities. Passed in 1986 and fully enacted in 1990 (Americans with Disabilities Act of 1990, as Amended, 2009), it protects people with disabilities from discrimination in public access and accommodations, employment, housing, and transportation. All public agencies and private businesses are required to make accommodations for people with disabilities unless they can prove that those accommodations create a financial hardship or fundamentally alter the nature of their business.

In 2008, the ADA Amendments Act (ADAAA) was passed (U.S. Equal Employment Opportunity Commission, 2008), in part to correct what Congress believed was the judiciary's misinterpretation of the law. ADAAA reverses several employer-friendly Supreme Court decisions by expanding the definition of a disability. It establishes that mitigating measures such as Assistive Technology or medication and remissions do not disqualify an individual from protection. Protection was also clarified for individuals "regarded as" having a disability.

For libraries, the key areas of ADAAA compliance involve:

- ensuring nondiscrimination in employment of persons with disabilities;
- ensuring equity of access to services and information;
- creating a physical environment free of barriers that restrict patrons with disabilities from using the library;
- having policies that can accommodate the needs of people with disabilities; and
- training staff and the general public in disability awareness issues and the regulations of the law.

Rehabilitation Act of 1973, Sections 504 and 508

The Rehabilitation Act of 1973 was passed to ensure that agencies receiving money from the federal government did not discriminate against people with disabilities. It is administered by the Office for Civil Rights. Two sections, Section 504 and Section 508, have particular relevance to children with disabilities and libraries (Compliance with Sections 504 and 508 of the Rehabilitation Act, 2013).

Section 504 requires schools to make accommodations for children with a medically diagnosed disability. Access to medications while in school, asthma or diabetes monitoring, testing accommodations, and sign language interpreters are all examples of accommodations available under Section 504. School library media centers are particularly affected by this law.

Section 508 requires that any entity that accepts money from the federal government have accessible communications. This requirement has been interpreted by the courts to apply to telecommunications, the Internet, and computers. So, for example, the website of a library receiving an Institute of Museum and Library Services grant, or any other federal money, must be fully accessible and compatible with commonly used screen reading software. This is a requirement that many libraries have been slow to meet, thus jeopardizing their eligibility for federal funds.

As a function of their size, many libraries are required to appoint ADA coordinators or 504 enforcement officers. These often have the responsibilities to:

- educate the administration and staff of the library as well as the general public in various aspects of the law;
- evaluate the environment and services of the library to ensure that they are free of barriers to access for patrons with disabilities;
- provide information about the services available in a variety of alternate formats (including Braille, sign language interpreters, large-print materials, and audio and computer discs); and
- ensure compliance with relevant laws.

Because many libraries have invested personnel and resources in ensuring equity of employment of access, they are in a good position to make the simple programmatic alterations necessary to include children with disabilities into their regular programs and services. Children's librarians can take responsibility and become key advocates within their own library to make their settings not only accessible but also welcoming to families of children with disabilities.

They can:

- assess the children's room to ensure it is accessible to people who use wheelchairs and identify potential barriers to inclusion and integration;
- develop collections including Braille, large-print materials, talking books, captioned videos, adaptive toys, exceptional parenting collections, and materials on disabilities for both children and adults;
- design programs for children with and without disabilities; and
- contact local agencies and organizations that work with families and young children and people with disabilities.

By working with parents at all levels, providing them with information resources, and developing connections with other professionals and organizations serving families, children's librarians have a strong role to play in the implementation of all of the laws that promote the inclusion of children with disabilities in our communities. In addition to meeting legal requirements, compliance with these laws can be immensely rewarding. One Brooklyn Public Library Hospital Storyteller found this out while giving away books at a local hospital. After reading a story to a child in an inpatient unit, the librarian offered to let the child pick a Reading Is Fundamental (RIF) book to keep. The girl's mother pulled the librarian aside and whispered, "You won't have a book for my child. She's blind." The Hospital Storyteller responded by pulling two Braille books out of her suitcase and letting the child choose which one she wanted, eliciting a huge grin from the child and tears of gratitude from the mother.

Resources

Council for Exceptional Children. 2010. "A Primer on the IDEA 2004 Regulations." Council for Exceptional Children. http://www.cec

.sped.org/Policy-and-Advocacy/Current-Sped-Gifted-Issues/Copy
-of-IDEA/A-Primer-on-the-IDEA-2004-RegulationsIDEA.

Dykema. 2008. "The Americans with Disabilities Act—New Amendments
Take Effect January 1, 2009." Dykema. http://www.dykema.com/
labor/news/empissues1208.pdf.

Foos, Donald D., and Nancy C. Pack. 1992. *How Libraries Must Comply
with the Americans with Disabilities Act (ADA)*. Phoenix, AZ: Orynx
Press.

Mulligan, Elaine. 2011. "The Facts on Charter Schools and Students
with Disabilities." National Dissemination Center for Children with
Disabilities. http://nichcy.org/publications/charters.

PACER Center. 2009. "Least Restrictive Environment (LRE): A
Simplified Guide to Key Legal Requirements." PACER Center Action
Information Sheets. http://www.pacer.org/parent/php/php-c7.pdf.

Wright, Pamela, and Pete Wright. 2007. "The Child Find Mandate: What
Does It Mean to You?" Wrightslaw. Last revised September 26. http://
www.wrightslaw.com/info/child.find.mandate.htm.

References

Americans with Disabilities Act of 1990, as Amended. 2009. U.S.
Department of Justice. Last updated March 25. http://www.ada.gov/
pubs/ada.htm.

Compliance with Sections 504 and 508 of the Rehabilitation Act. 2013.
U.S. Department of Health and Human Services. Accessed January
16. http://www.hhs.gov/web/508/training/508_508.html.

NYSED: Special Education. 2011. "Individuals with Disabilities Education
Improvement Act of 2004." NYSED.gov. Last updated March 28.
http://www.p12.nysed.gov/specialed/idea/.

U.S. Equal Employment Opportunity Commission. 2008. "ADA
Amendments Act of 2008: PL 110-325 (S 3406)." U.S. Equal
Employment Opportunity Commission. http://www.eeoc.gov/laws/
statutes/adaaa.cfm.

Developmentally Appropriate Library Services

3

> Where I come from kids with Down syndrome don't learn to read. I heard they can here. Show me.
> —*Barbudian-American aunt of a child with Down syndrome*

Library services for children must be viewed within the context of the child's development. Babies begin life completely dependent on their families and gain independence as they get older. Young children use the library with their families. As children get older they are sometimes with their families and sometimes on their own. As teens, they are often on their own or in groups with other teens. Successful library service is designed with this process in mind.

When designing services to meet the needs of children, librarians need to integrate the developmental needs of the child into the library environment. The creation of programs and services that meet the needs of children with disabilities and their families can be successful only when the librarians understand the basic concepts of developmental appropriateness for all children.

Developmentally Appropriate Practice

Developmentally appropriate practice applies our knowledge of child development to making decisions about how we provide library service to children. It is not a set of rigid rules and procedures but a framework or philosophy of service that means providing services that are child centered, based on data and information about what children are like at different stages of development. It demonstrates a fundamental respect for a child's developmental needs and cultural background.

Many factors come into play when looking at services within a developmentally appropriate framework, including developmental milestones, the relationship of the child to the parent/caregiver, the child's understanding of his environment and surroundings, and the child's relationship to the library and librarian. Basic principles of child development that all professionals who work with children need to understand include the following (Gestwicki, 1995: 8–9):

- There is a predictable sequence in development.
- Development at one stage lays the base for later development.
- There are optimal periods in development.
- Development results from the interaction of biological factors (maturation) and environmental factors (learning).
- Development proceeds as an interrelated whole, with all aspects (physical, cognitive, emotional, social) influencing the others.
- Each individual develops according to a particular timetable and pace.
- Development proceeds from simple to complex and from general to specific.

Every Child Ready to Read is one good example of developmentally based programming.

It must be remembered that nothing is clear-cut or absolute when applying these principles to practice. Librarians need to examine their programs and practices based on the whole environment and determine whether they enhance or diminish the quality of the child's and family's experience within the library.

Children with disabilities develop continuously too. However, they may differ from their typically developing peers in the pace or sequence of development or in their preferred leaning formats. For example, someone with an intellectual disability may learn more slowly and require more opportunities to practice a skill than his typically developing sibling. A child with autism spectrum disorder may learn to read, a receptive language skill related to listening, before he learns to write, an expressive language skill related to speaking (Bau-

Every Child Ready to Read
The Every Child Ready to Read initiative is a family literacy model developed by the Association for Library Service to Children and the Public Library Association. The principles of six early literacy skills and five early literacy practices are the key to Every Child Ready to Read. Early literacy skills were discussed earlier. The five early literacy practices include talking, singing, playing, writing, and reading. Key to the success is incorporating information about literacy development into all library programs so parents learn how they work and how to implement them at home. Focusing on the process and skill level rather than age helps make the program appropriate for children with disabilities. You can find out more at http://www.ala.org/everychildreadytoread/.

man, 1999: 16). A young child who is blind needs exposure to Braille as well as to print.

Keep in mind that what we know about children's development changes every day. Fifteen years ago, the concept of Multiple Intelligences was new. Now it is an established precept of educational psychology. Likewise, 20 years ago, we did not expect children with Down syndrome to learn to read. Now they go on to college (Kumin, 1998: 132).

Developmental Milestones

Every child develops differently and according to his or her own timetable. The unique vantage point of librarians, who have many experiences with young children and families, offers the possibility of the librarians noticing "something different" about a particular child or of parents asking the librarians questions regarding their children's development. Although not in a position to give advice, it is appropriate for the librarian to understand the basic developmental milestones and assist parents if there are concerns, referring them to appropriate services when necessary.

Being familiar with developmental milestones is important for librarians when they are designing programs for young children. Jean Piaget laid out the principle of cognitive development after observing his own son's intellectual growth. Erik Erikson looked at psychosocial development and expanded our understanding of developmental psychology to encompass an individual's entire life span. Table 3.1 presents a very brief outline of their developmental stages.

Table 3.2 provides a quick checklist of developmental milestones for children from birth through 21 years of age. This list of milestones will assist librarians in designing age-appropriate activities. These are other guidelines to keep in mind:

- Young children, with and without disabilities, should be engaged in activities that allow them to become aware of, explore, inquire about, and utilize new concepts, skills, and materials. Any activity or material should be meaningful, engaging, and relevant to the child.
- No activity should require a very young child to separate from the parents or caregiver.

TABLE 3.1 Stages of Development

Piaget	Erikson
0-8 months	**0-1 year**
Sensorimotor Stage • Learns via senses and reflexes • Manipulates things	Trust vs. Mistrust Stage
18 months to 6 years	**2-3 years**
Preoperationals • Forms ideas based on perception • Can focus on only one thing • Overgeneralizes	Autonomy vs. Shame and Doubt
	4-5 years
	Initiative vs. Guilt
6-12 Years	**6-12 Years**
Concrete Operations • Forms ideas with reasoning • Limits thinking to objects and known events	Industry vs. Inferiority • Develops competence
12 years and up	**Adolescence**
Formal Operations • Thinks concretely • Thinks hypothetically	Identity vs. Role Confusion • Fidelity develops

Note: Jean Piaget and Erik Erikson's work form the underpinning of the field of developmental psychology. If you are interested in the topic, it is well worth examining the work of Lev Vygotsky, Arnold Gesell, and Maria Montesorri. David G. Meyers (2004), in his introductory text *Psychology*, provides a good overview of developmental psychology in Chapter 4, "The Developing Person" (pp. 134-191). Chip Wood (2007) offers a concrete, easily accessible outline of children's development in *Yardsticks: Children in the Classroom Ages 4-14*.

- Activities need to consider the parent/child dyad as the essential factor when designing library-based early childhood programs and the child's increased need for independence as he grows.
- Each child should be allowed to move at his or her own pace in skill acquisition.
- The process, not the product, is what matters in young children's learning.
- Library programs must consider the child's cognitive and developmental stages as well as his or her chronological age.

TABLE 3.2 Developmental Milestones Checklist

Age Range	Milestones	
1-3 months	Lifts head and chest briefly when on stomach Wiggles, kicks with arms and legs Turns head to bright colors/lights Eyes track moving object together Pays attention to face in direct line of vision	Reacts to sudden sounds and noises Smiles and coos Makes fist with both hands; can grasp toys or hair
3-6 months	Recognizes familiar faces/objects Turns toward sounds Turns over from back to stomach Stretches out arms to be picked up	Babbles and laughs out loud Reaches for and holds objects Can switch toys from one hand to another Helps hold bottle during feeding
6-12 months	Sits without support Pulls to a standing position Creeps or crawls Finger-feeds self Drinks from a cup Plays peek-a-boo and patty cake Waves bye-bye Looks at person speaking	Uses crying to show different needs Responds to name Uses five or six words, including "mama" and "dada" Picks up objects with pincer grip Puts objects in containers Stacks two blocks
12-18 months	Pushes, pulls, and dumps things Pulls off shoes, socks, and mittens Walks with help Steps off a low object Follows simple directions	Imitates simple words Listens to music and dances in rhythm Likes to look at pictures Makes marks on paper with crayon or marker
18-24 months	Carries something while walking Feeds self with a spoon Refers to self by name Turns pages two or three at a time Listens to stories with pictures Uses two- to three-word sentences Has an expressive vocabulary of 300 words Carries on "conversations" with self and toys Builds a tower of four blocks	Recognizes familiar pictures Plays independently for short periods of time Imitates parents and everyday activities Identifies hair, eyes, ears, and nose by pointing Shows affection Begins to run and jump Likes to scribble and draw Puts squares and circles into puzzles
24-30 months	Kicks a ball Turns pages one at a time Helps to dress and undress Turns doorknob and unscrews lids	Feeds self well with spoon Uses many new words Names objects in books Knows at least one color

(Continued)

TABLE 3.2 Developmental Milestones Checklist (*Continued*)

Age Range	Milestones	
30-36 months	Walks up stairs (alternating feet) Rides a tricycle Puts on shoes Plays with other children for short periods of time Repeats common nursery rhymes Says first and last name Follows two- or three-step directions Begins to count	Begins to draw circles and vertical lines Uses three- to five-word sentences Has vocabulary of 1,000 words Uses words to relate observations, concepts, and relationships Understands night/day, big/little, summer/winter, yesterday/today Can stay with one activity for 8-9 minutes
36-48 months	Speaks in short sentences within the context of conversation Asks how, why, when, what, and where questions Gradually replaces parallel play with cooperative play Opens and turns pages of a book Knows front/back of a book and if book is upside down	Likes to hear same story over and over Listens to a book with a simple storyline Counts using a one-to-one correspondence Begins to draw a stick figure Is toilet trained Is able to dress and undress independently Is able to put toys or materials away when asked
48-60 months	Has expressive vocabulary of about 1,500 words, more if read to Understands spatial language (over, under, in, out) Actively engages in conversations with other children Follows sequential directions Orders object by size, number, and shape	Strings beads in a pattern Begins to use scissors Engages in more elaborate and sophisticated dramatic play Follows a story with full storyline Sits in a group for 15 or more minutes Separates from parent or caregiver for longer periods of time
6-8 years	Rates of typical development can vary more Rapid development of cognitive skills Understanding of right and wrong increases Sense of future develops Likes structure Knows right and left Focus is on self Has strong likes and dislikes Is physically sensitive to pain Mistakes loom larger	Develops understanding of broader world and place in it Importance of friendship grows; strong friendships develop Need for peer acceptance increases Facility to talk about experiences, thoughts, and feelings increases More outwardly focused Developmental differences may become more pronounced

TABLE 3.2   Developmental Milestones Checklist (*Continued*)

Age Range	Milestones	
8-11 years	Lots of energy, needs fuel/snacks Fine motor skills increase Tends to test physical and cognitive limits Use of expressive language includes more description Abstract thinking grows More easily adopts perspective of other Moves from enjoying mastery more to enjoying learning new skills Sense of fairness becomes acute	Group activities become important Friendships become more complex Same-sex friends predominate Peer pressure grows Independence from family continues to increase Moves from learning to read to reading to learn Academics become more challenging Awareness of body and changes develops Differences in social development related to a disability may become more pronounced
Girls: 8-13 years; Boys: 10-15 years	Puberty begins Sex organs develop Hormone production increases Major growth spurt occurs Skin problems appear Feels physically awkward and sensitive about it Body hair appears Concern about appearance increases Is moody	Is more self-absorbed Has tendency to be impulsive Has difficulty with decisions Same-sex peer groups, sometimes as cliques or gangs, predominate Adult personality characteristics emerge Word play becomes sophisticated; sarcasm and slang used more Can become more organized May challenge authority
Girls: 8-13 years	Begins menstruating	Develops close friendships
Boys: 10-15 years	Voice deepens and may crack Adam's apple grows Tends to prefer group friendships	
Adolescence	Girls reach full height between ages 14 and 15 Boys reach full height between ages 16 and 17 Academic differentiation continues to increase Vocational tracking may occur Comprehension of abstract concepts increases Ethics get more nuanced Openness to emotional intimacy grows Mature sense of identity develops Has ability to question previous values Emphasis may move from same-sex peer groups to romantic relationships	Sexual identity is established May become sexually active Decision-making skills develop less rapidly than physical strength and agility Risk-taking behaviors may increase Adult connections remain important, but often not parental ones Vocabulary deepens and broadens Logic becomes more secure May be more willing to admit mistakes Awareness of larger world issues grows and takes on importance

Young Children and Family-Centered Principles

The family, as the basic unit of our society, bears the responsibility for raising its children. For families who have a young child (newborn to five years old) with a disability or medical needs, this responsibility can be daunting. The simple tasks and activities of daily living are often complicated and fraught. Medical, educational, and financial concerns may be overwhelming. Relationships can become both more important and more strained. Yet not only the early years but also the early months are crucial to children's readiness to learn. Interaction with other family members and observation of their family's activities prepare children for lifelong openness and the ability to learn. The family-centered principles presented in this chapter support and respect the pivotal role of the family in the lives of children and ensure family participation in the provision of services to the child.

Libraries have an opportunity to join with other family-serving organizations in their community to develop and provide family-centered library services. Grounded in a basic respect for individuals, quality library service already assumes many of the fundamental tenets and guidelines found in the family-centered practices. Librarians are committed to lifelong learning, educational enrichment, and satisfying the informational, cultural, and recreational needs of patrons. While acknowledging and embracing nontraditional families from single parents to grandparents and same-sex couples raising children to foster parents and children being raised in congregate living situations, the libraries can use these principles to better serve exceptional families. The Association for Library Service to Children's early literacy initiative Every Children Ready to Read is one exciting example of how these principles can be used in a library setting.

The underlying principles of the family-centered approach, adopted in 1987 by the Association for the Care of Children's Health, with support from the Division of Maternal and Child Health of the U.S. Public Health Service, are the bases for the principles in this chapter. They are:

- recognition that the family is the constant in the child's life, while the service systems and personnel within those systems fluctuate;
- facilitation of parent/professional collaboration;

- sharing of unbiased and complete information with parents about their children on an ongoing basis in an appropriate and supportive manner;
- implementation of appropriate policies and programs that are comprehensive and provide emotional and financial support to meet the needs of families;
- encouragement and facilitation of parent-to-parent support;
- recognition of family strengths and individuality and respect for different methods of coping;
- assurance that the design of comprehensive, coordinated, multidisciplinary service delivery systems is flexible, accessible, and responsive to family-identified needs; and
- understanding and incorporating the developmental needs of infants, toddlers, and preschoolers and their families into service delivery systems.

In addition, librarians must recognize the needs and issues of siblings of people with disabilities in order to achieve true family-centered service.

To better serve the needs of children with disabilities and their families, librarians need to understand family-centered principles and their relationship to quality library service for all families. Exploring these principles from a library perspective helps to form the development of inclusive policies, programs, and services. This analysis enables us to cultivate the library's potential to serve families and children with special needs and foster family-centered communities.

Respect the Importance and Integrity of the Family Unit

The family is the constant in the child's life, and the family's awareness of the variety of services and resources a library provides is essential to the family's ability to make use of the library as a community support. To design services that meet the needs of young children, librarians must reach the parents or caregivers and include them.

Siblings are an important part of families. And siblings of children with disabilities have their own issues and informational and support needs. Furthermore, the brothers and sisters of a child with a disability will likely have the longest relationships with that child. Positioning the library to support siblings is key in maintaining a lifelong relationship with the family.

Working with families not only is in the best interest of the child but also is critical to the stability of public libraries. Strong library support is grounded in regular and consistent use of services by patrons, starting at their very earliest ages. The most effective way to make library users of the youngest community members is through family participation. If a family leaves one community, librarians want to ensure that the family will use the local library in the next community. We want all children and families to become lifelong users and friends. At the end of a workshop on transition planning sponsored by The Child's Place for Children with Special Needs at the Brooklyn Public Library, a mother stated that when her son with a disability was starting preschool she had attended a library program on preschool special education services. Now, 10 years later, he was in high school and beginning the transition to adult services. "You helped me then, and I knew you would help me now," she said.

Treat Families as Partners

Building a partnership with the parents is necessary if the librarian is to effectively support the individual development of each child. Parents understand and know their child best. Librarians need to respect this knowledge and build on the parent/child relationship to encourage family literacy and learning. Successful inclusion and integration of children with disabilities is based on a strong collaboration between the parent and the librarian.

This idea of parent/professional collaboration is not foreign to traditional library practice. Librarians, whether conducting a reference interview or working with young children in a program, have a natural tendency to recognize the parenting role required to elicit what it is the patron (child) needs. Every Child Ready to Read is also based on this partnership. The premise of Every Child Ready to Read is "to enlist parents and caregivers as partners in preparing their children for learning to read and to provide the most effective methods to achieve this end" (Meyers and Henderson, 2011). It is this form of respect and recognition that is required to effectively initiate and sustain the parent/professional partnership.

Siblings too have a role to play. They have ideas about the needs of their brother or sister with a disability and are often both experienced and adept at meeting those needs. Ignoring the input of siblings would mean losing an important resource for librarians.

Provide Balanced and Complete Information for Families

When first informed of their child's disability, parents of young children may experience many emotions. Their feelings of love and joy are often tinged with or overshadowed by disappointment, grief, and anger. As one parent put it: "Our world is shaken to the core. . . . The hope, the dream and the bright future we pictured for our child is gone, replaced by a very scary unknown world" (Snow, 2001: 55).

After a period of time, parents usually accept the fact that their child faces certain challenges. The first stage in this process often begins with parents questioning their own abilities to parent their child. To ease these doubts, many parents will seek information regarding their child's disability and the community resources available to assist their child. The parents' information needs are paramount.

Bailey and Simeonsson (1988) documented this need in their article "Assessing Needs of Families with Handicapped Infants." They surveyed 34 families using their recently developed Family Needs Survey and found that the most frequently cited parental needs were access to:

- information about how to teach their child;
- currently available services;
- services that their child will need in the future; and
- reading material about parents who have a child similar to theirs.

Other topics that were of interest to families included information on financial assistance, trained child care providers, explaining their child's disability to others, and assistance in family functioning.

Where do parents find this information? The New York State Developmental Disabilities Council found that parents, especially those of children with special needs, frequently report going to the public library for information soon after being told of their child's special need(s) (Cohen and Simkin, 1994: 1). Parents of children with disabilities found that public libraries are ideal places to obtain information that is balanced toward a particular approach or service. More recently, research indicates that parents, particularly mothers, turn to the Internet for information (Porter and Edirippulige, 2007). It is important to note that this need for information by parents is ongoing, comparable to the need of parents of typically developing children when faced with a new developmental stage of their child.

Helping parents locate information is central to the library's basic mission. Providing access to resources for parents and adults with children enhances the role of the children's librarian and provides the community support all families need raising children. Families who have children with disabilities are particularly in need of information regarding the disability, how to advocate for their child to receive services, and the management of day-to-day tasks of caring for their child. Exceptional parents who are not proficient in English have additional needs. Helping those parents who are doubly isolated, first by a language barrier and then as a parent of a child with a disability, is imperative.

Siblings need age-appropriate information. "Siblings have a unique need for honest, direct and comprehensible information" (Gallagher, Powell, and Rhodes, 2006: 109). Young siblings are more likely to be focused on the mechanics of the disability at first. Is it painful? Will I get it? Fiction and nonfiction books are available to answer these questions. Older siblings need more detailed information and support. Issues such as embarrassment, future care, and identity separate from their sibling may arise. "Siblings need an information system that is longitudinal . . . , one that adapts to their changing needs and is readily available throughout their lives" (Gallagher, Powell, and Rhodes, 2006: 109). By establishing that libraries can be reliable sources of information, we will make lifelong customers of siblings.

How the librarian provides service to families is critical. Developing active listening and communication skills is a must. Families need to know we are open to their questions and concerns. The diagnosis process itself necessarily emphasizes the child's deficits, not his strengths (Snow, 2001: 54). We can help balance that view of the child. Find out the child's name. Ask to see pictures; compliment his eyes or her smile. Let the family members know you are an advocate for their child. Talk about the importance of reading to the child. Let them know you have high expectations for their child. Housing the parenting collection in the children's room reduces barriers and makes it convenient for parents to approach with questions and concerns. It also allows parents and children to search for information in proximity. Providing information in a variety of formats and languages, covering all aspects and sides of an issue in a nonjudgmental, unbiased way, is particularly important for parents who need to make decisions regarding their children. Librarians are especially attuned to this need to present all sides. Information must be current and understandable. If it is written in a language the parent does not read or at a level the parent does not understand, it is useless.

Develop Programs, Policies, and Services to Facilitate Family Literacy and Learning

Babies, toddlers, preschoolers, and early elementary-age children do not visit the library independently. They are usually accompanied by an adult, such as a parent or caregiver. Sometimes they are in the care of an older sibling. This presents a wonderful opportunity for librarians to serve children within the family unit, focusing on the child's as well as the parent's or caregiver's needs. Services should reflect a family approach, recognizing that the parent's comfort with the library will be reflected in the child's comfort level.

Programs need to be designed with that dyad in mind. In storytime or a parent/child workshop, librarians need to focus on the parent and child learning together and support the parent-as-teacher role. The librarian serves as a facilitator of family learning, encouraging the parent to become involved in the child's earliest learning activities. Every Child Ready to Read is one such program.

Para los Niños, developed by the Houston Children's Museum and the Houston Public Library, is an outstanding model of family learning. Bilingual workshop leaders guide parents through literature-based units on topics such as play, nutrition, and literacy. Using common household materials, they offer the skills parents need to teach their children effectively (Children's Museum of Houston, 2010). In adapting the Houston program for its own use, the Brooklyn Public Library considered the needs of children with disabilities, and its program reflects that.

Facilitate Parent-to-Parent Support

Building community, though not a traditional role of the public library, has increasingly become part of children's services. Every Child Ready to Read recognizes this development. Incorporating parent services within the children's department allows the librarian the opportunity to assist in developing networks among parents. The library itself provides a common meeting ground for children and families. It is a place to meet other parents and talk. A library's parent/child workshop or storytime often stimulates the formation of local play groups or the initiation of new friendships. We have often seen this phenomenon at the inclusive Read and Play programs at the Brooklyn Public Library. Families adjourn to nearby parks or McDonald's to celebrate birthdays and regularly get together outside of the library.

Assisting in the development of babysitting cooperatives, playgroups, parent support groups, or parent-to-parent networks, especially for parents of children who have disabilities, is a natural extension of traditional children's services. Why not let parents use your meeting room? Create a community bulletin board that parent volunteers help maintain. Help families develop bibliographies on the day's discussion subject. Increase circulation with topical book displays on autism in April for Autism Awareness Month or heart health for February's Heart Health Awareness Month. And don't forget the books for children! Provide links to community blogs and wikis. The Brooklyn Public Library has partnered with a local sibling support network to maintain a wiki and support that community. Offer parenting workshops on needed topics. Parents of children with disabilities often feel that the medical and educational systems criticize them or at the very least fail to offer support (Snow, 2005: 59). Libraries can provide neutral support in a natural setting for all members of the family.

Build on Family Strengths and Recognize Cultural Diversity

The library's mission is to serve the entire community, respecting and celebrating the diversity it represents. The Library Bill of Rights states:

> I. Books and other library resources should be provided for the interest, information, and enlightenment of all people of the community the library serves. . . .
>
> V. A person's right to use a library should not be denied or abridged because of origin, ages, background, or views. (American Library Association, 1996)

Libraries pride themselves on being democratic institutions, encouraging use of the library by all individuals. This fundamental characteristic of public library service dovetails with family-centered principles.

This is particularly true as librarians work with families who exhibit a variety of special needs. As is true of all library patrons, the child with a disability and the family are recognized for their individual needs and differences, and appropriate service is provided accordingly. This tradition of public library service, where no one is denied access to the library's resources, fosters inclusion.

Cultural diversity is a complex issue, especially as it overlaps with disability issues. Language is often the first barrier. It is important to provide material and services in the language of the communities you work with. Hiring interpreters for workshops or using teachers or agency staff to interpret are options if you do not have staff with the languages you need. Written material should be proofread by native speakers. And remember, usage can vary from one country to another. The word *disability* can be translated into Spanish using at least three different words: in Mexico it is *incapacidade*, in Puerto Rico it is *invalidez*, and in New York's Spanglish it is *disabilidade*. Getting it right is important.

However, language competency is only the beginning. Cultural competency is a larger, and in some ways more important, issue. Perceptions of disability and what it means to have a disability change from culture to culture. For example, in Puerto Rico the values of *agunete*, or endurance and the centrality of the family, affect the expectations for the child with a disability. The emphasis may be less on getting services and pursuing independence than on creating a supportive family environment (Gannotti et al., 2001). Among the Hmong, epilepsy is "an illness of some distinction," and people with epilepsy often become shamans (Fadiman, 1997: 21). Cultural background can strongly influence how families perceive a disability and how they interact with service-providing agencies, the medial and educational systems, and librarians. We need to be sensitive to their reality and take it as our starting point. Keep in mind that "[f]amilies who find programs consistent with their personal needs and cultural values are more likely to follow through" (Batshaw, Pellegrino, and Roizen, 2007: 609).

Establish Links with Community Agencies That Serve Families and Children

By listening to and establishing relationships with families, the librarian is in a position to help parents find the local resources they need for themselves and their children. This information is not always easily available. Librarians need to build coalitions and networks with the larger community of family service providers and learn about what other services are available for families. It is only through this coordinated effort that librarians can give families the information they need, when they need it. Likewise, these relationships increase awareness about the library among service providers who will refer families to the library.

The librarian can be not only a key link between families and the resources that the professional community provides but also a critical partner in providing coordination and continuity for family support professionals. The librarian's skills in developing and organizing collections, accessing resources, and providing reference service enhance community networks. The library can serve as a central place for storing materials, sharing information, and providing meeting space.

Cultural competency comes into play here as well. While many of the traditional disability agencies have some Spanish-language capacity, Spanish-speaking families tend to be more comfortable with culturally competent agencies. These may be the multiservice agencies they are familiar with that also address disability issues rather than disability-specific agencies (World Institute on Disability, 2006). So it is important to reach out to these agencies as well.

School-Age Children and Teens: Growing Independence

The Elementary School Years

As children grow through the elementary school years, their families remains foremost in their lives. Parents and caregivers continue to accompany their children to the library but gradually may play less of a role in their library experience. Six-year-olds may have lists of suggested reading from school or strong ideas about books they want to read, including series, that may differ from their parents' ideas. Seven-year-olds have homework assignments. Eight-year-olds are preparing for state and national standardized tests, and they may start to come to the library in the care of older siblings or on their own. Children in the early elementary years have their own information needs, including information about disabilities. Now it is often the child's choice about whether to attend a program or even whether to go to the library. While some children with disabilities are unable to attend programs on their own, offering the opportunity is important and can serve as a bridge to independence.

It is often in these early elementary years that previously unrecognized academic issues come to the forefront, and subtle difference in the capabilities among children can become more obvious. Learning disabilities are traditionally not diagnosed until this age and frequently not until third grade. Children with intellectual disabilities are slower to learn to read and do math. The behavior of children on the autism spectrum can become relatively more bizarre. Some children with mild autism or Asperger's syndrome do not get diagnosed until now. Children with sensory disabilities such as blindness or deafness may also have academic and social issues resulting from late diagnosis or a limited independent exploration of the world.

Children without disabilities are relatively accepting of differences at this age, where they may have been oblivious at an earlier age. Braille or American Sign Language can be seen as cool secret codes. Children are intrigued by Assistive Technology, often seeing it as another aspect of game systems and cell phones, and can even be jealous of it. They are curious about disabilities and their peers. Their questions have progressed beyond the "does it hurt" stage, and they are open to honest explanations.

At this point, children still take their attitudinal cues from adults. If adults are open about differences, the children will respond in kind. If adults are defensive about them, children will learn that there is something wrong with having a disability. If adults ignore the question or punish the questioner, the children will get the message that the child with a disability is taboo and, if punished for asking questions, may become resentful of the other child. Any teasing by the adult, however playful, gives children permission to tease and bully the child with the disability. Remember, you set the tone and behavioral standards for your library.

Children with disabilities become more self-aware during the early elementary years. Their understanding of their strengths and weaknesses is improving and their need for information increasing.

Parents of children with disabilities will continue to need medical information. Some parents will be dealing with new diagnoses. School-age services now loom large and can be more complicated than previous special education services. The question of inclusion in general education programs with typically developing peers is more urgent. It is often at the kindergarten or first-grade level that students

Disability Self-Awareness

Preschool	Little or no knowledge of disability/difference
School-age	Increasing awareness of differences and challenges
Adolescence	Sometimes hyperawareness of differences; sometimes denial of differences

with a special education classification are tracked into "self-contained" or segregated settings. Helping the child with a disability negotiate social issues becomes both more important and more challenging. The support networks laid down previously continue to be significant.

Siblings of school-age children have their own issues. Depending on their ages, the differences between their brother or sister and other children are becoming more obvious. They need accurate information on their sibling's disability. Embarrassment, teasing, and bullying may come into play, especially if they attend the same school; they need information and support to help deal with these challenges.

Meeting these changing needs is imperative in order to keep children with disabilities and their families connected to the library. Building on the groundwork laid when the children were younger, we can continue to serve them. Family-centered practice is still important, but we must keep in mind that the needs of the individuals in the families may be diverging. Children are more independent at the library. Now is the time to ask them what they want. Later chapters will address materials issues and designing inclusive programs and services.

Upper elementary school sees these trends accelerate. In fourth and fifth grades, the transition from learning to read to reading to learn begins. Math becomes much more complex. Literature and social studies use new skills. For the first time understanding social dynamics is an academic requirement, part of the subject matter. Socially, there can be a tendency of students, often girls, to take care of the student with the disability. The child who is blind may be seen as cute. Pushing a child in a wheelchair can be a status symbol. By middle school, students often tire of this role. It can be a rude awakening for someone with a disability who is used to thinking of friends in this context.

The Middle School and High School Years

Middle school is a time of intense peer pressure to conform and a growing need for independence. The student with a pimple on her nose can be ostracized, let alone the one who cannot make eye contact or struggles with reading. The electronic recorder that was cool in elementary school may now be geeky and a cause for derision. A sign language interpreter may impede socialization. Secret codes have become weird. In some areas, gang issues may come to the forefront in middle school. Academics continue to be more challenging, and the gap between students with and without disabilities can grow.

Students with disabilities and their parents are beginning the transition process. What will the children be doing after high school? What skills do they need to develop in order to do that? How those skills can be developed in the school is reflected in the IEP. What transition and job training services are needed, if any? Youth at this age may want to become more involved in the IEP process or want no part of it whatsoever.

Dating and sexuality issues can be significant. Parents of children with disabilities can be slow to see their child's developing sexuality, particularly if the child has a developmental disability. The questions of sexual orientation and sexual health care may never even be considered by the youth's caregivers. Peers can also be unforgiving on these issues. Dealing with an unrequited crush is difficult for a typically developing youth. For one on the autism spectrum it can be completely incomprehensible.

The medical needs of the individuals with a disability are changing as their bodies change. Asthma may get better, get worse, or remain unchanged in adolescence. Hormonal changes can intensify behavioral issues. Some mental health issues first become apparent during this time. Teens can rebel against the medical regimens, such as blood sugar monitoring. Significant absences from school have a higher academic and social toll.

In the library, privacy and confidentiality come into play more. Young teens may want information on homosexuality or birth control or on careers that their parents are not considering for them. They may want more information on their disability or may distance themselves from it. Finding material on the individual's reading level that is age appropriate gets more difficult and more important. The library can support the teens' need for independence by offering the information that they need in a format that is accessible to them. Requiring teens to use their own library cards, regardless of their grasp of the finer points of the privilege, can support these needs. Providing volunteer opportunities for teens with and without disabilities is another way to support teens' need for autonomy.

Adolescence is often a trying time for parents as well. The child's emotional need for a more separate life may conflict with the parents' fears, both reasonable and unreasonable, about abilities and maturity. There is a dearth of information for parents on the development of teens with disabilities or their health care needs. One mother described standing in front of the parenting section of Barnes and Nobel with tears streaming down her face as she looked in vain for information on the possible effects of multiple surgeries on the parent–child relationship. When formal resources are not available, libraries that link parents with other parents in person or electronically can help meet these types of needs.

Of course the needs of brothers and sisters of an individual with a disability also change with adolescence. Now is the time they may begin to think about genetic, financial, and guardianship issues. Providing straightforward information in response to questions about these things is important but so is being able to link them to the many sibling networks that exist.

Using these basic guidelines, librarians can assess the programs they are currently offering for children and their families as well as initiate new services or programs. By weaving together basic library service with developmentally and educationally appropriate practice and family-centered principles, librarians will maximize the learning process and enhance the effectiveness of a child's experiences within the library setting.

Resources

Association for Library Service to Children and the Public Library Association. 2011. *Every Child Ready to Read @ your library.* 2nd ed. Developed by Susan B. Neuman and Donna Celano. Chicago: American Library Association. http://www.everychildreadytoread .org/.

Diamant-Cohen, Betsy. 2010. *Early Literacy Programming en Español: Mother Goose on the Loose Programs for Bilingual Learners.* New York: Neal Schuman.

Diamant-Cohen, Betsy, and Saroj Nadkarni Ghoting. 2010. *The Early Literacy Kit: A Handbook and Tip Cards.* Chicago: American Library Association.

Feinberg, Sandra, Kathleen Deerr, Barbara A. Jordan, Marcellina Byrne, and Lisa G. Kropp. 2008. *The Family-Centered Library Handbook.* New York: Neal Schuman.

Ghoting, Saroj Nadkarni, and Pamela Martin-Díaz. 2005. *Early Literacy Storytimes @ your library: Partnering with Caregivers for Success.* Chicago: American Library Association.

Jarombek, Kathy, and Anne Leon. 2010. "Leadership at Its Best: Library Managers Spearhead Successful Special Needs Programming." *Children and Libraries* 8, no. 2: 54–57.

Marino, Jane. 2007. *Babies in the Library!* Lanham, MD: Scarecrow Press.

Winson, Georgia, and Courtney Adams. 2010. "Collaboration at Its Best: Library and Autism Programs Combine to Serve Special Audience." *Children and Libraries* 8, no. 2: 15–17.

Wojahn, Rebecca Hougue. 2006. "Everyone's Invited: Ways to Make Your Library More Welcoming to Children with Special Needs." *School Library Journal* 52, no. 2: 46–48.

References

American Library Association. 1996. "Library Bill of Rights." Chicago: American Library Association. http://www.ala.org/ala/issuesadvocacy/intfreedom/librarybill/index.cfm.

Bailey, D., and R. Simeonsson. 1988. "Assessing Needs of Families with Handicapped Infants." *Journal of Special Education* 2, no. 1: 117–127.

Batshaw, Mark L., Louis Pellegrino, and Nancy J. Roizen. 2007. *Children with Disabilities.* 6th ed. Baltimore: Paul H. Brookes.

Bauman, Margaret. 1999. "Bauman Discusses the Neurobiology of Autism." *Advocate* 35, no 2: 15–17.

Children's Museum of Houston. 2010. "Para los Niños." Children's Museum of Houston. http://www.cmhouston.org/losninos/.

Cohen B. P., and L. S. Simkin. 1994. *Library-Based Parent Resource Centers: A Guide to Implementing Programs.* Albany: New York State Developmental Disabilities Planning Council and New York Library Association.

Fadiman, Anne. 1997. *The Spirit Catches You and You Fall Down: A Hmong Child, Her American Doctors, and the Collision of Two Cultures.* New York: Farrar, Strauss and Giroux.

Gallagher, Peggy A., Thomas H. Powell, and Cheryl A. Rhodes. 2006. *Brothers and Sisters: A Special Part of Exceptional Families.* 3rd ed. Baltimore: Paul H. Brookes.

Gannotti, Mary E., W. Penn Handwerker, Nora Ellen Groce, and Cynthia Cruz. 2001. "Sociocultural Influences on Disability Status in Puerto Rican Children." *Physical Therapy* 81, no. 9: 1512–1523.

Gestwicki, Carol. 1995. *Developmentally Appropriate Practice: Curriculum and Development in Early Education.* Albany, NY: Delmar.

Kumin, Libby. 1998. "Literacy and Language." *Down Syndrome News* 21, no. 10: 132–133.

Meyers, Elaine, and Harriet Henderson. 2011. "Overview of Every Child Ready to Read @ your library®, 1st Edition." American

Library Association. http://www.everychildreadytoread.org/project-history%09/overview-every-child-ready-read-your-library%C2%AE-1st-edition.

Myers, David G. 2004. *Psychology*. 7th ed. Hopeland, MI: Worth Publishers.

Porter, Ann, and Sisira Edirippulige. 2007. "Parents of Deaf Children Seeking Hearing Loss-Related Information on the Internet: The Australian Experience." *Journal of Deaf Studies and Deaf Education* 12, no. 2: 518–529.

Snow, Kathie. 2001. *Disability Is Natural: Revolutionary Common Sense for Raising Successful Children with Disabilities*. 1st ed. Woodland Park, CO: Braveheart Press.

Snow, Kathie. 2005. *Disability Is Natural: Revolutionary Common Sense for Raising Successful Children with Disabilities*. 2nd ed. Woodland Park, CO: Braveheart Press.

Wood, Chip. 2007. *Yardsticks: Children in the Classroom Ages 4–14*. 3rd ed. Turners Falls, MA: Northeast Foundation for Children.

World Institute on Disability. 2006. "Latinos with Disabilities in the United States: Understanding and Addressing Barriers to Employment." Proyecto Visión. http://www.proyectovision.net/documents/pvreport.pdf.

Resource-Based Practice and Inclusion

4

Library service is about building relationships and listening.
—*Pilar Martinez, Executive Director, Public Services, Public Services Department, Edmonton Public Library*

How do individuals react when they encounter a serious personal problem? To whom do they turn for support? A significant other or best friend? The immediate family? Their religious leader, coworkers, bowling partners, or neighbors? Chances are they would seek support and help from one of these trusted and familiar "community" members before going to a mental health or medical professional. Families of children with disabilities feel similarly. Unfortunately, families of children with disabilities often do not receive the support they need from these informal community sources. Why not?

Why Community Support Is Lacking

When families of children with disabilities do not receive community support it is not because it is impossible to provide this support. The two main reasons that such support is not forthcoming are that the community has become accustomed to leaving the care of children with disabilities to institutions or other professionals and, furthermore, that community members are simply not used to interacting with these children and are anxious about their own behaviors. However, these conditions need not persist and have been slowly changing.

Reliance on Professional Help

Traditionally, children with disabilities have been institutionalized, cared for by multiple professionals, or educated in special, self-contained classes and schools, segregated from their peers without disabilities. This has often led to isolation and a lack of connection to the informal support networks that exist within all communities.

These families need the technical and therapeutic advice and support of specialists on how to position a child, elicit language, develop cognitive skills, and facilitate gross motor development, but just because such professionals are "experts" does not necessarily mean they are supportive. There is often a clinical distance between education and medical professionals and their clients. Too often the relationship can feel clinical or tinged with condescension. Parents and librarians meet as equals in a warm environment. Just like any other family, families of children with disabilities sometimes need a good listener, another parent who is willing to share practical ideas, or a friendly neighbor who will invite a child to a birthday party. These networks remain important as a child grows. For example, one librarian got her first job because her next door neighbor's cousin needed someone to help in her frozen yogurt shop. An informal community support network, so necessary to a family's sense of being included, may not fit easily into the lives filled with a complex web of appointments, therapies, and treatments.

Need to Educate the Public

In some instances, community members shy away from giving help and support out of an anxiety of not knowing what to do or how to behave toward the child with a disability. Although antidiscrimination laws such as the ADA have broken through legal barriers, social situations are often difficult and awkward for those individuals who have had few encounters with people with disabilities. The generation that has grown up since the passage of the Americans with Disabilities Act in 1990 is the first to grow up with the expectation of people with disabilities living and working in the community. So there are few good role models.

More and more children with significant disabilities are surviving birth because of medical and technological advances. Community members, unaccustomed to seeing children with oxygen machines, tracheotomies, or communication devices may be uncomfortable and fearful of what is unfamiliar. Prior to 1990, many people never had the opportunity to interact with a person with a disability in a meaningful way. Immigrants often come from countries where there are few services for people with disabilities and isolation is the norm.

Fear and ignorance frequently lead to stereotypes about children with disabilities. Children who have physical disabilities are often assumed to have a cognitive disability as well. Sometimes people talk loudly to those who are blind or have low vision, and some view a child in a wheelchair as someone who will never live an independent life. Librarians frequently refer Deaf patrons to the National Library Service for the Blind. Stereotypes and ignorance about disabilities can often be eliminated or even avoided in the first place through experience, open communication, increased contact, and a broader knowledge base.

By embracing inclusive practices, the library can be an effective agent in reducing fear and prejudice toward children with disabilities. It can create a comfortable environment for families to get together. Familiarity leads to comfort and trust. Trust is necessary to build friendship and support.

Defining Resource-Based Practice and Inclusion

When a child is diagnosed with a disability, sometimes after a long period of the parent feeling that something was "not right," the family is often thrust into a complex, service-based system. The child accesses professionally delivered services at a special school, in a special class, or at a clinic that isolated him or her from typically developing peers and the network of informal community supporters. This system is expensive to maintain and unnatural.

Developed within the past 20 years, "resource-based practice" is an approach to service delivery that focuses on the identification and utilization of all resources with the community. In this model, a resource is defined as "the full range of possible types of community help or assistance—potentially useful information, experiences, opportunities, etc.—that might be mobilized and used to meet the needs of an individual or group. Resources are a means to accomplishing a desired outcome including, but not limited to, different kinds of community learning opportunities for enhancing and promoting child and family competence" (Trivette, Dunst, and Deal, 1996: 7). This approach to providing services is an opportunity for libraries.

Consider that all children and families belong to multiple communities. These communities—which include extended families, neighborhoods, places of worship, workplaces, child care settings, schools, libraries, sports leagues, scouting organization, and others—have the potential to provide support. The goal of resource-based practice is to increase utilization of these community resources, rather than just professionally provided services, as a way to enhance and support child, parent, and family functioning. Research has demonstrated that parents of children with disabilities, exposed to a resource-based approach, feel that their children achieve greater gains and that they themselves have more control over service provisions (Trivette, Dunst, and Deal, 1996: 15). In addition, resource-based practice allows for the needs of all family members to be met, not just the child with the disability but his parents and siblings as well.

Inclusion is both a prerequisite and a logical corollary of resource-based practice. It starts from the premise that people with disabilities are just as much a part of society as people without disabilities. If we look at disabilities as a part of the natural spectrum of the human condition, then the problem is less with the individual and more with the society that creates barriers to that individual's participation. Before modern building techniques existed, buildings were shorter, even sometimes all on one floor. In a community of single-floor buildings, not being able to walk is not necessarily a handicap. In a classroom filled with Braille and auditory cues, being blind is not a hindrance. It is only when we create an environment that relies on a single sense or a single way of getting around that someone with a disability is handicapped. "When we shift the paradigm and see that the 'problem' of disability resides in the environment and not the child, we can easily move in a different direction" (Snow, 2000: 215).

How the Library "Fits In"

A public library is one of the community's greatest assets. Librarians can provide families with a valuable source of information and support by using their information retrieval, technological, programmatic, and referral skills. For families of children with special needs, this support does not depend on the child meeting eligibility criteria, often deficit based or income limited and therefore stigmatizing. The library's capacity to provide access to information and an array of programs and resources for children, youth, and their families, in a natural community environment, makes it particularly applicable within the resource-based model.

The Library as a Community Place

Many libraries offer services that provide informal support for families of children with disabilities. Parents have access to valuable information and an opportunity to gain emotional and social support from their peers. Inclusive library programs offer a child with a disability the chance to learn from and play with children who are developing typically. Many libraries have created minienvironments with toys and learning materials that are aimed at young children. These areas are especially welcoming to young children. Programs for teens provide a natural environment for interaction, socializing, and job experience. Resources and programs for siblings of children with disabilities can create a safe place for them to explore their own issues and even meet other children who have siblings with disabilities. Or the library can provide an escape for siblings. The library can be especially helpful for families looking for a familiar community environment in which to interact with other children.

As a community place, the library also offers a variety of opportunities for service providers. Proactive marketing can encourage providers of Early Intervention (EI) and special education services to utilize the library's resources. The following strategies are just a few of the many ways in which providers can use the library to integrate children with disabilities within the community:

- Use the library as an alternative site for the provision of services.
- Bring a child with a disability to a library program.
- Visit the library with the family members and help them access the resources.
- Ensure that the children have library cards.
- Serve as a resource to the library staff so they can more effectively serve children with disabilities in their settings.
- Invite librarians to make presentations on library resources, summer reading, and literacy at parent meetings.

Serving Children and Youth with Disabilities around the Country

- Accessibility Arcade at the District of Columbia Public Library: http://dclibrary.org/node/32538
- The Child's Place for Children with Special Needs at the Brooklyn Public Library: http://www.bklynpubliclibrary.org/only-bpl/childs-place
- The Ferguson Library Special Needs Center: http://www.fergusonlibrary.org/kids/special-needs/about
- Libraries and Autism: We're Connected: http://www.librariesandautism.org/

- Invite librarians to in-service staff trainings to talk about library resources.
- Assist in designing a barrier-free setting.

A speech pathologist regularly brought her school-age client to an inclusive after-school program at the Brooklyn Public Library to provide speech therapy in a natural environment. Over the course of two years he got to know the other children and eventually became a volunteer. A librarian there conducts workshops for parents on literacy and children with disabilities at several schools in Brooklyn on an annual basis. At each workshop she finds one or two or three parents who have never had a library card and registers them.

The library can work with other child service providers as well. It can be a neutral place for child welfare officials to offer mandated parent training. Or a local medical center can conduct outreach on community health concerns, such as immunizations, the genetics of sickle cell disease, or diabetes management for children.

The Librarian as a Community Resource Person

Resource-based practice provides librarians with a wonderful opportunity to exhibit their professional skills. Traditional library roles are exactly what are needed for providing community services: information and referral specialist, program developer, special collections manager, coalition builder and networker, and educator and advocate for parenting services and for children.

Information and Referral Specialist

One of the key elements of the resource-based approach is the identification of community services, a natural fit for the information role of the public librarian. Skilled at locating resources within the community through access to collections, community databases, interlibrary loan, and the Internet, librarians can empower parents to use the area's resources and not just professionally based services.

As the survival of children with profound disabilities increases, more parents are in need of often hard-to-locate information and resources. A family of a child with a disability may need resources in areas of medicine, EI and special education services, public and private education, entitlement programs, Assistive Technology, inclusive child care, respite care, sibling support, insurance, custom-made vehicles, lifelong planning, living wills, trust funds, and advocacy training and services. Identifying these resources can be exhausting and may fall at the bottom of a long list of necessary caregiving tasks for parents. As information specialists, we can assist parents by helping them locate much-needed sources of reliable information and assistance.

Identifying these supports will not be a once-only task. Because the library is one of the most stable organizations within the community, librarians should anticipate that the family may turn to them for support throughout the child's entire life. The librarian, in her role as information and referral specialist, may be called on repeatedly by parents as their child grows and new experiences require different information and strategies. The value of this kind of support cannot be overemphasized. As one parent put it after finding a book on wheelchair repair, "You saved me again! Thank you."

Program Developer

Including families and children with disabilities in library service requires designing appropriate programs. Successful designs require planning and collaboration with parents and other family support agencies. These plans must respect and incorporate the needs of library patrons and potential patrons without disabilities while encouraging the inclusion of patrons with disabilities. Librarians, who already appreciate the complexities involved in delivering programs to the community at large, must take the lead in designing programs to meet the needs of children and youth with disabilities and their families. The principles of Multiple Intelligences and Universal Design can guide librarians in the development of successful, inclusive programs. Chapter 5 elucidates these principles.

Special Collections Developer

To better serve families of children and youth with special needs, librarians should consider developing exceptional parenting collections. Parent Resource Centers, journals and magazines, materials in alternate formats, adaptive toy lending collections, information kits, electronic resources, and Assistive Technology are just some of the collection possibilities. Chapters 10 through 12 provide specific guidelines on how to develop special collections for this audience.

Coalition Builder and Networker

Building coalitions among agencies and organizations is a critical role for librarians and key to impacting the lives of library patrons with disabilities and their families. In *Serving Families and Children through Partnerships* (Feinberg and Feldman, 1996: 13–14), the authors emphasize that

> through the development of coalitions and networks, librarians can expand their horizons, become more-informed professionals, and be alerted to trends in youth services, early childhood, and parent educations. They can integrate the library's youth and parenting services with the greater community of services and increase the library's potential for reaching families. In addition to what the librarians will gain, parents and professionals will learn
>
> - to recognize the library's ability to organize and disseminate information to the community;
> - to understand the role of the library in providing free access to information;
> - to look toward the library as a primary community center serving families and young children;
> - to place the library and children's librarian in a leadership role in advocating for youth and family services; and
> - to appreciate the library's role in sharing community resources . . . and beginning the lifelong learning process.

Building coalitions and partnerships is essential for librarians who wish to effectively implement inclusionary practices within their libraries. Chapters 6, 8, and 9 discuss ways to develop collaborative services, including resources to improve networking skills.

Educator and Advocate for Parenting Services

Recent trends in children's librarianship have acknowledged the role of parents and our role in supporting them. National initiatives such as the ALSC/PLA program Every Child Ready to Read emphasize that librarians can be most effective when they work with parents to support children's learning. "Because of our intermittent contact with each child, we have limited direct impact. However, by teaching parents and caregivers about early literacy skill and ways to incorporate them in their daily lives, we make a difference in the child's development by supporting the parent/caregiver" (Ghoting and Martinez-Díaz, 2006: ix).

Resource-based practice has opened up a window of opportunity for libraries and librarians. Establishing the library as a main player in providing services and a natural environment for young children, including those with disabilities, and their parents will ensure long-term survival as community centers that are truly responsive to the needs of all segments of its community.

Resources

Prendergast, Tess. 2011. "Beyond Storytime: Children's Librarians Collaborating in Communities." *Children and Libraries* 9, no. 1: 20–26, 40.

Wemett, Lisa. 2007. "The Building Bridges Project." *Children and Libraries* 5, no. 3: 15–20.

Working Together Project. 2008. *Community-Led Libraries Toolkit*. Vancouver: Libraries in Communities. http://www .librariesincommunities.ca/resources/Community-Led_Libraries _Toolkit.pdf.

References

Feinberg, Sandra, and Sari Feldman. 1996. *Serving Children and Families through Partnerships*. New York: Neal-Schuman.

Ghoting, Saroj Nadkarni, and Pamela Martinez-Díaz. 2006. *Early Literacy Storytimes @ your library: Partnering with Caregivers for Success*. Chicago: American Library Association.

Snow, Kathie. 2000. *Disability Is Natural: Creating New Lives for Children and Their Families!* Woodland Park, CO: Braveheart Press.

Trivette, Carol M., Carl J. Dunst, and Angela G. Deal. 1996. "Resource-Based Early Intervention Practices." In *The Contexts of Early Intervention: Systems and Settings*, edited by S. K. Thurman, J. R. Cornwell, and S. R. Gottwald. Baltimore: Paul H. Brookes.

Multiple Intelligences and Universal Design

5

[A]ll avenues to learning need to be open and available. Whether through drawing, writing, or performance, a person can eventually be lead by his own growing enthusiasm to science, mathematics, history, or whatever it is he might need to know. My career is the proof.

—*David Macaulay (2008: 10)*

Providing programs is an important part of what children's librarians do. Librarians connect children to stories, guide parents and caregivers to literacy activities, and entice families to come to the library. When she was a child, one librarian sat outside the storyhour room in the library and watched the other children enjoying the stories the librarian was reading. It was very clear to her that she should be outside and could not go in because all the children were there with their mothers, and she had only a father. Just in case she did not get the message, the program was called "Mother and Child Storyhour." When children are not comfortable in a program or cannot participate, it sends the message they are not welcome in the library. So, programs need to be clearly accessible to all from the beginning. Scrambling to change the craft project so the unexpected child who is blind can participate stigmatizes the child. Having a craft project that does not rely entirely on vision already set up sends a completely different, welcoming message.

Designing programs and services to be accessible to all requires thinking about how people learn and how people use things. Multiple Intelligences theory allows that there are many ways to learn. Universal Design suggests that in designing to make something accessible to one group, we make it easier for many groups. Both principles are necessary to accomplish the full inclusion and participation of children with disabilities and their families.

Multiple Intelligences Theory

What Is Multiple Intelligences Theory?

Multiple Intelligences theory holds that "we each have eight or more intelligences and we can use them to carry out all kinds of tasks" (Gardner, 2006: 26). Intelligence itself is a "biopsychological construct" (Gardner, 2006: 32) that has eight criteria; it:

- is brain based and has potential for isolation by brain damage;
- has a set of core operations or an information processing system;
- has stages of growth and can improve with teaching;
- has evolved over the course of human history;
- can be tested;
- is supported by research in psychology and cognitive science;
- can be encoded in a symbol system; and
- can be observed in isolated forms such as in prodigies. (Gardner, 2004: 63–66)

Intelligences operate together, and individuals may be stronger in one or another. Each intelligence also has the capacity for genius, as well as deficits. Finally, intelligence is in many ways only a potential. People must be given the opportunity to develop the multiple intelligences or they will be lost.

What Are the Eight Intelligences?

Howard Gardner posited the eight basic intelligences. The two intelligences we are most familiar with are linguistic and logical/mathematical. These are the ones that our schools emphasize and in which our children are tested every year. Being strong in either or both of these two areas is considered in our society as being smart. Linguistic intelligence refers to the reception of, processing of, and expression of ideas most comfortably through the use of language. Facility with words and being able to solve word problems more easily than a standard equation are traits of strength in linguistic intelligence. Logical/mathematical intelligence relies more on observation, analysis, and deduction. Scientific thinking is a subset of the logical/mathematical intelligence. Strong logical/mathematical thinkers conceive of things through cause and effect and relationships. A child who is strong in this area may arrive at the solution to a mathematical problem easily but have a difficult time using words to explain how she got there. Patterns, quantitative data, empirical relationships, and logical connections are all more important than words. The linguistic and the logical/mathematical intelligences are the primary foundation for what we traditionally think of as IQ.

Musical and spatial intelligences are both traditionally associated with the arts, and most people have some familiarity with them. However, here the concepts refer to the broader way of understanding. People with strong musical intelligence understand the world most easily through rhythm, timber, tone, and pitch. They may perceive patterns as harmony or disharmony. One librarian first understood the ability of music to tell a story when she listened to Burl Ives narrate "Peter and the Wolf" as a child. For someone with a strong musical intelligence, that connection would have been intuitive. Spatial intelligence involves a deep understanding of the relation of bodies in space and is sometimes described as "thinking visually." It is more than visual arts, although that is part of it. Spatial intelligence can also be used to communicate. One high school student choreographed the battle of Pearl Harbor for his senior year project, and there was no doubt as to the story behind the dance. Strong spatial thinking is also required for navigation, architecture, leading troops in battle, the games of Go and chess, engineering, and many other fields where relative physical positions are important.

Interpersonal and intrapersonal intelligences are generally less well understood. Interpersonal intelligence refers to a sensitivity to the uniqueness of individuals and their connections with each other. The social world is paramount in interpersonal intelligence. Strong interpersonal learners will learn best through discussion, perhaps in a study group. One librarian had a three-and-a-half-year-old daughter, Sally, who had a friend, James, who was just three years old. James was constantly aware of Sally's needs, waiting for her to catch up if she was lagging behind and sharing his food and toys without prompting. When he was four and she was five, the librarian and her family moved and did not see James again for many years. Eleven years later, the librarian was sitting on a bus when she heard someone say, "Look, there's Sally's mom, Mrs. B." The librarian turned and saw James. At the puzzled look of his companion, James went on to explain that they had lived across the hall from Sally and her mother. Sally took the school bus to preschool and liked to read *Mike Mulligan and His Steam Shovel* and eat cucumbers. Clearly James lives in the social world.

Intrapersonal intelligence is in many ways complementary to interpersonal intelligence. The in-depth understanding of the inner lives of others that someone with a strong interpersonal intelligence has is applied to oneself in someone with a dominant intrapersonal intelligence. He has as strong and accurate a sense of himself as James has of others. It is through this understanding that he navigates the world. A method actor who draws on his own emotions to portray those of a character is one example of the manifestation of this intelligence. That psychiatrists and psychologists must themselves undergo therapy is an application of intrapersonal intelligence.

Bodily/kinesthetic intelligence draws on both the vestibular (sense of balance) and proprioceptive (sense of movement and spacial orientation) senses and involves a keen awareness of one's body in space and how to coordinate and move it. A kinesthetic learner thinks with her body. From this understanding comes the ability to solve problems with one's body. Soldiers, dancers, video-game designers, athletes, and surgeons all rely on this intelligence.

The last intelligence Gardner identified was natural intelligence. People with a strong natural intelligence understand the world most easily, communicate most efficiently, and solve problems using the tools of nature. A person for whom ratios are a mystery may easily and intuitively comprehend that if he has ten seeds, only three will germinate and only one of the three that germinate will survive to bear fruit.

Table 5.1 summarizes the various intelligences. It is important to remember that the intelligences work in concert. Any given task or profession may require us to draw on more than one intelligence.

People may be stronger in one than another, but they can use any of the intelligences to learn about a given subject. As noted at the beginning of the chapter, David Macaulay's experience exemplifies that different points of access can lead to the same result. Gardner himself suggests:

TABLE 5.1 Multiple Intelligences

Intelligence	Characteristics	Associated Activities/Fields
Linguistic	Words	Reading Oral storytelling Writing
Logical/mathematical	Numbers Patterns	Physics Puzzles Computer programming Cryptography
Spatial	Aesthetic Spatial relations	Visual arts Chess Architecture Mechanics
Bodily/kinesthetic	Movement Body smarts	Dancing Athletics Ironwork Physical therapy
Musical	Music Rhythm Cadence	Drumming Composing
Intrapersonal	Feelings Self-smarts	Running Meditation Acting
Interpersonal	Relationships People smarts	Team sports Diplomacy Teaching Interpreting
Natural	Nature	Animal husbandry Gardening Medicine Biology

We might think of the topics as a room with at least 7 doorways. Students vary as to which entry point is most appropriate for them and which routes are most comfortable to follow once they have gained initial access to the room. (Gardner, 2006: 149)

As librarians we need to keep this in mind: the more doors and pathways we provide, the more children we will reach.

Librarians have another important role to play with regard to multiple intelligences. Linguistic and logical/mathematical intelligences are the ones we know best and that society values the most. These are the ones the schools test for each year starting in third grade. Musical intelligence and interpersonal intelligence are also well known and understood. Spatial intelligence combines an understanding of the physical world and an aesthetic sense. These three are less valued by society and often the first to be cut from school curriculums. Bodily/kinesthetic intelligence gets lip service, but with gym classes of over 30 students and recess an endangered species, it cannot be said to be really valued. Finally, natural and intrapersonal intelligences struggle to find a place in our schools. Children whose strength lies in areas outside of logical/mathematical and linguistic intelligences experience less success in school. We can give these children a chance to shine at the library.

Universal Design

Universal Design is a concept borrowed from architecture. It suggests that when something is designed to work well for one person it will also work well for another. Curb cuts are a good example of the concept. They were designed to give people who use wheelchairs access to sidewalks, and they are very successful in that. However, they are more often used by adults pushing children in strollers or shopping carts. In the library world we see an analogous phenomenon with audiobooks. Once the sole preserve of the National Library Service for the Blind and Physically Handicapped for use by people who were blind, audiobooks are now found in most libraries and often listened to by people traveling in cars.

Multiple Intelligences theory and Universal Design are combined in the concept of "Universal Design for Learning." The precepts are simple: multiple means of representation, engagement, expression, and assessment. The first three are more important to librarians. By providing children with more than one way to interact with the material, we allow more children to become engaged and provide them with a comfortable point of access. Providing students with websites, books, and the battlefield sketches of Thomas Nash represents information on the Civil War in multiple ways. Adding a discussion after a lecture gives another point of access. Multiple means of engagement means using their strengths and interests to make a connection between them and the material. Demonstrating math concepts with sports models for an avid fan is one example of this. Allowing students to demonstrate their knowledge through drama, music, and sculpture as well as words supports multiple means of representation. Adding portfolio-based assessment, where examples of a student's work are compiled and examined, to standard tests expands the means of assessment.

Designing Accessible Library Programs

So, what does Universal Design for Learning look like in a library program? Table 5.2 describes a program with a farm theme. In this program we are engaging all of the intelligences and using many forms of expression and representation. Several of the activities, such as using clay to model bread and the Chicken Dance, draw on more than one intelligence. In other words, we provide children with a choice of routes to the farm.

In addition, we are reaching out to children with a variety of abilities. By using books at different levels of complexity, we engage children on a variety of grade and cognitive levels. There are activities for children who are blind, children who are deaf, and children who are neither. The movement in the Chicken Dance may appeal to children who have a difficult time sitting still. But it is general enough to be adaptable to any child's physical abilities. The dance can be done sitting or standing.

The difference between poor design and Universal Design is often a simple thing. It would have been easy to call the program mentioned at the beginning of the chapter "Adult and Child Storytime," opening it up to children with one parent, orphans, foster children, and children being raised by grandparents or two fathers. When we use Multiple Intelligences and Universal Design to create our programs, design our physical spaces, and select our materials, we have the opportunity to reach all the children in our communities.

Resources

Blue, Elfreda V., and Darra Pace. 2011. "UD and UDL: Paving the Way toward Inclusion and Independence in the School Library." *Knowledge Quest* 39, no. 3: 48–55.

TABLE 5.2 Farm Program

Intelligence	Activity	Content
Linguistic	Reading	Pinkney, *Little Red Hen*
		Morris, *Bread, Bread, Bread*
Logical/mathematical	Finding patterns	Three responses to each question
	Sequencing	Deconstruct steps of making bread
	Discussion	Ratios: How many seeds become plants?
Spatial	Looking at pictures	Pinkney, *Little Red Hen*
	Arts and crafts	Morris, *Bread, Bread, Bread*
	Exploring	Make clay bread
		Chicken toy
Bodily/kinesthetic	Dancing	Chicken Dance
	Miming	Knead bread; sniff baking aromas
	Touching	Feel wheat, flour, and bread
	Exploring	Chicken toy
	Planting	Wheat berries
Musical	Dancing	Chicken Dance
	Call and response	Structured around animal responses to questions
Intrapersonal	Reflections	Feelings about growing, farms, bread
	Diary writing	Garden or personal diaries
Interpersonal	Discussion	Experiences with farms, growing, or food
		How things grow
Natural	Touching	Feel wheat, flour, and bread
	Watching	Videos of chickens
	Discussion	How things grow
	Planting	Wheat berries

Brown, Ann, and Molly Meyers. 2008. "Bringing in the Boys: Using the Theory of Multiple Intelligences to Plan Programs That Appeal to Boys." *Children and Libraries* 6, no. 1: 4–9.

CAST: Universal Design for Learning. 2011. "About UDL: What Is Universal Design for Learning?" CAST: Universal Design for Learning. http://www.cast.org/udl/index.html.

Rupp, Rebecca. 2009. "What's the Big Idea? Science and Math at the Library for Preschoolers and Kindergarteners." *Children and Libraries* 7, no. 3: 27–31.

Schiller, Pam, and Pat Phipps. 2006. *Starting with Stories: Engaging Multiple Intelligences through Children's Books.* Illustrations by Kathy Ferrell and Debi Johnson. Beltsville, MD: Gryphon House.

Williams, R. Bruce. 2002. *Multiple Intelligences for Differentiated Learning.* Thousand Oaks, CA: Corwin Press.

References

Gardner, Howard. 2004. *Frames of Mind: The Theory of Multiple Intelligences.* New York: Basic Books.

———. 2006. *Multiple Intelligences: New Horizons.* New York: Basic Books.

Macaulay, David. 2008. "Thirteen Studios: 2008 May Hill Arbuthnot Honor Lecture." *Children and Libraries* 6, no. 3: 9–15.

PART 2
Getting Your Library Ready

Assessing Your Staff and Library

They referred another Deaf patron to me today.

—*Librarian in Charge of a Regional Braille and Talking Book Library*

Assessing staff attitudes and competencies, understanding the characteristics and needs of children with disabilities and their families as a patron group, and training staff are some of the initial steps to consider before embarking on service development. Creating a welcoming place is the goal of inclusionary practices when examining library readiness. A ramp, multiple formats, Assistive Technology, and the proper nomenclature are not enough. Library staff generally understand that modifying the physical environment to accommodate people who use wheelchairs, adapting a program to include all children, or adding screen reading software to a computer makes libraries more accessible. What we struggle to understand is that staff attitudes and competencies are more important and set the framework for an inclusive, and truly welcoming, library.

People with disabilities often cite insufficient staff training, awareness, and sensitivity rather than costly architectural modifications or expensive equipment and services as key issues when addressing barriers to inclusion. A library can have the best written policies, Assistive Technologies, resources, and collections, but unless the staff have a genuine understanding of and commitment to inclusion, children with disabilities and their families will not feel welcomed. Achieving this level of understanding and commitment is a process that involves the reexamination of the attitudes, comfort levels, expectations, and skills of all library employees, not just those providing direct service to children.

Staff Attitude

Traditionally, children's staff strive to provide a nonthreatening, nonjudgmental atmosphere within the library, offering a wide range of services specially designed for children. A child's smiling, inquisitive face is like a magnet that brings out the librarian's best qualities—warmth, solicitude, and nurturing. A cute, pleasant child can bring out the best in all of us.

When a child has a disability, however, the initial response may not be so positive. While most library staff support the concept of including children with special needs in theory, when faced with the reality, they often have mixed feelings. Each library employee brings his or her own life experiences, skills, and comfort levels to the workplace. For inclusion to work, librarians need to acknowledge personal attitudes, feelings, and experiences and the reactions they may engender in response to a child with a disability and his family. Library readiness for inclusion begins with honest personal assessment.

Different disabilities often generate different responses. Working with children who have a visible disability is probably the least anxiety-provoking for staff. They recognize immediately that a disability exists. The presence of physical clues helps the librarian and other staff assess the situation and anticipate the patron's needs. When a library is able to meet those needs, the comfort level is high for both the library staff and the patron. For example, if a child is blind, the librarian may suggest a talking, Braille, tactile, or twin vision book or introduce the child to a listening station. The parent may be directed to a variety of books and local resources that focus on parenting a child who is blind. This situation is ideal and a positive one all around.

A child who looks different may evoke a different reaction. For example, people are often reluctant to look at a child with extensive burn scaring, either because it makes them uncomfortable or because they are afraid of being accused of "staring." They may avoid the family altogether or deal only with the parent, not acknowledging the child. The response to a child with a speech impairment is often similar. This avoidance response limits the child's ability to interact with her environment and relegates her to the status of a nonentity.

Common Negative Attitudes toward People with Disabilities

- **Fear:** Fears of contagion and of being made sad by seeing a disability are common. Fear can also be the result of the equation of disability and amorality, as in the physical must be an outward manifestation of an inner deficit.

- **Sympathy:** Sympathy is an expression of pity and requires objectifying the person. It is distinct from empathy.

- **Avoidance:** Avoiding people with disabilities results from feeling uncomfortable around them.

- **Repulsion:** Repulsion, a reaction to an unwanted interaction, is often tied to fear, avoidance, and lack of understanding.

- **Overprotection:** Protecting people with disabilities from the world ill prepares them to live in it independently.

- **Tolerance in absentia:** Again, this view requires the objectification of people with disabilities and creating a separate category for them. This attitude, once common, is antithetical to inclusion.

(Adapted from Walling and Karrenbrock, 1993, pp. 4-5.)

Alternatively, staff may be overly sympathetic or have an overprotective attitude. This reaction also prevents the child from using the library in a natural way. Either strategy on the part of library staff can make communication with the individual and the family awkward and strained. These interactions will produce frustration for all parties.

Children who look different often encounter another reaction, too: the assumption that they have functional limitations. A child whose large head may indicate hydrocephalus or "water on the brain" is assumed to have an intellectual disability. Likewise a child with wide-set eyes and a cleft lip is taken for someone with Down syndrome. These assumptions, like many of the other assumptions we make, lead to poor customer service and negative feelings all around.

Children whose disability is invisible face different issues. They may include children who have a learning disability such as dyslexia, low vision, or a heart or other medical condition that limits exertion such as climbing stairs. In these cases, library staff may fail to consider the possibility that the child is anything but typically developing. When children behave unexpectedly, in a manner other than would normally be anticipated for their age, they and their parents may be judged and blamed. Staff may feel angry, resentful, and apprehensive about having the child visit the library.

The assumption that a child or a teen is typically developing, that is to say does not have a disability, can lead to misunderstandings and negative experiences for everyone involved. Early in the career of a branch librarian, an eight-year-old boy entered her library asking for a book for school. She showed him all the "third grade boy books"; he did not want any of them. She showed all the "third grade girl books"; he did not want any of them. They were both starting to get frustrated when he said to the librarian, "It's not your fault. I have learning disabilities and I'm stupid." When she replied, "Well, I have learning disabilities too and I'm not stupid, just dense sometimes," they both relaxed and were able to find several books for him. An hour later, five minutes before closing, he returned to the library with his mother in tow pointing at the librarian while averring, "Her, she's the one. She has learning disabilities and she's not stupid." Although the librarian was able to turn the situation around, her initial assumption that the child was typically developing was a mistake that caused needless anxiety.

With a child who has an apparent mental illness or emotional disability, expectations for behavior and cognitive ability are often ambivalent. If speech is too loud and/or difficult to understand or behavior is viewed as disturbing to other children, the librarians may feel uncertain about how to approach the parent and determine the needs of the child and family. There may be a tendency to interact only with the parent, avoiding direct contact with the child, or make the interaction as brief as possible, sending the family on its way before anything "unpleasant" happens. In these situations, the staff's feelings of inadequacy, helplessness, and lack of control will often be conveyed and are not conducive to promoting inclusion.

Personal attitude assessments can be a valuable tool in establishing a baseline for inclusion at your library and changing attitudes. Before a change in attitude can occur, the staff need to honestly assess their individual attitudes regarding disabilities and the library's role in the inclusion process. The Personal Attitude Checklist (Figure 6.1) and the corresponding Response to Staff Issues and Concerns section in Chapter 7 can serve as catalysts for the exploration of feelings and attitudes and guide staff to an understanding and awareness of their own biases, the ones that many of us share.

Involving the entire staff in this process is key to making it an effective one. Security personnel who believe that children with autism spectrum disorder are just bad and custodial staff who blame a child for a toileting accident beyond his control will negatively affect your ability to fully include children with disabilities. Likewise, the attitudes of administrators, managers and directors, policy makers, and financial planners are essential to making inclusion work.

Competencies

In *Competencies for Librarians Serving Children in Public Libraries*, the Association for Library Service to Children (2009) recommends mastery of core competencies for all library staff working with children in a public library. In the first section, "Knowledge of Client Group," the association includes as a competency "[i]dentifies patrons with special needs as a basis for designing and implementing services, following the Americans with Disabilities Act (ADA) and state and local regulations where appropriate," making it clear that all of the competencies apply to children with and without disabilities (Association for Library Service to Children, 2009).

FIGURE 6.1 Personal Attitude Checklist

	Agree	Disagree
1. Other professionals, agencies, and organizations are already in place to serve children with disabilities and their families. The library should not compete with them.		
2. Children with disabilities cannot attend regular library programs because they are receiving services in an agency-based program during regular library hours.		
3. I am a librarian, not a special education professional. If I wanted to work with children with disabilities, I would have become a special education teacher.		
4. I can't become an expert on every type of disability.		
5. It is the parents' responsibility to control the behavior of their children while in the library. It is not the librarian's job to intervene.		
6. Serving children with special needs consumes a disproportionate amount of resources and takes away from the majority of children needing the library.		
7. Parents of typically developing children feel uncomfortable in an inclusive setting.		
8. Parents of children with disabilities feel uncomfortable in an inclusive setting.		
9. Typically developing children feel uncomfortable in an inclusive setting.		
10. Children with disabilities feel uncomfortable in an inclusive setting.		
11. Siblings of a child with a disability are usually embarrassed by their brother or sister.		
12. Parents don't want their children to learn the inappropriate behaviors that some children with special needs may exhibit.		
13. Librarians are not trained and feel inadequate when working with children with disabilities and their families.		
14. Children with disabilities are best served in special settings such as the National Library for the Blind and Physically Handicapped.		
15. It is natural for children without disabilities to tease children with disabilities.		
16. The library is in a unique position to offer opportunities for children with disabilities and their families.		

A librarian who wants to become comfortable working with children with disabilities and in the disability community will need additional competencies. She will need a basic understanding of:

- special education laws, the referral process, and families' rights;
- Augmentative and Alternative Communication systems;

- Assistive Technology; and
- the extraordinary confidentiality needs of children with disabilities and their families.

Finally, she will need to be able to define and communicate the needs of children with disabilities and their families so that administrators, library staff, and members of the larger community understand how inclusion works at the library.

Using the competencies set forth by the Association for Library Service to Children, librarians can examine their own skills and behaviors relevant to service for families of children with special needs.

Physical Library

Evaluating the physical plant of your library is less emotionally fraught and more straightforward. The Americans with Disabilities Act (ADA) lays out clear standards for barrier-free design. Checklists such as the federal government's Checklist for Existing Facilities 2.1 (Adaptive Environments Center and Barrier Free Environments, 1995) are readily available to help with this process. In addition, the ADA National Network and its regional offices can provide assistance with this part of the process. They can be contacted at http://www.adata.org/. Finally, Amy Watson and Rebecca McCarthen (2009) have developed an excellent checklist for preschool and kindergarten providers that is easily adapted for the library environment. It can be found in their article "Supporting All Kinds of Learners: Including Children with Special Needs: Are You and Your Early Childhood Program Ready?"

Virtual Library

Taking stock of your virtual library and telecommunication systems is the next step. Start with the simple things like ensuring that there is a text enlargement feature on your website and that the website is compatible with basic screen reading technology. A truly inclusive library also considers the accessibility of the sites it links to. The Association of Specialized and Cooperative Library Agencies (2010) includes a useful tipsheet in its "Library Accessibility—What You Need to Know" toolkit series called "Assistive Technology: What You Need to Know, Library Accessibility Tip Sheet 11." All of the various aspects of your library's technology need to be evaluated: hardware, software, and website design.

Community Needs

We cannot undertake an effective assessment of our libraries without involving the community we wish to reach. Needs assessments are a traditional tool of library service, and our existing skills in this area can easily be extended to the disability community. This process follows these steps:

1. Identifying the population
2. Locating children with disabilities and their families
3. Finding out what they want by developing the questions and the tools to ask the questions

Identifying the Population

Before library services and programs can be planned and appropriate materials obtained, it is important to identify the target audience. What age range are you seeking to serve? Federal education mandates provide a useful framework for library services to children and youth. IDEA–I allows for service to children birth to age 3 and requires it for children and youth ages 3 to 21. Are you going to work with children and youth in institutional settings such as congregate foster care and inpatient units in hospitals and psychiatric facilities?

Locating Children with Disabilities and Their Families

The size, location, and type of your library will influence how you locate your target group. A school library media specialist in a small elementary school has a fairly defined population. A generalist in a small rural library may already know many children with disabilities in her community. But she may not, and she does not have the advantage of having access to the type of support groups you may find in even a small city. In addition, it is often the case that it can be difficult to reach the families of migrant workers. A children's librarian in a large urban area may be overwhelmed by the number of children and families she needs to reach. So, a variety of strategies are necessary to find children with disabilities and their families:

- Contact your local education authority or school district. They may be able to give you demographic information about the children they serve, such as how many children have a disability and the types of those disabilities. Meet with school personnel assigned to administer special education services. They may be willing to assist the library in reaching these families by sending home information about the library's initiative or organizing a joint meeting.
- Find out which state agency administers the EI program. The local/regional representative of this agency, as well as the special education department of the local school district for children ages three to five, will be important contacts and sources of information about local services. They may have access to information about families living in your district. You can find them via the National Early Childhood Technical Assistance Center (http://www .nectac.org/). They may be able to provide some of the same assistance as your school district.
- Get in touch with the advocacy and self-advocacy agencies in your communities. For a list of federally supported Parent Training and Information Centers (PTIs), go to http://www.parentcenternetwork.org/. For self-advocacy organizations, start with http://www.virtualcil.net/cils/.
- Reach out to local hospitals, clinics, and service providers. Like the education agencies, they may be able to assist with demographic information and distribute information to their consumers and their families.
- Speak with a variety of types of social service agencies, including adult literacy and English-language instruction

programs, immigrant groups, legal aid providers, and so forth.

- Talk to parents who are already patrons. They often know of families within the library's service area or may be aware of parent organizations.
- Advertise an open forum on how the library can be more inclusive and open it up to the entire community.

Think broadly. Anywhere you find adults you may find children, grandchildren, godchildren, nieces, nephews, and children of friends who have disabilities. Fraternal organizations, veteran's groups, and professional organizations will all likely have members who have a connection with a child with a disability. A branch manager once asked a patron about a T-shirt he was wearing that announced a walkathon for the Juvenile Diabetes Foundation. It turned out he was president of the local chapter, and the next thing she knew she was hosting the group in the library and speaking to members about library services.

Finding Out What They Want

Developing the Questions

When meeting with professionals or parents, use these questions as a starting point to garner information about the characteristics and needs of children with disabilities and their families:

- How many children and teens have disabilities in your community?
- What types of disabilities do they have?
- How might various disabilities affect the stages of child development and age-appropriate practice?
- Where do the children receive services?
- What is a typical day like in the life of a child with a disability and his family?
- When are families available to come to the library?
- How and where can the library provide outreach to these families?
- What library services do parents want for their children and teens?
- What library services do the children and teens want?
- What library services do the parents want for themselves?

- If children with disabilities and their parents and caregivers have not been using the library, why not?
- What are the barriers to using the library?

Remember that people may not be aware of the range of services modern libraries offer. Therefore, it is important to let people know what is available when asking them what they want. A librarian at The Child's Place for Children with Special Needs in Brooklyn offered a workshop on sensory integration that included Spanish interpretation and was heavily advertised in the Spanish-speaking disability community. Afterward, she saw one of the participants wandering around the central library looking slightly awestruck. When the librarian approached to ask if the mother had enjoyed the workshop, she said, "Nunca sabia que se habla español en la biblioteca. Ahora puedo usar la biblioteca!" ("I didn't know you spoke Spanish, and I can use the library.")

Developing the Tools to Ask the Questions

Once you have decided on the questions you want to ask, you need to find a way to ask them. There are several ways to go about this process. Surveys are a time-honored tool frequently used in the social services arena. They have four major limitations:

- The bias of the person who writes the survey
- Getting answers only to the questions you ask
- Sample bias
- Format limitations

The first issue of researcher bias can be partially alleviated by having the survey reviewed by more than one library staff and by including community members in its drafting and reviewing. In addition, it should be administered by someone without ties to the library. Including open-ended questions such as "What do you need to use the library easily?" and "How can the library best meet your needs?" will allow you to get unanticipated suggestions, ameliorating the second issue. Sampling bias is slightly thornier. If we survey people in the library, or current library users, we are hearing only from people who are relatively comfortable with library service as it is. Going outside the library can be time consuming and overwhelming if we are not already involved in the communities we are seeking to reach. However, it can also be the first step in outreach. "Nothing about us without us" is one of the seminal tenets of the disability rights movement, and by involving the disability community in the assessment process we honor that tenet. Finally, in order to reach our intended audience, the survey must be available in a variety of formats at a variety of locations. SurveyMonkey and other online survey tools require access to a computer, and not all such tools are ADA compliant. Paper surveys exclude people with print disabilities. So, if you use a survey, make sure that it is available online, in standard print, in large print, in Braille, and in audio formats. And offer everyone all of the options. Not only will you get more responses but also you will concretely demonstrate your library's commitment to full inclusion.

Focus groups and advisory boards are another strategy for needs assessments. A focus group convenes a manageable group of people from the community and poses a series of questions to elicit discussion. Generally, they meet once and then are disbanded. Attendees are usually offered some form of compensation, such as lunch, a gift certificate, or babysitting and travel reimbursement. Advisory boards are ongoing and usually set the agenda themselves rather than only responding to the library's questions. Focus groups have the advantage of being to the point and time limited. An advisory board can provide ongoing, free consultation and follow-up but can also develop its own, independent agenda. Both are good ways to make new community contacts and friends.

When considering a focus group or advisory board, remember that children and youth with disabilities often have a different perspective than their parents and the other adults involved in their education and care. For example, it was from a focus group made up of teens that one library system discovered that a strong residual smell from the cleaning fluid it used prevented some people on the autism spectrum from using the library. Likewise, a local hospital had failed to consider the need for short toilets in the pediatrics unit until a child on its family advisory board mentioned it. The designers had never considered the patients' need for independence. In neither case were the parents aware of the issues.

Thoroughly evaluating your library's readiness to include children with disabilities can be a stressful process. However, if you take the time to do it well, you will be able to eliminate the barriers faced by children and youth with disabilities and their families. In so doing, you lay a solid foundation for the eventual success of inclusion at your library.

Resources

Biblarz, Dora, Stephen Bosch, and Chris Sugnet. 2001. *Guide to Library User Needs Assessment for Integrated Information Resource Management and Collection Development*. Collection Management and Development Series, no. 11. Lanham, MD: Scarecrow Press.

Dudden, Rosalind Farnam. 2008. *Using Benchmarking, Needs Assessment, Quality Improvement, Outcome Measurement, and Library Standards: A How-To-Do-It Manual*. New York: Neal-Schuman.

Rubin, Rhea Joyce. 2001. *Planning for Library Services to People with Disabilities*. ASCLA Changing Horizon Series No. 5. Chicago: Association for Specialized and Cooperative Library Agencies.

References

Adaptive Environments Center and Barrier Free Environments. 1995. *The Americans with Disabilities Act Checklist for Readily Achievable Barrier Removal*. U.S. Department of Justice. http://www.ada.gov/racheck.pdf.

Association for Library Service to Children. 2009. *Competencies for Librarians Serving Children in Public Libraries*. Chicago: Association for Library Service to Children. http://www.ala.org/ala/mgrps/divs/alsc/edcareeers/alsccorecomps/corecomps.cfm.

Association of Specialized and Cooperative Library Agencies. 2010. "Library Accessibility: What You Need to Know." American Library Association. http://www.ala.org/ascla/asclaprotools/accessibilitytipsheets.

Walling, Linda Lucas, and Marilyn H. Karrenbrock. 1993. *Disabilities, Children, and Libraries: Mainstreaming Services in Public Libraries and School Library Media Centers*. Englewood, CO: Libraries Unlimited.

Watson, Amy, and Rebecca McCarthen. 2009. "Supporting All Kinds of Learners: Including Children with Special Needs: Are You and Your Early Childhood Program Ready?" *Beyond the Journal*, March. http://www.naeyc.org/files/yc/file/200903/Watson_BTJ309.pdf.

Staff Training

It's all about attitude.

—*Response of a New York City disability rights advocate
when asked what the most important training issue is
for children's librarians*

Learning does not stop when we graduate from school. It is a lifelong process. No job is static. It evolves and grows in response to community and library needs. In the past 20 years electronic reference evolved from being an elective course with extra fees in library school to become a core part of what librarians do. Back then, knowledge of computers was a bonus for a job applicant. Now it is mandatory. As our jobs change, so must we. To implement inclusive practices, it is critical for all levels of library staff, from the custodian and part-time page to the coordinator of children's services and the library director, to gain new skills.

Before you can design effective staff training, you need to answer the following questions:

- Why are you conducting the training?
- Whom are you training?
- What are the goals of the training?
- What form will the training take?
- Who will conduct the training?

Why Are You Conducting the Training?

Staff training is often sparked by a new initiative, such as outreach to a new special education school. Other times, it starts because of failure or a complaint from the public. Perhaps a patron with arthritis complained about the self-check system when trying to check out books or a parent complained that someone overreacted to the raised voice of a Deaf child. When that is the case, it is important to involve the individual or institution in the design process. Alternatively, the assessment process may have identified weakness that needs to be addressed, or your legal counsel has advised you of a recent court decision related to the Americans with Disabilities Act that could impact on your library. Whatever the case, remember to keep this initial spark in focus so that it gets addressed.

Whom Are You Training?

All staff need basic training. There is a tendency in libraries, particularly in larger library systems, to categorize training by job title. So, librarians and clerical staff get the customer service training and custodial staff get the safety training. However, ultimately we are all responsible for both customer service and safety. A custodian who is rude to the public and a librarian who blocks an exit with a display both harm their library. At the very least, all staff members should be part of a formal Americans with Disabilities Act training workshop to make them aware of the law and its ramifications for providing library service. Depending on the type of responsibilities and amount of patron interaction, additional training will be needed for successful inclusion.

Besides the training common to all staff members, people do need information and resources related to their job titles. For example, maintenance and custodial staff need to be aware of issues related to the physical plant:

- natural light florescent bulbs are less likely to trigger seizures;
- the aisles are required to be certain widths for people who use wheelchairs; and
- some cleaning materials are not friendly to people with chemical sensitivities.

Security staff need to be aware of the behavioral issues associated with autism spectrum disorder (ASD) and mental illness and of effective ways to address these behaviors. A basic understanding of the communications issues inherent in ASD and learning disabilities and coping strategies is important. Communications issues are also important for clerical staff as are issues of people with intellectual disabilities.

What Are the Goals of Your Training?

This question is intimately tied to the first one, why you are offering training, and should take into account in your answer. Is there a problem with service as it is currently being offered? Do you have existing policies and procedures that need to be reinforced? Have you developed new, more disability-friendly policies and procedures? Is there something specific that you want to get across, or are you trying to open a broad discussion about an issue? The basic question here is: what do you want people to do after the training?

At a minimum any staff training should cover the following topics:

- A basic overview of the types of disabilities
- Attitudes about people with disabilities
- Requirements of the Americans with Disabilities Act
- Your library's expectations for staff
- Job-specific issues
- The tools to implement inclusion
- Resources for further investigation

Respond to Staff Issues and Concerns

Address the Assessment

As we discussed in the previous chapter, examining an individual's feelings and attitudes regarding children with disabilities and their families is a critical first step in building inclusive practices. The Personal Attitude Checklist (see Figure 6.1, p. 77) is a tool to begin this process. Discuss staff concerns and issues together, referring to this section on response to concerns. These discussions often lead to the breakdown of barriers and increased sensitivity and awareness among staff. They can also help you pinpoint a starting point for further training. The following suggestions will help you encourage your staff to be open to inclusive practices.

ATTITUDE

Other professionals, agencies, and organizations are already in place to serve children with disabilities and their families. The library should not compete with them.

RESPONSE

Early Intervention (EI), preschool, and school-age special education programs do not provide library services. EI personnel need access to community-based resources in order to fulfill their legal requirement to provide services in the Least Restrictive Environment. Alongside day care centers and nursery schools, library-based early childhood services help fill this need. They need us, and we need them. Just as we complement services provided by Head Start and day care programs and schools, so do we complement services provided by EI and special education programs. They provide direct education and therapeutic services. We provide families with early literacy support, recreational opportunities, and books as well as a portal to other resources. Library service supplements and enhances EI and special education services, providing an opportunity for lifelong learning and skills development using the local library. These relationships are mutually beneficial and strengthen all of our institutions, leaving us better equipped to serve children and teens with disabilities and their families.

ATTITUDE

Children with disabilities cannot attend regular library programs because they are receiving services in an agency-based program during regular library hours.

RESPONSE

Many children with disabilities receive their EI and special education services in the natural setting of their homes and schools. This type of service delivery allows for greater flexibility in a family's ability and motivation to attend library programs. Parents and providers often schedule special services around or within the child's community activities, such as swim programs, storytimes, and playgroups. The library is another natural setting in which children can receive services. Attendance at the Brooklyn Library's Read and Play program has been written into more than one Individualized Family Service Plan (IFSP). Here children and their peers, family members, and therapists can work on social, speech, educational, or other goals in an everyday, familiar setting.

Many children are unable to attend library programs because of full-time enrollment in preschool, day care, or after-school programs. In this aspect of modern life, children with disabilities are more like their typically developing peers than not. According to the U.S. Department of Health and Human Services, 77.2 percent of mothers of children ages 6 to 17 worked in 2007, while 63.1 percent of mothers of children under age 6 worked (U.S. Department of Health and Human Services, 2009). Clearly, children's librarians need to rethink some program models to accommodate this changing demographic, if they have not already. Librarians may need to consider outreach services, providing on-site programs or training for center staff. Weekend, evening, and vacation programs, designed for children who cannot attend programs during the school day or work day, need to become a part of regular program offerings.

ATTITUDE

"I am a librarian, not a special education professional. If I wanted to work with children with disabilities, I would have become a special education teacher."

RESPONSE

If libraries are to remain vital, significant institutions within their communities, it is essential that they anticipate and respond to needs and changes in society. The roles of the library and the children's librarian are constantly evolving. The 1970s brought an array of audiovisual collections and services. The 1980s saw the lowering of the age requirements for children's programming and recognition of our role in servicing adults who live and/or work with children. The 1990s brought ever-changing technology and the centrality of computers in libraries and the beginnings of virtual libraries for children, teens, and adults. In the 2000s there was the normalization of bilingual children's library services, as seen, for example, in the growing popularity of Dia de los Niños/Dia de los Libros celebrations. In the beginning of each of these changes, the expansion beyond traditional services and client groups was uncomfortable for many librarians. Today these services and audiences are considered standard fare for public libraries.

This evolution is still in process regarding library service to children with special needs. Their participation in the full range of library programs and routines is new and largely untested. However, the

Dia de los Niños/ Dia de los Libros

The Dia celebrations, sponsored by the American Library Association, bring attention to the importance of literacy to children and families from all backgrounds through the following goals:

- "Celebrate children and connect them to the world of learning through books, stories and libraries.
- Nurture cognitive and literacy development in ways that honor and embrace a child's home language and culture.
- Introduce families to community resources that provide opportunities for learning through multiple literacies.
- Recognize and respect culture, heritage and language as powerful tools for strengthening families and communities."

(Association for Library Service to Children, 2013)

role of the librarian has not fundamentally changed. Just as we are distinct from general education teachers and guidance counselors, we are distinct from EI providers, special education teachers, and social workers. Our job continues to be literacy support, programming, information, and referral. As library professionals, our role is clearly to provide library service to *all* of the children and families within our community, including those with disabilities.

ATTITUDE

"I can't become an expert on every type of disability."

RESPONSE

Librarians must obtain a basic knowledge of the various clientele they may encounter in the library so that they can provide quality community service. The knowledge of any client group is the keystone of appropriate service. Knowledge, however, does not imply in-depth knowledge or expertise. Few children's librarians are expert in every aspect of child development, but they do have enough knowledge to deliver library service in a developmentally appropriate manner. Acquiring general knowledge about children with disabilities is part of this process. The previous chapter on assessment addresses ways to start this process.

ATTITUDE

It is the parents' responsibility to control the behavior of their children while in the library. It is not the librarian's job to intervene.

RESPONSE

Legally, library staff are not *in loco parentis*. And although it is not their job to intervene in a manner that oversteps parental authority, librarians often experience two emotions when children are disruptive. First is the need to provide a safe and pleasant setting. Second is the desire to support parents whenever possible. Because of these feelings, most librarians are motivated to become involved.

It is clear that staff should intervene if someone needs help or they see a child doing something that would result in possible self-harm or injury to another child. Staff members routinely assist parents by opening doors for caregivers with strollers and heading off darting toddlers before they get into unsafe situations. In talking and working together with parents, libraries and staff can be an integral part of a strategy that supports the authority of the parents. Modeling good communication techniques for parents through conveying expectations in a clear and consistent manner helps the children understand appropriate library behavior and allows families to feel comfortable in the library setting.

Creating a welcoming environment will also support parents and can help avoid behavioral issues before they arise. Making a social story that introduces all aspects of a library visit available to families before they come can let children know what to expect during the first visit and reduce their anxiety. One example of such a story can be found at http://www.bklynpubliclibrary.org/sites/default/files/files/pdf/childsplace/tcpsn_read_and_play_social_stories.pdf. Having a quiet, private space where a child can go when she feels overwhelmed can prevent acting out. Accurate signage will prevent frustration. Making expectations and schedules clear is another way to prevent behavioral outbursts in the library. These strategies all contribute to preventing behavioral issues from arising in the first place, reducing the burden on the child, the parent, and the librarian.

ATTITUDE

Serving children with special needs consumes a disproportionate amount of resources and takes away from the majority of children needing the library.

RESPONSE

Whenever a library expands services to a particular group, some may feel it is taking resources away from those already served. It was thus when libraries first began to serve children and share resources with adult services. Children with disabilities are patrons with the same right to library service as other children. The Americans with Disabilities Act is in place to ensure this, mandating the provision of "reasonable accommodations" to all persons with disabilities. Inclusion of children with disabilities broadens the ranges of service and fulfills the library's mission as a public institution.

Furthermore, as we have discussed in previous chapters, adhering to good design principles broadens access for everyone. An elevator in your library will make it easier for everyone accompanying young children to use the upper floors. Using picture schedules for programs will help engage younger children as well as those with developmental and attention issues. And reaching out to an inclusive Head Start program will publicize your program to a wide swath of the community, not just the 20 percent with a disability.

ATTITUDE

Parents of typically developing children feel uncomfortable in an inclusive setting.

RESPONSE

People fear what they do not know. Educating the community on the benefits of inclusion for all children and families and providing opportunities for families to voice their concerns will pave the way for inclusion. The best method to alleviate anxious feelings and fears is to have families with typically developing children participate in inclusive settings. Observing the acceptance that their own children exhibit toward children with disabilities can diminish the discomfort and often engenders a sense of pride.

ATTITUDE

Parents of children with disabilities feel uncomfortable in an inclusive setting.

RESPONSE

Families may fear that the needs of their children will not be met or that their children will face ridicule or rejection. In all likelihood these fears are based on past experiences. How many times has the family gotten the message, directly or indirectly, "Your child doesn't fit in here"? Involving children with disabilities and their families in your needs assessment and design processes can alleviate some concerns. Being open to ongoing feedback is also important. Your own acceptance of the children will address others'. Above all, creating an environment in which parents feel willing to at least give it a try will be the best antidote to these issues.

ATTITUDE

Typically developing children feel uncomfortable in an inclusive setting, and children with disabilities feel uncomfortable in an inclusive setting.

RESPONSE

These are attitudes that children pick up from those around them. Modeling more inclusive attitudes will go a long way toward changing the attitudes of the children. Including role models with disabilities such as teen volunteers and library staff members or characters in the books and toys we share can also help. Allowing children to ask questions about disabilities and discuss issues that come up conveys the message that "disability is natural" and not the unspeakable, embarrassing elephant in the room. Furthermore, we know from past experience that segregation and separation breed ignorance and fear. The best way to get rid of these prejudices is to let the children play together in a safe and supportive milieu and experience things for themselves.

ATTITUDE

Siblings of a child with a disability are usually embarrassed by their brother or sister.

RESPONSE

Taking it at its face value, we can see that perpetuating the artificial separation of children with disabilities from the natural environment of the library will only reinforce this embarrassment, when it exists. Siblings have issues with each other. They may focus on age, birth order, parental expectation, or even disability. Brothers and sisters have a lifetime to address these issues. Modeling inclusion can help typically developing siblings accept their brothers and sisters with a disability. Creating a place where children with disabilities can function effortlessly, where print, audio, and Braille books are equally legitimate, and where dolls use wheelchairs gives the child with a disability an opportunity to be just another child rather than an object of embarrassment and can help the typically developing siblings to understand that disability is natural. And you just might find that siblings of a child with a disability are proud of the accomplishments of their sibling and happy to have the opportunity for the rest of the world to see them as they do.

Furthermore, examining this attitude allows us to consider that we may be the ones who are embarrassed. Providing staff with the opportunity to ponder this idea, and perhaps even discuss it, will help obviate it.

ATTITUDE

Parents don't want their children to learn the inappropriate behaviors that some children with special needs may exhibit.

RESPONSE

There is no evidence to suggest that typically developing children regress or learn inappropriate behaviors from their peers with disabilities. In actuality, children often become more sensitive or empathetic. The more opportunities children have to interact with children of different ages, cultures, and abilities, the more accepting and understanding they will become and the more aware they will be of similarities rather than differences.

ATTITUDE

Librarians are not trained and feel inadequate when working with children with disabilities and their families.

RESPONSE

Inclusion requires not only developing new skills but also learning how to apply existing skills to new situations. Some type of initial training, as well as ongoing support, may be necessary, as it is with all areas of service. Very few librarians are immediately comfortable with a new circulation system or policy regarding overdue books. Reading this book and discussing it with peers provides a first step in determining training needs and figuring out how to meet them.

ATTITUDE

Children with disabilities are best served in special settings such as the National Library Service for the Blind and Physically Handicapped.

RESPONSE

The National Library Service for the Blind and Physically Handicapped, now usually called the Braille and Talking Book Library, is a network of regional libraries established by the federal government and administered by the Library of Congress to serve people with print disabilities such as blindness and dyslexia. It is not equipped to serve people with other types of disabilities. Furthermore, it does not provide convenient, community-based service. Some states have only one. The majority of its materials are circulated by mail. In short, it cannot replace local libraries, whether public, school, or academic, as a community center and destination for literacy.

ATTITUDE

It is natural for children without disabilities to tease children with disabilities.

RESPONSE

Teasing and bullying, like other social interactions, are learned and decidedly not natural. It is modeled by and accepted by others, usually adults or powerful peers. In other words, it starts with us and needs to stop with us. Creating an inclusive environment that welcomes children with disabilities is a good first step. Using person-first terminology and refusing to tolerate offensive words such as "retard" is another. Modeling tolerance, refusing to participate in teasing, even so-called playful teasing, and intervening to stop teasing and bullying whenever we see it are further important steps.

Most formal antibullying programs are school based. However, we can adapt relevant strategies for our libraries. Successful antibullying programs tend to rest on four principles:

> (1) warmth, positive interest and involvement from adults; (2) firm limits on unacceptable behavior; (3) consistent application of non-punitive, non-physical sanctions for unacceptable behavior and violation of rules; and (4) adults who act as authorities and positive role models. (American Psychological Association, 2011)

We can use these principles to guide our response to disability-based harassment. Teasing recently erupted in a program at the Brooklyn Public Library's The Child's Place. The programming specialist intervened at the time to end the inappropriate behavior. Then she planned a program about bullying the next week, which included reading stories and allowing some time for discussion. The teasing stopped. Using the combination of adult involvement, limits on unacceptable behavior, and positive role models, she was able to nip this in the bud.

ATTITUDE

The library is in a unique position to offer opportunities for children with disabilities and their families.

RESPONSE

As a voluntary institution where all people can come for information and recreation, we indeed are in this unique and wonderful position.

Person-First Terminology

When referring to a person with a disability, it is important to put this person first and then the disability. For example, we say "a person with mental illness" rather than "a mentally ill person" or even "a crazy person." By putting the person first, we are emphasizing our shared humanity and putting our possible differences in the secondary position. We are also avoiding objectifying the person with the disability.

One significant exception to this rule occurs when referring to someone who is culturally Deaf. Because many people in the Deaf community identify deafness as a linguistic and cultural difference, they prefer to use the uppercase "D" in the same way that Americans use an uppercase "A." For more information on person-first terminology and specific words to avoid, see the PACER Center information sheet at http://www.pacer.org/parent/php/php-c31.pdf.

The PACER Center in Minneapolis, Minnesota, is one of the federally funded Parent Training and Information Centers. It is an excellent source for material about many aspects of exceptional parenting and special education.

Antibullying Resources

As research has validated the lifelong negative effects of bullying, on both the bully and the victim, many antibullying programs have been developed. Some are well studied and tested; others are not. To find out more about validated programs, check out these resources:

- **Be BRAVE Against Bullying:** Building Respect Acceptance and Voice through Education is a project of the United Federation of Teachers. Its goal it to provide parents, educators, and students with tools to combat bullying. Their resource guide can be found at http://www.uft .org/files/attachments/brave -resource-guide.pdf.

- **National Bullying Prevention:** This PACER Center landing site at http://www.pacer.org/landing/ anti-bullying-activities/?gclid= CKHkmPi68LUCFYXc4AodpTw ADg provides links to resources for children, teens, and adults on separate websites. While it has universal applicability, the issues that are unique to people with disabilities are also addressed.

- **StopBullying.gov:** This website (http://www.stopbullying .gov/), managed by the U.S. Department of Health and Human Services, offers a comprehensive overview of bullying for adults. It includes sections on defining bullying and cyberbullying, identifying who is at risk for bullying, preventing bullying, and dealing with bullying. This site is also available in Spanish.

Provide a Climate That Supports Staff as They Go through This Process

Although staff may have difficulties in adapting to these changes, there are ways to set a tone that will make the process easier. Allowing staff to voice their concerns validates their feelings and is critical to the process of accepting and working with families and children with special needs. Through this inclusion process, as they adopt new roles and learn new skills, staff need the opportunity to vent frustrations and anger. This exchange of feelings can be done in an open forum where as many staff members as possible, not just children's staff, can attend. The forum needs to provide an open atmosphere where staff can share both positive and negative feelings. They must be able to do this honestly and without fear of their job being impacted or how fellow workers, supervisors, and administrators may view them. Having a disabilities specialist or someone trained in EI and special education conduct the forum helps set an impartial and nonjudgmental tone. Because they are acknowledged experts and are not in a position to impose change in the library, staff may be more accepting of their suggestions and viewpoints.

Validation of staff feelings is heightened when staff have an opportunity to articulate their concerns to supervisors and explore strategies together. Interdisciplinary teamwork involving many staff members strengthens inter- and intra-agency collaborations, increases the number of people with a vested interest in promoting the process of inclusion, and provides a network of interdisciplinary expertise and resources that team members can draw upon. It may be the case that "experts" emerge from these forums. You may find that your staff have more personal experience with people with disabilities than you were previously aware of.

Offer this forum regularly. Those who in theory support the concept of inclusion may feel differently as they experience real-life challenges. The forum provides an ongoing opportunity for staff to share their frustrations as well as their positive, heartwarming, and inspiring stories. Positive stories about real children and families having successful library experiences are wonderful motivators and morale boosters. A wiki may also be an effective venue for staff to share and support one another.

Attitudinal changes take time and patience. When a staff member who initially expressed anxiety and perhaps even anger shares a positive experience that influenced the development of the family and the child, other staff can observe the impact of the library's role in the inclusion process. The individual staff member feels personally gratified, and supervisory staff can take this opportunity to point out how all staff contributed to this positive development.

In one library, a set of nonverbal, antisocial, two-and-a-half-year-old twins were viewed by staff as "terrors with a permissive mother" when they came into the library. The twins pulled books and toys off the shelf and left the room in complete disarray. The mother paid little attention to them and the disruption they caused and appeared herself to be in need of support and assistance. The librarian realized that this was a complex problem that required intervention.

She listened to her staff's feelings of frustration and provided enough support to handle the extra work the children generated. She spoke to the mother directly about the children's behavior, explaining that they needed supervision and constant assistance and could not be left to roam the library or destroy materials. She suggested that when the children came in, a gate be used to keep the children safely within the early childhood area. She asked that the mother stay in the area with the children and that they pick up materials along with the staff. She offered assistance to get additional library materials for the family as needed. This intervention required creative thinking and good communication skills on the part of the librarian and the rest of the staff.

The family continued to use the library and began to successfully acclimate to the library environment. After several months, one of the children responded to a staff member's greeting by looking directly at her and saying "book" for the first time. The staff member was thrilled. The librarian pointed out how much the entire staff had supported this family during the prior months by their direct or indirect roles in the process. Everyone felt positive and could appreciate the benefits of their new or expanded roles.

Set the Tone

Attitudes and Behaviors

To foster an environment that supports inclusion, nurture the following staff behaviors:

- *Acceptance and respect.* A welcoming atmosphere for families and children with disabilities is a must. Greet them with smiles and the same good customer service provided to all library patrons.

- *Nonjudgmental attitude.* Apply this attitude to both the child and the parent. For example, if library staff view the parent of a child with attention deficit disorder with hyperactivity as ineffectual and have a critical attitude that implies, "If I were that child's parent, she would behave," this attitude could undermine a successful inclusionary experience. Staff need to remain neutral and supportive.
- *Flexibility.* Look beyond policies, procedures, and rules and identify the purposes behind them. Reexamine policies to meet the needs of children with disabilities while adhering to the basic intent of the rule or policy.
- *Empathy, not sympathy.* Feeling sorry for families does nothing to support and empower parents. Offer genuine understanding, caring, and a willingness to partner with the parents and other specialists in the child's life.

Communication

The following communication guidelines, while benefiting all children, are particularly critical to keep in mind when working with children with disabilities:

- See the child as a child first, the disability only secondarily and only if necessary.
- Always acknowledge the child by speaking directly to him or her.
- Be patient. It may take extra time for a child with a disability to say or do things.
- Relax. Don't worry about using common expressions like "See you later" or "I recently heard that . . ." when talking with children with disabilities.
- Use people-first language that refers to the child first and then to the disability.

Ideas on how to better communicate with children who have specific disabilities can be found in the Association of Specialized and Cooperative Library Agencies' (ASCLA, 2010) online tool kit, "Library Accessibility: What You Need to Know." In addition, *Disabilities, Children, and Libraries: Mainstreaming Services in Public Libraries and School Library Media Centers* by Linda Lucas Walling and Marilyn H. Karrenbrock (1993) is a classic work that offers many useful suggestions. Chapters 9 and 10 in this book address communication issues in more depth.

What Form Will the Training Take?

Modern technology has opened up a slew of new avenues for education. Previously we were limited to in-person training or asking people to read something or perhaps having a conference call. These days we can offer training in person, through video conferencing, on the web, one-on-one, in a group, privately, and publicly with any number of variations on these methods. Discussions can be in person and time limited or online and ongoing.

However you offer training, try to keep the relationship between the content and the format in mind, as well the learning styles of your teachers and audience. For example, it is difficult to adequately address social skills and attitudes in a self-directed virtual course. Learning about interacting with others ultimately requires interacting with others. On the other hand, a virtual course may be the ideal format for a fact-based review of recent changes in disability rights laws.

The learning styles of the audience are also central to the design of any training. As we discussed in Chapter 5, people do learn in many ways and effective teaching allows for that variety. Many people, even those who love computers, are uncomfortable with technology-based learning. Others get anxious in group discussions. Self-directed training is a great tool for many people. Staff can be provided with resources to read, view, or listen to on library time. The previously discussed forums or wiki can reinforce this process. A comprehensive bibliography of resources related to the inclusion of children and teens with disabilities can be found at the end of this book.

Consider nontraditional training formats. Observation combined with information and follow-up discussion can provide a rich learning opportunity. Librarians can visit EI or special education programs or arrange for the library to host a program, such as a sensory storytime, that focuses on meeting the needs of children with disabilities. Find out what is going on in your area. Does your regional Braille and Talking Book Library offer programs? Would the school for the Deaf allow you to visit? Does a hospital rehabilitation center have recreational programs?

Who Will Conduct the Training?

Much of the anxiety of not knowing what to do or how to respond in a particular instance when working with children with disabilities is lessened if an EI professional, special educator, therapist, or knowledgeable parent of a child with a disability participates in the library staff development. Because these providers are looking for a natural community setting for their children, they are often very willing to participate in a joint program, modeling for the staff and other families and children in a group setting. Furthermore, tapping existing resources is an inexpensive way to bring experts to your training.

Community Resources

Related to what form the training will take is the question of who will conduct it. Training need not be costly. This is a good opportunity to reach out to community organizations and members who have expertise. There are many potential resources, including these:

- Local education authorities
- Regional technology training centers
- Federally financed parent training centers
- Parent support groups
- Local affiliates of national organizations
- Individuals in your community with disabilities
- Individuals in your community with experience with people with disabilities

The appendix to this book provides online portals for finding agencies such as those listed here.

Libraries in small communities and rural libraries may be able to work with people and agencies remotely through webinars and basic teleconferencing such as Skype. Supplementing this with onsite discussions can actively involve different types of learners. Sharing resources with other libraries on a regional or countywide basis can broaden both your pool of presenters and the kinds of training provided.

In-House Resources

In addition, look to your in-house expertise. It is more than likely that someone in your library has direct experience with a person with a disability or has one himself. Brooklyn Public Library staff have learned from the experiences of staff who have learning disabilities, staff who are parents or siblings of people with disabilities, and staff with special education backgrounds. However, it is important to keep in mind that when expertise comes from personal experience staff should be offered the opportunity and may be willing to share their knowledge but should never be pressured to do so.

Training the trainer is another cost-effective way to enhance training. Arrange for key staff members to attend formal trainings and bring the information back to staff in large or small group settings. At The Child's Place for Children with Special Needs at the Brooklyn Public Library, we regularly send staff to local and regional conferences and workshops to enhance all kinds of all skills. These venues are often free, with fees waived because of ongoing partnerships or through quid pro quo arrangements. Topics covered in this manner include literacy and people with autism, managing problematic behaviors, and composting in an inclusive garden. A team of trainers spanning all positions within the library (security, custodial, page, clerk, paraprofessional, librarian, and administration) can relate training to their particular job responsibilities. They can also discuss the interaction of various position responsibilities and how best to work together when assisting families.

Best Practices

Libraries have been including children with disabilities and their families for some time now, and there are solid examples of "best practices" programs. Libraries and Autism: We're Connected is a library-wide program developed by the Scotch Plains (NJ) Public Library and the Fanwood (NJ) Memorial Library along with extensive community partners. In 2008 they made an outstanding training video, which is available for free on their website at http://www.TheJointLibrary.org/autism. The Skokie (IL) Public Library's Come On In! . . . The Library Is a Special Place for Children with Disabilities (http://www.skokie.lib.il.us/s_kids/kd_COI/index.asp) is another example. Both of these programs are recipients of the ASCLA/Keystone Library Automation System (KLAS) and National Organization on Disability (NOD) Award. Additional award winners can be found at http://www.ala.org/ala/mgrps/divs/ascla/asclaawards/asclanational.cfm. The Child's Place for Children with Special Needs at the Brooklyn Public Library (http://www.bklynpubliclibrary.org/only-bpl/childs-Place) serves over

18,000 children with disabilities and their peers, family members, and educators each year and has been awarded its county's Developmental Disabilities Council's best practices designation.

Many of us are already comfortable with listening skills, customer service, and information and referral techniques. By including children with disabilities in the library setting and supporting their families with information and referral services, materials, programs, and resources, libraries have the opportunity to give these families not only access to resources but also a sense of belonging. A secure base empowers families to seek additional means of informal support—such as friends or child-care providers—and to learn about government and private agencies, advocacy groups, and community networks.

Effective staff training is the foundation for any successful library initiative. It must be an ongoing process to address new issues as they arise and to ensure the training of new staff members. The library is in a unique position to offer opportunities for children and teens with disabilities and their families. Unlike many other public and private institutions, we have no age limits, screening requirements, membership dues, or other eligibility criteria that can exclude rather than include these patrons. Few community-based institutions offer as many positive and supportive options for youth with disabilities as libraries. And it all starts with an aware and knowledgeable staff.

Resources

Akin, Lynn, and Donna MacKinney. 2004. "Autism, Literacy, and Libraries: The 3 Rs = Routine, Repetition, and Redundancy." *Children and Libraries* 2, no. 2: 35–43.

Banks, Carrie. 2004. "All Kinds of Flowers Grow Here: The Child's Place for Children with Special Needs at the Brooklyn Public Library." *Children and Libraries* 2, no. 1: 5–10.

Biech, Elaine. 2010. *ASTD's Ultimate Train the Trainer: A Complete Guide to Training Success.* Chicago: ALA Editions.

D'Orazio, Antonette K. 2007. "Small Steps, Big Results." *Children and Libraries* 5, no. 3: 21–23.

Gray, Carol, and Abbie Leigh White. 2002. *My Social Stories Book.* Illustrated by Sean McAndrew. Philadelphia: Jessica Kingsley.

Heinrichs, Rebekah. 2003. *Perfect Targets: Asperger Syndrome and Bullying—Practical Solutions for Surviving in the Social World.* Overland Park, KS: AAPC Publishing.

Holt, Cynthia, and Wanda Hole. 2003. "Training Rewards and Challenges of Serving Library Users with Disabilities." *Public Libraries* 42, no. 1: 34–37.

The Libraries of Fanwood and Scotch Plains. 2008. *Libraries and Autism: We're Connected.* DVD. 19 min, 40 sec. EngelEntertainment. http://www.thejointlibrary.org/autism/video.htm.

National Library Service for the Blind and Physically Handicapped. 2011. *That All May Read.* National Library Service for the Blind and Physically Handicapped, Library of Congress. http://www.loc.gov/nls/.

Skokie Public Library. 2011. Come On In! . . . The Library Is a Friendly Place for Children with Special Needs. Skokie (IL) Public Library. http://www.skokie.lib.il.us/s_kids/kd_COI/index.asp.

Whelan, Debra Lau. 2009. "The Equal Opportunity Disorder: Autism Is on the Rise, and It Can Affect Any Family. Here's What You Need to Know." *School Library Journal* 55, no. 8. http://www.schoollibraryjournal.com/article/CA6673570.html.

Winson, Georgia, and Courtney Adams. 2010. "Collaboration at Its Best: Library and Autism Programs Combine to Serve Special Audience." *Children and Libraries* 8, no. 2: 15–17.

Wojahn, Rebecca Hogue. 2006. "Everyone's Invited: Ways to Make Your Library More Welcoming to Children with Special Needs." *School Library Journal* 52, no. 2: 46–48.

Wong, Peggy, and Allen McGinley. 2010. "Rated E for Everyone: Expanding Services to Children with Special Needs." *School Library Journal* 56, no. 12: 22–23.

References

American Psychological Association. 2011. "School Bullying Is Nothing New, but Psychologists Identify New Ways to Prevent It." American Psychological Association. http://www.apa.org/research/action/bullying.aspx.

Association for Library Service to Children. 2013. "Dia de los Niños/Dia de los Libros: Many Children, Many Cultures, Many Books." American Library Association. http://dia.ala.org/.

Association of Specialized and Cooperative Library Agencies. 2010. "Library Accessibility: What You Need to Know." American Library Association. http://www.ala.org/ascla/asclaprotools/accessibilitytipsheets/.

U.S. Department of Health and Human Services. 2009. "Child Health USA 2008–2009: Working Mothers and Child Care." U.S. Department of Health and Human Services. http://mchb.hrsa.gov/chusa08/popchar/pages/106wmcc.html.

Walling, Linda Lucas, and Marilyn H. Karrenbrock. 1993. *Disabilities, Children, and Libraries: Mainstreaming Services in Public Libraries and School Library Media Centers*. Englewood, CO: Libraries Unlimited.

Community Involvement

Nothing about us without us!
—*Seminal rallying cry of the disability rights movement*

Seizing their own destiny and in reaction to the lack of control over their own lives, early disability rights activists adopted the slogan "Nothing about us without us." It speaks to the fundamental need we all have to make our own decisions. And it is important to keep this tenet in mind when designing inclusive library services.

Community involvement happens at three levels. As librarians, we can work on inclusion with individuals, whether they are individuals with a disability or their peers, parents, or other family members. We can work with professionals, or those people who work with or represent individuals with disabilities and their families. Finally, we can work at the institutional level in formal partnerships with organizations such as service providers, government departments, and advocacy groups.

Working with Individuals

Working with individuals is something that comes naturally to librarians. From the reference interview to signing someone up for a library card, our focus has always been on the person in front of us. When planning and implementing services for youth with disabilities, "individuals" refers to youth with disabilities and their families. In many respects, their concerns will be similar.

Collaboration with the child or teen and her family is essential for the delivery of quality service, particularly when working with children with disabilities. After all, it is usually the parents who bring the child to the library and who knows their child best. It is critical that we develop a general sensitivity to the emotional needs of families, practice active and reflective listening skills, and implement strategies to encourage families to trust and partner with the library.

Understanding Needs and Feelings

Needs and Feelings of Parents

As discussed in Chapter 3, there are as many reactions to the diagnosis of a child's disability as there are parents. Grief, anger, relief, confusion, guilt, and stoicism are all common and valid reactions. Our job is to discover and meet these parents' information needs. Remember to empathize, not sympathize, and to follow the parents' lead. Asking the child's name and even asking to see a picture of the child can go a long way toward supporting parents and establishing trust. It is often the case when a child has a disability that acquaintances neglect to do these simple and affirming things.

Needs and Feelings of Children and Teens with Disabilities

Although preschool-age children are usually unaware of their disability or that they are different from their peers, school-age children are aware and teenagers can be hyperaware (Batshaw, Pellegrino, and Roizen, 2007: 606). We must take these developmental issues into account both when we are designing our programs and services and when we are working with children individually.

Meeting the needs of youth with disabilities is usually as simple as asking a question. Anthony was a teen volunteer with an intellectual disability. While we were setting up a craft project, a librarian asked Anthony to cut out a template. He told her he did not want to. When she asked why not, it turned out that he could not use the scissors. When she showed him scissors that were operated by squeezing rather than with a pincer grip, he was intrigued. When he tried cutting a piece of paper, he was excited. When he successfully cut out the template, he was thrilled. In his entire 11-year school career, he had never enjoyed participating in crafts because he had not had the proper tools. In this case, asking the question "why not?" solved a lifelong problem.

Needs and Feelings of Siblings

Brothers and sisters of people with disabilities will usually have the longest lasting relationships with them. They will often know each other better than anyone else. Like siblings of people without disabilities, their relationships are complex and often rich. However, siblings of people with disabilities have unique components to their relationships.

In Chapter 2 of their book *Sibshops*, Don Meyer and Patricia Vadasy (2008) identify the following common concerns of siblings:

- Fear of developing the sibling's disability
- Embarrassment
- Guilt
- Isolation
- Resentment
- Increased responsibilities
- Pressure to achieve for both of them

Guilt can take the form of feeling responsible for the disability, survivor's guilt, guilt about relative abilities, guilt over typical sibling conflicts, guilt over limitations in caregiving, and shame. Siblings may feel isolated from their parents, from their sibling, or from peers. Their experiences are, after all, unique and difficult to comprehend from the outside. Relative lack of attention, unequal treatment by parents, and parents' failure to include them in decision making or provide for the future can all lead to resentment (Meyer and Vadasy, 2008: 7–33).

Having a sibling with a disability can foster positive qualities as well (Meyer and Vadasy, 2008: 51–65):

- Maturity
- Social competence
- Insight
- Tolerance
- Pride
- Caretaking skills
- Advocacy
- Loyalty

These attributes may develop from coping strategies and from practice negotiating the world with a brother or sister with a disability, but their application is much broader.

Providing Information and Referral

Satisfying the individual's request for information, either through referral to other community resources or by providing services within the library itself, is a primary task of children's librarians who wish to create an inclusive library environment. The reference interview is often the starting point for our interaction with library users. It is where we get to ask questions in order to meet the user's needs.

As information and referral specialists, children's librarians need to practice good listening skills, remaining compassionate without becoming overly involved or becoming "family counselors." Being prepared for questions and understanding how to appropriately engage individuals in the reference interview helps to alleviate discomfort or uneasiness while successfully meeting their needs. It can be helpful to keep the following guidelines in mind.

Be ready for inquiries of a sensitive nature. Provide staff training on how to provide referral information, where such information can be found in the library, and what policies exist regarding confidentiality. Because support staff are often most visible and first asked for assistance, include them in the training. They need to know how to assist parents and connect them to the librarian. When children, teens, and parents request help, all library staff need to be prepared to provide the information.

Confidentiality is central to building trust. Sometimes families do not discuss an individual's medical condition in the family as a whole or even with the affected child or teen. Many children and teens who are HIV positive or who have other serious medical conditions are not aware of their status. Likewise, youth with disabilities have the same right to privacy as other library patrons, even with respect to their parents.

Finally, keep it age appropriate. A 7-year-old looking for information on cerebral palsy has different needs than does a 15-year-old, and both have different needs than their parents do.

Be Empathetic

Imagine how the individual with the disability or parent may be feeling. Conduct the reference interview using reflective listening techniques, restating the question or concern. Be nonjudgmental, and verbally communicate support.

Base Advice on Your Qualifications and Experience

Although librarians may have degrees and credentials in related fields, our role is clearly defined. We are not personal friends, counselors, or social workers. Acknowledge when you are not the best person to answer a question, and be ready to refer them to the person who is.

Support Parents

Having good listening skills, being nonjudgmental, and letting families know you are available will help parents be more comfortable asking questions. Having a parents' collection in the children's room, displaying posters and brochures of children with disabilities, and offering an array of services for parents, children, and teens demonstrates to parents that the library cares.

Librarians need to be flexible and creative in the partner/professional exchange. Being comfortable with a wide array of material and community resources enhances the exchange and provides the librarian with alternative strategies to satisfy the information need. Some parents may be looking for a support group, and others are more comfortable looking things up on the Internet. Some will learn best by watching a DVD or YouTube video. Reading a book or short article or pamphlet may be just what another parent needs. It is incumbent upon us to be knowledgeable about alternative learning styles and to offer a variety of formats and venues for information. We must also provide them with tools for evaluation of the information, regardless of the format.

Information is not the only need of parents of children with disabilities. As with all families, these parents need support in their parental role. Many families today are separated from their extended families. Parents of children with disabilities often feel a sense of isolation from families of typically developing children. They may look to other families who have children with special needs in order to find support and a sense of community. Librarians may be the only people outside of medical and educational professionals who come into contact with their children. As such, they may also look to us for this type of support.

Support Children and Teens with Disabilities

It is sometimes more difficult to assess the information needs of children and teens. Children may not have the words to express their questions, and teens may be self-conscious. When your patron is the

Parents as Adult Learners

Providing information to parents and developing the parent-professional partnership requires that librarians understand the characteristics of an adult learner. Adult learners learn at their own pace and in their own way. They want to incorporate their own knowledge about themselves and their child, usually preferring a facilitated exchange of ideas rather than a didactic or professional exchange. Librarians should be prepared for those times when they will provide information that parents will choose to ignore. They may prefer one or another point of view on a topic. For example, they may support the culturally Deaf model and insist on material friendly to American Sign Language usage rather than cochlear implants. They may feel overwhelmed by options and say "enough." The important thing here is to respect the parents' learning style and point of view, even if you do not agree with it. Providing information they can use and keeping the channels of communication open lay the basis for a future relationship built on trust.

child or teen with a disability, consider the following in addition to your standard questions:

- "Do you read with your eyes, ears, or fingers?" to get at the preferred format
- "What was the last book you read and liked?" to get at the comfortable reading level
- "Do you want help with that?" as opposed to "Do you need help with that?" to avoid stigma
- "How can I help?" only after he or she has responded affirmatively to the previous question

Chapter 9 discusses communication issues that may be helpful to think about in reference interviews with a youth with a disability. Following the individual's lead and not imposing your "help" on her will let the child know that you respect and value her.

Support Siblings

Siblings of individuals with disabilities have information needs independent of the rest of their family. And these needs change over the course of their lives. Children as young as three have some understanding of the differences and may have magical thinking about the condition. The snippets of hushed conversations they overhear may contribute to misunderstandings. They need basic facts in a concrete way (Meyer and Vadasy, 2008: 38). School-age children may or may not have a more accurate understanding of the issues involved. They are likely to have very specific questions (Meyer and Vadasy, 2008: 41). Teens will also have specific questions about the disability and may be wondering about the future, such as the implications for their offspring and who will care for their brother or sister after their parents are unable to do so (Meyer and Vadasy, 2008: 45).

Developing Listening Skills

As our relationships with families develop, good communication is essential. The most important communication technique is listening. The ability to listen well improves communications, conveys a caring attitude, and helps the listener to better understand and be in control of a situation. Good listening enables librarians to provide better and more accurate assistance.

Listening is more than hearing. Hearing is a physical act. Listening is an intellectual and emotional act. And it starts with curiosity. Hearing acknowledges sounds. Listening requires understanding what is said, getting the whole message, including that which is beyond just the words. Active listening is a learned activity. And it must be authentic. Here are some things to keep in mind:

- Begin from genuine curiosity. Understanding the person's experience can only help you communicate with him.
- Ask questions in order to learn. Do not disguise statements as questions; use them to clarify meaning.
- Use paraphrasing to check your understanding and demonstrate that you have heard.
- Acknowledge the person's feelings. Problem solving is much easier once feelings have been acknowledged. And remember that acknowledging the feelings is not the same as agreeing with them. (Stone, Patton, and Heen, 2010: 72–83)

Applying these listening skills when working with children with disabilities helps us to be better information specialists. By listening, librarians will more accurately interpret an individual's information needs and can ease the parent's anxiety. By being aware of our own nonverbal communication and emotional filters, librarians can control their own tendencies and diffuse a difficult situation. This awareness and sensitivity sets the stage for us to partner with our patrons, adults and children alike, and helps them begin the process of acquiring the resources, services, and supports they need.

Be Approachable, but Establish Limits

We cannot solve all problems for all families. Tell the questioners, whether they are adults or children, that the library is pleased to assist them with their request. Listen long enough and ask pertinent questions in order to uncover what is actually wanted, for example, a support group, health information, or a therapeutic service.

Personal boundaries are equally important. There is a delicate line between being a family support professional and a personal friend. And if you are interested in inclusion because of your own relationship to someone with a disability, as many of us are, it can be even more difficult to maintain a purely professional relationship. We must be clear in our own minds about the limits we need and want to establish and clearly communicate them when needed.

One librarian was a trained and certified newborn intervention counselor and advocate for families of children born with certain congenital conditions. This meant when the need arose, hospital personnel, among others, could give her home number to parents in crisis because of their child's medical condition. Families could, and from time to time did, call her in the middle of the night with practical or emotional needs. However, this is not the type of relationship she has with the families who come into the library. If they need a counselor or an advocate, she sends them to someone else. Finally, it is worth mentioning that very few people want to hear about your second cousin twice removed who had a similar condition.

Be Nonjudgmental

The families who come to the library may have issues with which we are uncomfortable or make different decisions than we would make. It is often difficult to distinguish impact from intent. Intent is what the person meant to do: the reaction or consequence that he wanted. Impact is the reaction or consequence that actually occurred (Stone, Patton, and Heen, 2010: 44). For example, a person tossing pebbles at a window intends to get the attention of the person inside. The impact, however, may be a broken window. Similarly, an alcoholic pregnant woman cuts down on her drinking while pregnant. Her intention is to protect her child by drinking less. Her impact may be fetal alcohol syndrome.

Parents may choose not to medicate a child with attention deficit disorder or to homeschool a child with an intellectual disability or not to get a cochlear implant for their deaf child or to try nonstandard treatments for a non-life-threatening condition. It is important to respect the parents' choices as long as they are not abusive. Any other course of action risks alienating the parents, depriving them of access to resources, and may isolate the child. The father of a child with serious learning disabilities (LD) who regularly attended one library's inclusive programs with her mother refused to acknowledge the LD, have his daughter receive services through school, or get tutoring for her outside of school. While the librarian strongly disagreed with his decisions in this situation, she did not discuss her feelings with the family. She continued to support the mother and child, letting them both know she had LD too and giving them resources when they needed them. As a teen, the daughter began volunteering at the library and brought her younger brother, who also had LD, to the library.

Children and teens may also make decisions with which we disagree. For example, a child may choose not to use his hearing aids when a parent is not around. Unless the behavior is so risky as to endanger the child or teen, we cannot voice or show our judgments. Here again, we want to maintain the relationship with our patron.

Collaborating with Families

To successfully include children with disabilities and their families, we need to be aware of their goals in using the library and the barriers to library use. While the specifics will vary from family to family, there are some general trends to keep in mind.

Identifying Family Goals

The family's goals for the child and themselves when using the library are of primary importance. So, what are likely goals for families? The list is as varied as the families themselves. Here are some typical goals, which have been identified through interviews with families of children with disabilities:

- I want my child to participate in the library's programming along with other children.
- I want my child to learn to read.
- I want my child to have playmates.
- I want my child's siblings to see that their brother or sister is a person who can be liked by others.
- I need to learn more about my child's disabilities.
- I need help in identifying emergency services and informing them of my child's disabilities in case I should ever need to call on them.
- I want to feel less isolated.
- I want someone who will talk to me and talk to my child.
- I need someone who can show me options and give my child choices.

Getting to know the family and the individual goals they have for the child will help staff understand what our best role is. Perhaps specific library activities can be added to the child's Individualized Family Service Plan (IFSP) or Individualized Educational Program (IEP). Or the librarian may be able to redefine a library program to fit the goals outlined in the child's existing plan. The Brooklyn Public Library's description of Read and Play, an early literacy program at The Child's Place for Children with Special Needs, as a language stimulation and socialization program, enabled several families to get the program added to their child's IFSP. The more familiar parents become with the library and the more familiar librarians become with the family, the more connections we can make between the child's goals and the library's resources.

Building a Parent-Professional Partnership

When working with families, it is also essential to recognize that the attitudes and beliefs that professionals bring to the partnership influence the relationship. It is too often the case that professionals believe they know best when it comes to other people's children. It can be helpful to the relationship to remember that parents are the professionals when it comes to their children—they know their children better than anyone. A doctor once told the mother of a young child that her daughter could not possibly have a vocabulary of 150 words. He argued his position in a fundamentally condescending way until the mother produced the list the she had been keeping. Very soon afterward the family changed doctors.

To be effective, we need to acknowledge parents' personal feelings about parental responsibility, accept them as individuals and adult learners, and assess their professional beliefs about serving children within the family unit. Considering the following questions can help us address our own beliefs:

- Do I allow families to speak freely by creating a supportive and comfortable setting?
- Do I use active listening and respect the family's opinions?
- Do I believe that families' perspectives and opinions are as important as those of other professionals?
- Do I consistently value the insights of parents?
- Do I believe that parents can look beyond their own child's and family's experience?
- Do I clearly state what is expected of families in the library?
- Do I understand the demands placed on parents and how these demands affect them?
- Do I believe that families bring a unique expertise to the parent/professional relationship?

- Do I believe in the importance of family participation in decision making at the program level?
- Do I believe that parents bring critical elements to library services that no one else can provide?

Variations on these questions are the basis for the partnership of parents and many kinds of professionals, including service coordinators and doctors. Project DOCC (Delivery of Chronic Care), a curriculum for teaching medical residents about the needs of children with disabilities and their families, includes home visits by the medical residents. During one home visit, the resident looked at the family's daily calendar and finally understood why the family needed a once or twice a day antibiotic rather than a five times a day one. His visit allowed him to truly understand the family's perspective, what their opinions were based on, the stresses in their lives, and the value of a true partnership in their daughter's care. Listening to individual families and creating venues for their input, such as family advisory boards, can help librarians grappling with this understanding. Actively involving them in the planning process can concretely demonstrate our respect for them as parents.

Identifying the Goals of the Children and Teens with Disabilities

Children's or teens' wishes, desires, and goals must be first and foremost in our planning for inclusion. If children or teens do not want to go to the library, all the planning in the world will not make it a pleasant experience for them. Children and teens want to:

- read books;
- get together with friends;
- play with toys;
- visit the fish or garden;
- learn about something;
- learn more about their disability; and
- have fun at the library.

These are the things we should be fostering.

Some common things they may not want are to:

- stick out or seem different;
- be singled out;

Project DOCC (Delivery of Chronic Care)

Project DOCC operates in teaching hospitals throughout the country. Its mission, according to the informally published *Training Manual for Parent Teachers* (1998), is to "provide pediatric residents with a comprehensive understanding of life with a child with chronic illness/disability." They do this by training families of children with disabilities to teach the residents about their lives. There are three components to the educational process:

1. Ground rounds panel presentation: A panel of parents discusses their personal experiences with their children and the medical systems.

2. Home visit: Residents visit families in their homes to get a sense of their daily lives.

3. Parent interview: The parent uses a Chronic Illness History questionnaire to discuss issues related to the child's care with the resident, including current political and medical debates.

At the end of the process, it is hoped that the residents have gained insights that will make them more attuned to the needs and capabilities of children with disabilities and their families, ultimately making them better doctors.

For more information, visit http://icpf.wordpress.com/2010/01/06/project-docc-delivery-of-chronic-care/.

- be embarrassed, especially in front of their friends and especially by parents;
- be teased or bullied;
- get in a fight; and
- need help with the bathroom or water fountain.

These are the things we should avoid. See the sidebar for one perspective on what kids want.

Involve children and teens with disabilities in the evaluation process discussed in Chapter 6, and continue to touch base with them. Consider a youth advisory board that includes youth with and without disabilities, or have two advisory boards: one for children and one for teens. Be open to their suggestions: Can we read this book? Try that craft? Have a fish tank? Ask individual patrons if they are finding what they want at the library. Ask if they had fun. If things are going badly, ask what you can do to help. Ask what you can do to make it easier next time. If you meet students who do not use the library, ask why not and try to fix it. Creating formal and informal alliances with youth with disabilities will go a long way in creating a fully inclusive library.

Providing Family Support and Education

Parent programs need to maintain a balanced focus on the needs of both the parent and the child. Focus on the social context of parenthood by strengthening parents' social networks and community ties, as well as assisting them to increase their general parenting skills and the specific skills they need as parents of children with disabilities. Offer to host a parent support group or to start an exceptional parenting bulletin board, or tell them about the great electronic discussion list that addresses local special education issues. Include exceptional parenting materials in your parent resource collections.

Offer workshops on a wide variety of topics, such as literacy and children with autism, educational advocacy, sexuality and teens with intellectual disabilities and autism, and Assistive Technology. Ask your parents what subjects they would like to see addressed in these workshops. Some of the Brooklyn Public Library's most successful workshops have been on behavior management for children with autism and emotional disabilities, sexuality and people with developmental disabilities, and communication. Consider hosting a sibshop (Meyer and Vadasy, 2008).

What Every Kid Should Have by Kyle Glozier, Age 12

Every kid wants:

- to have friends
- to get As or A+s
- to give a helping hand
- a television of their own
- a million dollars
- toys
- a pool to swim in
- a birthday every day
- cool bikes and motorcycles and snowmobiles.

Every kid who uses a wheelchair wants:

- to walk, sometime
- to go to the bathroom by themselves
- to eat without help
- to go inside a friend's house—ACCESS!
- to have their own chores
- to ride bikes whenever they want
- to not have an adult around ALL the time.

Every kid wants to have a LIFE. What do you want for your kid?

(Glozier, 1997: 16)

Addressing Extraordinary Issues

Families of children with disabilities are in an extraordinary situation. This situation is acknowledged in the medical and social work fields by referring to them as "exceptional families." Sometimes, however, things can get even more complicated. You may suspect that the child has a disability but the parent is unaware, or one of the parents may have a disability. The following sections address these and other circumstances.

Identifying Children Who May Need Services

From time to time, children's librarians find themselves observing behaviors during programs or in the library that alert us to the possibility that a particular child may have a delay or a disability. A toddler who does not show interest in the toys or respond to his mother as other children do, or a preschooler with very limited expressive language, may draw our attention. Sometimes when this occurs, a parent will approach us and ask, "Is this right?" Observing their child with their peers for the first time in a library may be the first opportunity parents have to compare their child with other children.

There are also times when we will notice a potential problem before the parent does. Even experienced librarians who may recognize atypical behavior are often unsure about how to broach the matter with parents. Indeed, many of us are hesitant to voice our concerns, feeling perhaps that it is not our role or responsibility.

As family service professionals, one can argue that we have a responsibility to advocate for children and to intercede on their behalf. The sooner a child's disability is recognized, the greater chance she has to reach her full potential. Most parents will welcome your interest and involvement with their child. Often they have observed the same behaviors at home and do not know where to turn for advice. Even if parents initially dismiss the librarian's concerns, when the issue arises in another setting, they may be more able to consider the information.

Of course it is easier to approach parents with a concern when we have a relationship with them. Perhaps they are regular patrons or you have talked about their families with them before. If you do not already have a relationship, now may be the time to establish one. If they regularly attend a program, make an effort to get to know them while you are preparing to speak with them.

Confidentiality

Confidentiality and privacy are at the heart of both the library and medical professions. Discussing children in front of or with other parents is never appropriate. Likewise, when speaking with professionals, use aliases and be careful not to mention identifying details. Sometimes it is helpful to speak with a professional who is involved with the child, but we may only do so with the parent's permission. It is surprising the number of medical and educational professionals who approach librarians wanting to talk about specific children and their disabilities. It is not appropriate.

There are additional privacy concerns when working with teens. Once an individual turns 18, the age of majority, it is important to get his or her permission before speaking to a parent or other adult about the individual, unless this person, usually a parent, has been appointed legal guardian by the court.

When speaking with parents about their child, we need to talk openly and honestly, focusing on the child's behavior. Consider the approach and setting in which the conversation will occur. Handle the discussion discreetly, with care and sensitivity. Here are some tips for a successful discussion:

- Find common ground with the parents.
- Describe what the child is doing or not doing.
- Never attempt to diagnose problems or make judgments about the child.
- Listen carefully to what the parents have to say.
- Try not to get defensive.
- Be open to the possibility that you are wrong.
- Respect confidentiality.

Examine what you are bringing to the conversation. We all notice different things and see them through the lens of our own experiences. Try to see things from the parents' point of view. Both sets of experiences can be "true." Accepting this can help you get past your own righteousness and the parents' defensiveness and can lead to a useful conversation about the child (Stone, Patton, and Heen, 2010: 39).

Speaking with parents about their child can be a painful process but well worth it. You may very well help a child and create a family of lifelong library supporters.

Welcoming Culturally Diverse Families

When communicating with parents, librarians need to recognize the roles that culture, ethnicity, race, religion, gender, income levels, and sexual orientation play in parenting and child rearing. The first step in working with a diverse constituency is to scrutinize one's own feelings and beliefs about groups other than one's own. Acknowledging stereotypes and biases is essential to being able to effectively work with *all* families. Cultural perspective may influence how families interact within the library environment as manifest in:

- child-reading techniques;
- language and communication styles;
- how people see assistance;
- availability of extended family and other informal helping networks;

- attitude toward bureaucracies, government-sponsored programs and services, and the so-called helping professions;
- attitude toward disabilities; and
- level of familiarity with American culture.

A diverse staff, reflective of the community that the library serves, is in the best position to meet the needs of a diverse constituency. It is essential for librarians to be aware of and educated about the array of cultures that make up their community. Bear in mind that while a parent may speak English well, reading it may be more difficult, particularly when encountering the technical jargon of the educational and medical worlds.

Having a strong collection of materials targeted to diverse audiences, displaying posters that depict the diversity of our society, being familiar with community resources for a variety of groups, and developing cooperative programs with agencies that work with diverse cultures are just some ideas for including families within the library setting.

Recognizing Parents with Special Needs

Parents with substance abuse problems or those who have an intellectual disability, teenage parents, and families who live in poverty are just some of the families considered at risk for having children with developmental disabilities. In addition, many disabilities have a hereditary component, including:

- learning disabilities,
- autism spectrum disorder,
- sensory integration disorder,
- emotional disabilities such as bipolar disorder, and
- some types of blindness and deafness.

Working with parents with special needs may require another level of understanding and commitment outside the scope and educational experience of the children's services staff. When librarians encounter a child whose parent appears to have a disability that seems to impact the ability to nurture and encourage the child's development, a referral to the local EI program or preschool special education program may be in the best interest of both the parent and child.

Working with Teenage Parents

Teenage parents present another unique set of challenges for librarians. Working with teen parents can be difficult because the young parents' own needs can sometimes overwhelm their ability to focus on their child's needs. Lack of transportation, understanding, and motivation may impact their interest or ability to bring their child to library programs.

Successful programs are often conducted in collaboration with a local agency that already serves these teenagers. Agency staff can work with the teens, their children, and the library staff and facilitate their coming to the library.

Sometimes librarians can go off-site, taking resources to the teen parents and their children. It helps to keep in mind that teenage parents, like their adult peers, usually want the best for their child. Through the Brooklyn Public Library's Hospital Storytelling program, one of the storytellers met the teenage parents of a one-week-old baby at their first healthy baby visit. She was giving away Reading Is Fundamental books, which the parents initially refused. After the storyteller explained that reading to the baby fed her brain in the same way that milk and formula fed her body, the mother took a book for the baby. Then she turned to the father, playfully slapped him with the book, and said, "And you're going to read to her too, right?!"

Regardless of the family situation that puts a child at risk, proper intervention designed to support the parents in caring for their children can help the child develop. Prevention and intervention strategies designed at the community level in agencies such as public libraries can aid these children in their struggle to grow into healthy adults. Librarians need to acknowledge that library programs and resources provide a preventative strategy to families and young children in need of healthy role models and appropriate learning environments. For young children, storyhours and library visits may present an opportunity to learn and practice positive social interactions.

Working with Families in Transitional Situations

MILITARY FAMILIES

Military families with children with disabilities face issues in addition to the ones typically faced by exceptional families. Many of these are related to the repeated moves they make. State variations in eligibility requirements for EI services, difficulty enforcing IEPs from a child's previous school, and income that fluctuates with standard-of-living adjustments that affect eligibility for Supplemental Security Income (SSI) are just three examples. Children attending Department of Defense Education Department schools are not covered by IDEA–I but by a separate legislation. DoDI 1342.12 is similar to IDEA in its requirement for a free, appropriate education in the LRE but does not impose a timeline. Parents of a child with a disability in the military are required to enroll in the Exceptional Family Member Program (http://www.militaryhomefront.dod.mil/tf/efmp) and are eligible for supplemental insurance benefits that can provide for additional therapies. Service members also have access to their own Parent Training Center, STOMP (http://www.stompproject.org/).

FAMILIES EXPERIENCING HOMELESSNESS

Families in transitional situations can be difficult to reach and are also at greater risk. For example, experiencing homelessness can magnify the effects of poverty. Children who experience extreme poverty and/or trauma can develop problems in interpersonal relationships, growth, sensory integration, information processing, and intellectual development (Oberg, 2003: 2–3). To reach out to these children, whose families are not likely to use the library, it may be necessary for librarians to work in partnership with other local agencies and organizations. In one such partnership, The Child's Place works with two agencies, a family homeless shelter and a volunteer agency, to provide one-on-one reading assistance to struggling readers living in transitional housing in one of Brooklyn's poorest neighborhoods. Often it is only in close partnership with community-based agencies and through unique strategies like home visitation programs that libraries can seek to support children and families at highest risk.

FOSTER FAMILIES

Children in foster care are another at-risk group who are difficult to find. You will most easily find them in group homes, through the foster care agency that works with them, or through your area's child welfare agency. Why not offer an early literacy workshop for foster parents in partnership with an agency? The Brooklyn Public Library has hosted mandatory parent training workshops for a foster care agency that the public is invited to attend. The latter partnership allowed parents to attend the training required to get their children back in a neutral setting without stigma.

Children in foster care often face an additional barrier to getting their library cards. In most states, foster parents are not the legal guardians of the child, the state is. Therefore, they cannot sign as "parent or legal guardian" as many children's library card applications require. In fact, they are expressly forbidden from doing so and can risk losing their foster care license if they do. Some libraries get around this by working directly with the child's social workers who sign the cards. Other libraries have a broad definition of "parent" that includes foster parents. Look at your policy with an eye to ensuring that it allows children in foster care to get cards. Then make sure that the library staff and the foster care community are aware of the policy.

CHILDREN OF INCARCERATED PARENTS

Whether they are in foster care, living with the nonincarcerated parent, or incarcerated with their parent in a prison or jail nursery, children of incarcerated parents are at risk—and they are difficult to reach. The New York Public Library provides services to these children and their families through their Daddy and Me program and, in partnership with the Brooklyn Public Library, by offering programs in the nursery of the Rikers Island jail. And both libraries offer reentry services while encouraging people to get library cards.

These family literacy programs are grounded in the Every Child Ready to Read philosophy; in both cases, parents are encouraged to read to their children. Daddy and Me, a family literacy program at the Rikers Island jail, begun by Correctional Services Librarian Nicholas Higgins, teaches fathers, and sometimes mothers, to read to their children. At the end of the five-week program, they are recorded reading a book. The book and a CD of the recording are presented to the children in person. In the nursery at Rikers, children's librarians read to children and their mothers, demonstrating early literacy skills and techniques. The mothers are then given board books to read to their children when the librarians are gone. Strong family ties have been shown to reduce recidivism rates (Visher and Travis, 2003: 101). These types of programs help incarcerated parents maintain those important ties.

Providing Outreach

Outreach is key to meeting children with disabilities and their families. One children's services librarian describes her job at the library as inviting parents in one at a time. They are used to not being welcomed, especially if their children have disabilities with behavioral issues. She feels it is her responsibility to let them know they are welcome and to ask them to tell their friends.

Libraries are not necessarily the first resource they think of. A librarian attending the national conference of the Association for Deaf Children came face-to-face with this reality. Throughout the first day she was asked, "Why are you here?" at least a dozen times. By the fourth and last day, people were saying things like, "Oh, you're the librarian. . . . Do you have books for Sally's older sister on learning sign language?"

Finding Families of Children with Disabilities

Families of children with disabilities can be found throughout our communities in many of the same places as families of typically developing children: PTA meetings, open school nights, grocery stores, houses of worship, playgrounds, parks, zoos, swimming pools, YMCAs/YWCAs, and so forth. Here are some additional places you can look for them:

- Hospitals
- Clinics
- Agencies that provide services
- Benefits offices such as SSI and Medicaid
- Residential schools
- Self-contained schools, school programs, and classes
- Support and advocacy groups
- Government offices that work with people with disabilities
- Electronic discussion lists, blogs, and online communities
- Self-contained recreation programs
- Sign language classes

These groups should be receiving publicity about your programs at the very least. In the best-case scenario, you are already working with them to plan and publicize library services.

Finding Children and Teens with Disabilities

Again, for the most part, you find children and teens with disabilities in the same ways you find typically developing children—through their schools, after-school programs, recreation programs, and families. You may also find them at medical and therapeutic centers, respite programs, and group homes. However, when you find them,

Virtual Parenting Communities

Virtual parenting communities are often associated with advocacy groups for specific disabilities. They take many forms: online discussions, e-mail relationships, blogs, and social media. What they all share is the ability to make a direct connection between one person and another. The following are examples of some of these types of communities; similar resources are available for many other conditions.

- CHARGE Syndrome has a Yahoo Group discussion list at http://health.groups.yahoo.com/group/CHARGE/ that connects families with this rare condition.

- Down Syndrome Blogs at http://downsyndromeblogs.blogspot.com/ is a clearinghouse for blogs on Down syndrome.

- My Child Without Limits, sponsored by United Cerebral Palsy, is open to parents of children with all types of disabilities; one such group can be found at http://www.inspire.com/groups/my-child-without-limits/.

- National Alliance on Mental Illness has a variety of online communities, including Twitter, Facebook, and peer-to-peer support, accessible at http://www.nami.org/Template.cfm?section=Find_Support.

they may not have the same frame of reference for the library as typically developing children do. They may not see it as a destination.

If you meet children and teens with a disability outside the library, find out if they use the library and if not, why not. It may be that they are not fluid readers and do not know that we have audiobooks, music, magazines, and movies that circulate. Let them know about the other services the library offers. If they say the library is too noisy, suggest a quieter time or noise-blocking headphones. If they say it is too quiet, suggest playing music on headphones. It may be that they have never thought of the library as a destination before.

Taking Every Opportunity to Involve Families

Encourage parent participation through one-on-one interactions at the reference desk and by honoring parents' requests for materials. Ask bilingual parents whose first language is not English for recommendations for books or to proofread your publicity in that language. Ask them to share information about library programs and services with their friends and family and on their blogs and discussion lists.

Getting Involved in Virtual Parenting Communities

Monitor local virtual communities, and be aware of national ones. The Internet has fundamentally changed the experiences of many parents of children with disabilities. Previously, a person with a rare disability might never meet another person with that disability. Now, they often meet online and share information and support. You can also ask these communities to publicize the library and your programs. Explore developing reciprocal links on webpages.

Working One-on-One with Other Professionals

Individual service providers, educators, and other professionals can be very helpful in fully integrating your library. These professionals include:

- service coordinators, aka social workers or case managers;
- physical, occupational, speech, and other therapists;
- teachers, EI providers, and other educators;

- one-to-one aides, such as personal care attendants (PCAs) or sign language interpreters;
- doctors, psychologists, and psychiatrists; and
- advocates and lawyers.

These individuals work with children and teens with disabilities and their families and are often eager to get involved. Our goal in working with other professionals such as teachers, social workers, advocates, and therapy providers is in large part to reach children and teens with disabilities and their families. This is a very different relationship than the relationship with the individual or family in which our goal is to provide service directly.

Like the parents' goals, the goals of service providers may be child specific, easily defined, and easy to meet. For example, one librarian was approached by a service coordinator about involving a teen who was blind and loved reading and libraries. While he volunteered with at her library, he would receive a salary from the New York City's summer youth employment program. The librarian met with Donald and his case manager to determine the supports he would need. He needed Braille books if he was going to read to the children, an audio input/output program for the computer, and a way to get to and from the library. The books they already had, and the case manager approached the New York Commission for the Blind to provide the Assistive Technology. Donald's grandmother, with whom he lived, spoke with the school about getting the travel trainer to negotiate the routes with him. When Donald came to the library for the first time it quickly became evident that he also needed the staff to push their chairs in when they were not sitting in them and to keep the pathways around the office clear. Donald spent 20 hours a week with them that summer reading to children in hospitals, helping with the garden program, inventorying the music collection, and developing a curriculum for manners in collaboration with the library and another agency, Art Education for the Blind. It was such a successful summer that he came back the next year.

Some professionals get more involved than others. One service coordinator and a librarian have worked together for over 12 years to support an adult with a disability, Jane, a volunteer at the library. The librarian has Jane's permission to speak with the service coordinator. The service coordinator has kept the librarian informed about unanticipated schedule changes due to hospitalizations, listened when the librarian told her Jane had asked for a referral to a housing advocate, and alerted the librarian to issues that might come up. The work that Jane does is useful and frees up staff to do other things. Volunteering is important to Jane, who told the librarian:

> I love being a volunteer at the library because I have a chance to change my lifestyle and contribute to other people when I'm needed. Usually, my life centers around therapy all week long. However, for two hours each week I have the opportunity to apply myself to my work skills and also socialize with the nicest people. I like gardening and I hope I am doing a satisfactory job. I like thinking that I am delighting children if the garden is flourishing.

Because Jane's availability to participate can be inconsistent, it is this partnership with her service provider than enables her to successfully volunteer at the library.

Professionals can represent groups of children or teens with disabilities rather than an individual. Teachers or respite care workers can represent a class of students or an after-school recreation group. They may want you to visit the children at their site or may be willing to visit you at the library. Setting this up on a one-to-one basis is really no different than scheduling a general education class visit or a boys and girls club visit.

There are some additional pieces of information that you may need to make the experience a successful one. After exploring the standard questions (e.g., How old are the children? What grade are they in?), ask these questions:

- What are the teacher's goals for the visit?
- What support do the children need?
- Do any of the children use wheelchairs?
- Is there anything that needs to be avoided? (This question can apply equally to allergies and phobias.)
- How do the children communicate? What languages do the children speak?

Also, do not assume that the children have library cards.

Because the professionals' goals are different, the working relationship is different. Consider these variations:

- The interactions may be more detached, less emotional.
- Confidentiality issues have to be negotiated.

- Professionals may be less available and harder to reach.
- There is more potential for misunderstanding, as the librarians are at one remove from the individuals they are ultimately serving.
- The librarians and the professionals need to establish respect for one another's expertise.

However, the relationships can be productive and rewarding.

Working with Institutions

Working with institutions is usually more complicated than working with the individuals within them. For one thing, some of the goals may be different. Some goals of a service provision agency that overlap with the previously discussed partners may include:

- helping a client achieve his or her full potential and
- helping the child meet an IFSP or IEP goal.

Institutional goals that may diverge from those of the individuals, families, or professionals include:

- demonstrating the effectiveness of a program through the success of individuals;
- implementing a new directive or mandate, such as "Get the clients out into the community more";
- meeting a placement quota;
- providing staff with an opportunity for training;
- developing new opportunities; and
- meeting funding requirements such as working with community partners.

When these goals are in accord with our institutions and those of the children or teens we are serving, we can form mutually beneficial partnerships.

At The Child's Place, library staff worked with an agency serving Deaf children to incorporate early literacy practices into their home visiting program. As part of a state-supported Parent and Child Grant, Brooklyn Public Library developed Family Literacy

PowerPacks, some of which were designed specifically with the needs of Deaf children and Braille readers in mind. They trained the staff of the Deaf Family Service Unit of the New York Foundling Hospital to use the kits with the families of the Deaf children they were visiting. The library circulated the Deaf Literacy PowerPacks to the agency, which showed parents how to use them. The PowerPacks were traded for new ones at each monthly visit. The social workers reported that there were more weekly literacy activities in the families they had trained to use the PowerPacks than in those they had not. Here we met both parties' goals. The library wanted to get increased use out of the PowerPacks, and the agency wanted to support early literacy in the home. The Cleveland Braille and Talking Book Library has had a long-standing mutually beneficial partnership with the Perkins School for the Blind. Both agencies are dedicated to helping people who are blind to read. Their joint programs have included virtual book discussion groups and mentoring programs for struggling Braille readers.

Forming partnerships can be more difficult when the goals of the agency are different or conflict with yours. A for-profit insurance company approached a library asking to demonstrate its product, special needs trusts. The agency's goal was to tell people about its product. The library was interested in the topic but felt that hosting just this one company would be seen as an endorsement. So they found other speakers, one from a not-for-profit and another from a competing company, and held a workshop on the topic. While the goals may have been different, advertising their services and providing information, the partnership was successful.

In some cases formal memorandums of agreement may be necessary. In these agreements, each institution clearly states its goals, expectations, responsibilities, and liabilities. Legal counsel should always be involved in approving the agreements, but it is often helpful if you have a draft to present first.

These categories—individuals with a disability, families, professionals, and institutions—can be fluid. A teen with a disability may speak on his own behalf but also represent a self-advocacy group. School librarians are in the unique position of representing the institution, in this case the school, when writing the IEP, and later the individual student when implementing it. Partnerships with individuals may evolve into partnerships with the entire agency. A successful class visit arranged by one teacher may result in the principal wanting to have all of the classes visit, or an institutional partnership may lead to an individual one if a staff person moves and is still interested in working together in her new position.

Partnerships add richness to libraries. They allow us to reach potential users we may not have otherwise reached. They bring us resources that we may not have had. And they help us get the word out about the great things we do.

Resources

Dewey, Barbara I., and Loretta Parham. 2006. *Achieving Diversity: A How-To-Do-It Manual for Librarians.* New York: Neal-Schuman.

Diamant-Cohen, Betsy. 2010. *Children's Services: Partnerships for Success.* Chicago: ALA Editions.

Holt, Leslie Edmonds, and Glen E. Holt. 2010. *Public Library Service for the Poor: Doing All We Can.* Chicago: ALA Editions.

Osborn, Robin, ed. 2004. *From Outreach to Equity: Innovative Models of Library Policy and Practice.* Chicago: ALA Editions.

Payne, Ruby K., Philip DeVol, and Terie Dreussi Smith. 2005. *Bridges out of Poverty: Strategies for Professionals and Communities.* Revised ed. Highlands, TX: aha! Process Books.

Schuchs-Gopaul, Elizabeth L. 2011. "Twelve Things Every JAG Should Know: Legal Issues Facing Military Families with Special Needs Children: A Primer and Introduction." *The Reporter* 38, no. 1: 20–26. http://www.wrightslaw.com/blog/?p=5891.

Smallwood, Carol, ed. 2010. *Librarians as Community Partners: An Outreach Handbook.* Chicago: ALA Editions.

Wrightslaw. 2011. "Military and Department of Defense (DOD) Special Education." Wrightslaw. http://www.wrightslaw.com/info/dod.index.htm.

References

Batshaw, Mark L., Louis Pellegrino, and Nancy J. Roizen. eds. 2007. *Children with Disabilities.* 6th ed. Baltimore: Paul H. Brookes.

Glozier, Kyle. 1997. "What Every Kid Should Have: A Birthday Every Day." *Mouth Magazine,* November/December: 16.

Meyer, Don, and Patricia Vadasy. 2008. *Sibshops: Workshop for Siblings of Children with Special Needs.* Revised ed. Baltimore: Paul G. Brooks.

Oberg, Charles. 2003. "The Impact of Childhood Poverty on Health and Development." *Healthy Generations* 4, no. 1: 2–3. http://www.epi .umn.edu/mch/resources/hg/hg_childpoverty.pdf.

Stone, Douglas, Bruce Patton, and Sheila Heen. 2010. *Difficult Conversations: How to Discuss What Matters Most.* New York: Penguin Books.

Visher, Christy A., and Jeremy Travis. 2003. "Transitions from Prison to Community: Understanding Individual Pathways." *Annual Review of Sociology* 29: 89–113. http://www.caction.org/rrt_new/professionals/ articles/VISHER-PRISON%20TO%20COMMUNITY.pdf.

Designing Library Services for All Children

9

"They played with Josiah!"

—*Grandmother of a child with osteogenesis imperfecta*
after an inclusive preschool storytime program

"Fun."

—*Josiah after the same storytime*

Librarians know more than they realize about meeting the needs of children with disabilities. Having a public service orientation and creating services for a wide variety of audiences are hallmarks of our daily work. As children's services specialists, we already design recreational and educational programs for children within a broad range of ages. Meeting the needs of individuals in a group has always been the norm.

Many parents of children with disabilities come to the library precisely because they want a normal community experience for their child. They are not looking for therapy, and when therapy is provided in the library, it is trained professionals who provide it, not the librarians. Because library activities are typically informal and self-selected, they are ideally suited for children with varying abilities and interests.

Within this framework, it is essential for librarians to see the child first and consider the disability only if it impacts the child's ability to participate in a desired activity. It is important that the experience be a normal one. We need to be ready to serve all children and not be casting around for a quick fix when an unanticipated child with a disability suddenly appears. Universal Design allows us to be prepared.

General Considerations

The behavior of the librarian and staff is the most critical factor in providing a successful library experience for a child with a disability. As the opening story illustrates, other children and their parents will take their cue from the sensitivity and comfort level of the staff as they acknowledge and accept individual differences among children. If we model appropriate behavior, children will often follow.

Be prepared to answer children's questions openly and honestly, using simple, matter-of-fact language. Involve the child with a disability to the extent possible. One day in the Read and Play program for children birth to age five, a four-year-old child pointed to the leg braces on the child next to the librarian and asked, "What's wrong with him?" The librarian responded by asking James, who was also four, if he wanted to answer the question or wanted her to answer the question. James indicated she should answer, and the librarian told the first child that she thought that they helped James to walk just like the librarian's glasses helped her to see. Had James indicated that he did not want the question answered, the librarian might have said something like, "James wants his privacy right now," and shown the first child where to find the dolls and leg braces for the dolls to let him get comfortable with the idea.

Take a page from literacy instruction and "presume competence" (Kluth and Chandler-Olcott, 2008: 33). Start by assuming the child can participate. If you have designed the service well, using a Universal Design and Multiple Intelligences framework, in all likelihood the child can participate. If not, determine the barrier and fix it. Ask the child, "What would make this easier for you?" If she does not or cannot answer, ask the parent. Bear in mind that we do not need to know the child's diagnosis, just what it takes to make the experience a successful one.

The Environment

Now is the time to correct any problems that became evident in your assessment of the physical and virtual libraries discussed in Chapter 6. How your library looks and feels will set the tone for your initial encounters and make a statement about your commitment to inclusivity. Wide, clear aisles, large signage with good contrast and graphic support, depictions of people with disabilities in your publicity and books, and toys and games children and teens with disabilities can use create a solid, visible foundation for your library service.

When preparing for your program, assess the physical arrangement of the program area and any ways the space could better meet the needs of all children. Would a different location provide easier accessibility or have better lighting? Could the space and surroundings be modified to reduce distractions and create a more enclosed environment for a very active, easily distracted child? Is there room for the child's wheelchair or positioning equipment? Having to move the program out of a sunken pit at the last minute when you realize that a child using a walker wants to attend would be embarrassing, drawing unnecessary attention to the child's disability.

Cube chairs work well for a variety of children. They rotate to provide different levels of support and accommodate children of different sizes. Bean bag chairs are great for many children but can be hazardous to infants: their use should always be supervised. Chapter 11 provides some examples of suppliers of these types of items.

Good lighting is important. It allows children who are blind to make the most of their vision. Avoid standing in front of a light source when speaking to people who are Deaf or hard of hearing or who have communication issues. They all need to see your face and your body language clearly. Natural light florescent lighting is better for people with epilepsy, as it seems to trigger seizures less often and people with sensory integration disorder tend to find it more tolerable.

Policies

Standard policies can inadvertently interfere with our ability to provide inclusive library services. These can be anything from accounting procedures that require purchasing from certain vendors to the prohibition on touching children. When designing inclusive library service, almost everything needs to be examined.

To be inclusive, consider the following policies:

- Examine age and other requirements to see if they are really necessary.
- Eliminate any program eligibility requirements that would have the effect of screening out children with disabilities.
- Schedule your programs to account for the extra time it may take a child with a disability to get home from school.

- Be flexible with time limits. If a child is taking extra time with his craft, let him take it home and finish it. Provide the materials and lend the tools. *The crayons almost always come back.*

- Permit parents to accompany their child into programs. Encourage parents to separate only when the child is ready.

- Be open to the possibility that the parent may want to bring the child's service provider into a library program. The service provider may want to work with the child within the context of the experience that is part of the child's regular routine. Or the service provider may want to give the parent or the library staff suggestions on ways for the child to participate in the program more fully. This can be a wonderful opportunity for the library staff to learn from the expertise of a specialist in another discipline. Take advantage!

- Keep the group size small. Smaller groups allow for individual attention when necessary and do not overwhelm children.

- Anticipate potential safety hazards. Not all children are equal in physical strength, coordination, or ability to assess risks.

Inclusive Literacy

Literacy is, after all, what libraries are about. In the past, it was not expected that people with disabilities would become literate. Fortunately, those expectations have changed. We understand that one teaching method will not reach all students and one definition of literacy will not fit all people.

Paula Kluth and Kelly Chandler-Olcott offer a model of inclusive literacy instruction that can be adapted for the library setting. They set forth seven principles for promoting inclusive literacy practices:

1. Maintain high expectations.
2. Provide models of literate behavior.
3. Elicit students' perspectives.
4. Promote diversity as a positive resource.
5. Adopt elastic instructional approaches.
6. Use flexible grouping strategies.
7. Differentiate instruction. (Kluth and Chandler-Olcott, 2008: 45)

One of the greatest gifts we can give a child or a teen with a disability is high expectations. We know that not everyone will learn to read. But we cannot know which children will not. We do know, however, that if we do not expect a child to learn to read and if we do not give him the opportunity to learn to read, he will not. We need to share our high literacy expectations with parents. Modeling literate behavior is one way of sharing with parents.

In the library, we must provide models of literate behavior for the individual and also for her family. Current research indicates that librarians need to model literacy behaviors for all families, including those of typically developing children. Once-a-week storytimes are not enough to influence literacy outcomes. This is the basis for the Association for Library Service to Children's (ALSC) Every Child Ready to Read program and the cornerstone of children's services since the early 2000s.

As discussed earlier, one of the fundamental principles of the disability rights movement is "Nothing about us without us." This is a sound educational principle too. Getting to know the child's view of his own literacy will help us support him. What books does he like to read? How does he read? Where does he like to read? Does he like to read? Perhaps a child hates reading and is only reading assigned books. Can you find something that he is interested in? Maybe he loves storytelling but hates reading. Can you suggest audiobooks? It may be the case that he does not see himself as a reader. However, you know he avidly explores gaming magazines or comic books. Point this out.

Point out literacy behaviors to parents to support modeling them. During a program the children's services specialist observed a four-year-old with Down syndrome following an arrow key. When she pointed out this developing literacy skill to the mother, the mother indicated that she had thought her daughter could not learn to read. Likewise, parents do not necessarily understand that using a pictorial communication system demonstrates an understanding of one of the fundamental concepts of reading—that symbols represent language—and can be a bridge to literacy.

As our understanding of cognition grows, we are more accepting of the diversity of ways to read. Reading print, or large print, with one's eyes, reading Braille with one's fingers, and reading audiobooks with one's ears are all legitimate ways of reading. New technology even allows some people to read print with their tongues! Having a variety of formats available gives us more literacy tools.

Determining audiences for programs, or grouping strategies, can be difficult. ALSC recommends very specific groupings that focus on clear skills. They identify those groups by both age and developmental markers. Generally speaking, it is best to group by chronological age, especially as the children get older. A 16-year-old with an intellectual disability is not a 4-year-old trapped in a 16-year-old's body. This image, often found in literature and the media, is wrong. A 16-year-old with the academic skills of a prekindergarten student may very well have the hormones of an average adolescent. She is most likely more interested in dating and cars than in *Frog and Toad* or *Sesame Street*.

So, what to do about grouping strategies? The following approaches can be helpful. First, use broad age categories such as preschool, school-age, and teen. Second, provide for a variety of intellectual levels within each program. For the preschoolers, one programmer targets the two-and-a-half- to three-year-old range and often uses pop-up books or books with songs; for a school-age program she uses three books, each pegged to a different academic stage. Poetry, traditional folktales, and nonfiction tend to interest older students and teens. And third, have a clearly defined role for teens, for example, encouraging teens with and without disabilities to help out when they attend storytime.

In recent years, schools have adopted Multiple Intelligences principles and differentiated instruction. Adopting these techniques in the library both aligns us more closely with schools and better meets the needs of our patrons. The outline of the Farm Program in Chapter 5 (see Table 5.2, p. 68) is one example of these techniques.

Programs

Flexibility is key to making library programs accessible to children with disabilities. Think simply and creatively: costly and complicated solutions are not usually necessary. Providing sponges for a child with tactile sensitivity to encourage him to participate in a "finger painting" activity is a simple, imaginative adaptation that requires little cost and no extra staff time or training.

In the best Universal Design fashion, many of the program design elements that allow inclusion are applicable in a number of situations. For example, avoiding an overstimulating environment is important for children and teens with sensory integration, attention deficit disorder with or without hyperactivity, and autism. Keeping activities focused, doing only one activity at a time, and not using background music help all of these too. Other planning considerations include:

- normalizing the disability experience;
- being aware of invisible disabilities;
- making the structure of the program explicit and offer the option of preparing the children for it;
- encouraging but not demanding participation;
- communicating clearly;
- using stories that appeal to a broad range of children and teens;
- enabling focusing;
- providing quiet areas;
- using multisensory, Multiple Intelligences strategies;
- having appropriate Assistive and Adaptive Technology available;
- encouraging socialization; and
- offering choices, but not so many as to overwhelm.

Normalize the Disability Experience

Fifty-six years ago, Augusta Baker urged us to reevaluate our collections: "Are there books on the shelves which will . . . perpetuate stereotyped ideas in the minds of your regular library users?" (Horning, 2010: 12). Baker was referring to racial and ethnic stereotypes. Now is the time to extend this sensitivity to people with disabilities. Chapter 6 looks at this issue in more depth.

Likewise, our toy collections must be inclusive. Have toys that reflect the backgrounds and abilities of all children. Dolls with a variety of ethnic backgrounds are easily available as are wheelchairs, mobility canes, glasses, and even hearing aids and other accessories. Chapter 11 also examines this issue.

Anticipate Invisible Disabilities

Most disabilities are invisible. When a child has a learning disability, autism, or an emotional disability, you will not necessarily know. People often make assumptions about other people based solely on their appearance. At a new job, one librarian encountered a brother and a sister who were attending one of the programs on a regular basis and appeared to be about seven and nine years old. After observing them for several weeks, she assumed the younger child had a developmental disability. You can imagine her shock when she learned that the boy was, in fact, three years old. His behavior had been age appropriate all along. Because she made an assumption based on appearances, she was the one who was out of line.

Provide Structure

Imagine getting on a bus and not knowing where it will go or when you will get off. You ask the driver and she tells you, "I'll let you know." You try to wait patiently for your stop but find yourself getting fidgety and anxious. When the driver finally announces your stop, you are so flustered you leave your favorite umbrella on the bus. All that angst could have been avoided if you'd had a map of the bus route, a global positioning system, or a more forthcoming driver.

In the library we are like the bus driver: we know the route and what will happen next. The person coming in the door does not. Our libraries have a plan that is obvious to us, fiction here, nonfiction there, bathrooms and program room in the back. When we create our programs, we have a certain structure in mind. The song flows from the story into the activity. Cleanup logically follows playtime. In order to fully include children with disabilities, and their young friends, we should extend them the courtesy of preparing them for their visit and letting them in on the plan.

Start before the family enters the building. Have a map of the building on your website. Let them know what to expect in the library by providing social story–like introductions. Social stories describe new experiences in detail and in advance, allowing individuals to prepare for them. The Joint Scotch Plains (NJ) and Fanwood (NJ) Memorial Public Libraries' Libraries and Autism project (http://www.thejointlibrary.org/autism/resources.htm) and the Brooklyn Public Library (http://www.bklynpubliclibrary.org/pv_obj_cache/pv_obj_id_EF6036D2DCD2433140EF6880FB291AD300B0C500/filename/Flatlands%20After%20School%20Stories.doc) both have sample social stories available on their websites.

Offer tours for newcomers. Children who are blind need to be oriented to their surroundings. Children with mobility issues can plan their routes in their own time. Being in a familiar place will lessen anxiety for children and teens with emotional disabilities, those on the autism spectrum, and those with intellectual disabilities. Deaf children will have visual cues in advance, and children with sensory integration disorder will know what to expect.

Encourage parents to arrive early for a program to allow their children to become acclimated to the environment and find their way around. Arriving early may help the child with autism or an intellectual or emotional disability get acclimated to the surroundings and achieve a certain comfort level before the larger group of parents and children arrive. Leaving early and gradually extending the amount of time a child participates can make a program successful for the child with a short attention span.

Like the fairy tales and folktales we often use, our programs all have a structure that is clear to us. Make that structure clear to the participants as well. Use picture schedules such as the one in Figure 9.1. You can also use photographs. Verbally explain the agenda, and refer back to the picture schedule. Anticipate that transitions—browsing to storytime, circle time to free play, active fingerplays and singing to quiet story, the end of the program—may be difficult for the child with an intellectual disability, autism, and many other disabilities. Keep program routines consistent, using repetitive cues, songs, or directions to ease transition from one activity to another.

Structure within the stories you use is also important. Books with rhyme and poetry are helpful to children with communication issues, hearing issues, and intellectual disabilities. Refrains that repeat throughout the book are likewise useful.

Remember that sudden or unexpected movements and unfamiliar textures and sounds may be frightening for children who cannot provide a context through the senses or understanding or who cannot use visual or auditory cues to anticipate them. Warnings about loud noises or new textures will minimize disruptions.

FIGURE 9.1 Picture Schedule

Source: The Picture Communication Symbol © 1981–2012 by Mayer-Johnson LLC. All Rights Reserved Worldwide. Used with permission.

Design for Active Participation

Make library activities active. Show patrons how to look up a book as you do it. Take them with you to the shelves. Encourage them to repeat the chorus of a book or song with you. Use call and response during programs. Have children turn the pages. Sing songs and do fingerplays twice so the children can become familiar with them. Engage children in conversation. The reciprocity will build social and communication skills, particularly in children with autism and communication disorders. Keeping children and teens actively engaged will support those with attention issues, communication issues, intellectual disabilities, and learning differences.

Find ways to engage a child and direct his energies. During storytime, ask the child to help turn the pages of the book. During regular class visits to the library, one child could not sit still long enough for the librarian to read one page of a picture book. By offering him the reward of turning the pages, she was able to get him to sit for longer and longer amounts of time before he would jump up and act. Gradually over the course of the school year, he learned to wait for one page and then two; eventually sitting for the entire book was not a problem. Holding a manipulative associated with the story can help some children with focus and self-regulation. More general fidgets may also be useful. One very small, unreplicated study showed that chewing gum may assist some students trying to focus (McGrath, 2004).

Communicate Clearly

Communication is key to everything we do. There are many potential barriers to effective communication when working with people with disabilities. In the previous chapter, we discussed some of the issues that may arise when speaking with parents. Although they have different causes and manifestations, the following conditions all have the potential for communication issues to arise when speaking with children:

- Autism spectrum disorder
- Intellectual disabilities
- Learning disabilities
- Physical disabilities
- Deaf and hard of hearing
- Attention deficit disorder with or without hyperactivity
- Sensory-processing disorder

- Emotional disabilities
- Speech and language delays

The following techniques will allow effective communication whatever the issue.

There is more than one way to "talk." People use spoken words, signed words, printed words, and pictograms to talk to each other every day. It is important to defer to the child's preferred mode of communication. If a child or family member speaks sign language or Spanish, bring in a staff member who speaks that language, learn some words, and get an interpreter. If a child uses a communication board, let her use it. If she uses a pictorial communication system, reinforce its use by using it yourself. Use picture schedules, and have symbols for key ideas available.

Learning to communicate a few core words in a variety of ways will go a long way toward making people feel welcome. Learn the signs for a few basic words, and share them with the other staff and children. Have someone else learn them in Spanish and share them. Have picture symbols of these words available (see, e.g., Figure 9.2). A vocabulary of fewer than 20 words will go a long way toward creating a friendly environment. Consider learning the following words in the languages you encounter:

- Hello/goodbye
- Yes/no
- Please
- Thank you/you're welcome

FIGURE 9.2 Mayer-Johnson Symbol for Book

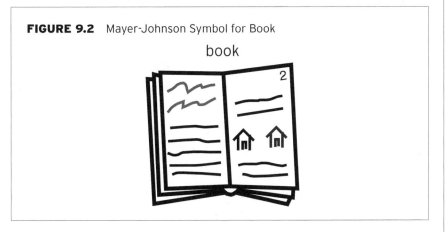

Source: The Picture Communication Symbol © 1981–2012 by Mayer-Johnson LLC. All Rights Reserved Worldwide. Used with permission.

- My/your
- Name
- Book
- Home
- Library
- Bathroom

For example, the word *book* can be rendered in the following synonymous ways:

- Book
- Libro
- Using the picture symbol in Figure 9.2
- Placing your palms together, thumbs up, in front of your chest and rotating them outward, keeping the pinky sides or your hands touching, until they are flat

The American Sign Language University has a free database of introductory signs and can be accessed at http://www.lifeprint.com/. On the Internet, Google translator, BabelFish, or Dictionary.com can provide basic, accurate phrases in many languages. Some children, family members, and interpreters may be willing to teach the group a word. Children who use PECS (Picture Exchange Communication System) symbols can share them with the others in the group.

One of the simplest techniques for good communication is rephrasing. If someone does not understand what you said, say it differently. Avoid figures of speech and humor unless they are explained. Allow children and teens time to process communication. Keep your verbal and nonverbal messages congruent. Ensure that directions are simple, and model them. Break down activities into small steps, demonstrating each step and providing one-on-one support if necessary. Reinforce each step with praise and encouragement. Refer to visual schedules. These will allow concrete learners, such as those with intellectual disabilities, and literal communicators, such as those with Asperger's, to understand more easily. They will also keep children with attention issues and learning disabilities on track.

Whatever the child's preferred mode of communication, do not rely on the parent to interpret. Approach the child on her level, getting the child's attention with eye contact. Do not interrupt or anticipate her response, no matter how long it takes. Make an effort to understand the child on your own. If this proves impossible, explain this to the child and ask if it's okay to include the parent in your conversation.

Keep It Real

For storytimes, select books with clear, representational illustrations and stories representing experiences and objects familiar to the children. Photographs work well, as do realistic drawings and paintings. For older children, look for hip cartoon illustrations that portray young adults and adults. Books with straightforward story lines can also be effective. Nonfiction is more concrete, and many people find it easier to relate to. It is not necessary for the entire program to be realistic. However, keeping at least part of your program grounded in the concrete will help younger children and those children with autism and intellectual disabilities. They will also serve as a bridge to the more complex and abstract stories on the same theme.

Read stories with flair and emphasis, diverting slightly to provide explanations when necessary: this helps children focus their attention. Clarifying what may be unknown or confusing can help the child with an intellectual disability stay with the story and may also be helpful for others in the group with limited attention spans.

Making the story tangible can also help. Enhance the storytimes with flannel boards, realia, puppets, and other thematic props. These strategies are helpful for concrete learners and children with attention issues and learning and intellectual disabilities.

Enable Focusing

Keeping the audience's attention is always difficult. Providing exciting, well-thought-out programs with lots of participation is an excellent start. The following strategies may also help.

Minimize sensory overstimulation by reducing background noise and loud voices, have a soft, noise-absorbing floor surface, and request that people not wear strong scents. Carpeted floors or those with soft tiles help to absorb distracting background noise. People with autism, sensory integration disorder, and attention issues will benefit from the ability to focus on the important sounds.

Have an FM amplification system available. FM systems use a microphone and transmitter that send the sound to the individual earphones of users. Youth who are hard of hearing and children with attention or sensory issues may benefit. These systems are also a good investment for programs that need to be simultaneously interpreted into other languages.

Offer Quiet Areas

Have a self-contained quiet area for children to explore. It can serve as a transition area for children getting used to the program, an area where an overstimulated child can retreat to, and a safe place for a blind child to explore. Exciting toys will encourage children to explore independently and safely. Capitalize on corner spaces, and use chairs, large blocks, low shelving, or pillows to create smaller spaces within the room. Put up "roadblocks" using large chairs or a table to inhibit running in an area that is usually wide open. The time-out area should be separate.

Provide Multisensory Experiences

We examined the rationale for multisensory presentation in Chapter 5 and reviewed a sample program. Now it's time to see how multisensory experiences can be integrated throughout the library.

Simple changes such as signage that includes pictures and shelf locaters with toys representing the subjects can make independently navigating the stacks much easier for people with intellectual or learning disabilities and those who are Deaf. Having magnifiers, signatures guides, large pens, and felt tip pens on hand for library card registration can enable children who are blind or have learning or physical disabilities to sign their own cards.

In programs, consider the engagement strategies described in Table 9.1. As you can see, each design element addresses a variety of needs.

Invest in Some Assistive and Adaptive Technology

To be fully inclusive, you will need some Assistive or Adaptive Technology (AT). Some things you may already have, such as toddler-sized crayons, will also work well for children with physical disabilities and sensory issues. Your computers have standard accessibility features such screen magnification, sticky keys, and speech output that assist youth with visual, physical, learning, and intellectual disabilities. Other things are commercially available, such as scissors that operate by squeezing that are useful for children with physical disabilities and tactile issues.

Other items, such as BIGmack communicators, which record short statements that can be played back by touching a large button, will require special purchase. BIGmacks help children with autism, speech and language delays, and emotional disabilities participate in choral reading or signing or answer simple yes/no questions. A text-to-audio

TABLE 9.1 Engagement Strategies

Use This Strategy . . .	To Involve Children and Teens with . . .
Music	Learning disabilities, autism, attention deficit disorder, blindness, speech and language issues, emotional disabilities
Props	Learning disabilities, intellectual disabilities, attention deficit disorder, sensory integration disorder, vision and hearing issues
Call and response	Speech and language issues, attention deficit disorder, learning disabilities, blindness and low vision
Limited choices	Emotional disabilities, attention deficit disorder, autism, sensory integration disorder, attention deficit disorder
Movement	Hearing issues, blindness, intellectual disabilities, attention deficit disorder, sensory integration disorder
Creative dramatics	Hearing issues, intellectual disabilities, attention deficit disorder, LDs, emotional disabilities

scanner, either as a stand-alone or as part of computer station, can assist older children and teens with visual disabilities, learning disabilities, and intellectual disabilities. These readers will become more popular as baby boomers age and develop age-related vision issues. Chapter 10 covers AT in more depth.

Encourage Socialization

Socializing, or having a good time with other people, is at the core of what makes an experience desirable for most people. There are many ways to encourage socialization. Introducing yourself to the children and the children to each other is a good start. Name tags are great and so are songs and having the children say their names, associating them with their voice as well as their visual schema. Having children say or sing their names helps those with visual impairments to identify the children by their voices.

Make play activities available that stimulate language, spark the imagination, and encourage interaction among children. Dolls, trucks, dress-up clothes, blocks, dramatic play areas, and a sand/water table all fit the bill. Make sure there are enough materials for all of the children, including duplicates of the most popular items, to head off squabbling.

Demonstrate basic concepts such as sharing and turn taking. You can join in the play to facilitate these skills. At the same time, you will offer an alternative parenting strategy to the all too frequent screeches of "Johnny, share!" or "Play nice, Jane!" from the parent across the room.

It may be necessary to promote and facilitate play by arranging toys in a variety of ways to help children get started. Start a puzzle. Initiate a block construction so children have a model to follow, group dolls together with some doll furniture, or place farm animals inside an enclosure of blocks, helping children make the cognitive connections.

During craft time, encourage socialization by providing fewer tools than children and assign specific roles to children, such as passing out paper or glue. Having to ask someone else to pass the glue becomes an opportunity for the children to get to know each other, and a shy child can sometimes interact more comfortably through a defined job. However, do not have so few items as to frustrate the children.

Explore Emotions

Understanding emotions is important to communication, behavior, and socialization. Using books that focus on feelings and self-awareness can be useful for children with autism, those with attention deficit disorder, and those with behavioral issues. It also gives children permission to talk about feelings.

Design Considerations for Specific Types of Disabilities

While most issues that come up in the library can be accommodated through the Universal Design methods earlier, some barriers will require specific solutions.

Blindness and Low Vision

The unfamiliar setting of the physical library is a barrier to children who are blind. Offer tours of the library in advance of a program, during a quiet time, or work with the Orientation and Mobility (O&M) specialist at the children's school to include the library space as part of the children's training.

Children who are blind or have low vision can easily become isolated. Those with very low vision may be unable to watch and observe other young children at play and to learn through imitation and modeling. They need the opportunity for hands-on exploration and exposure to materials that stimulate all of their senses. Sometimes one-on-one guidance in developing new skills is necessary.

Describe what you are going to do before you launch into a rhythm activity or fingerplay. Table 9.2 describes how you might support a child who is blind when using the fingerplay the Itsy Bitsy Spider. If the parent is there or you have a volunteer, they can guide the child through the fingerplay the first time. Or, teach it in advance. Be sure to do it twice so the child has the opportunity to do it herself.

Use big books and oversized flannel board pieces in bright colors that contrast distinctly from the background color. Although fine details will not be apparent, it is worth keeping in mind that most children who are blind have some vision. Choose books in which the language carries the story and illustrations are of secondary importance. Describe the pictures. This will also assist verbally oriented learners and concrete learners. And have plenty of books with tactile illustrations. If possible, have individual copies of the books you are sharing with the group in Braille or in large print so the child who is blind can follow along.

In craft programs, increase visual contrast to aid a child in distinguishing between the table and the drawing paper. Use glue sticks

---

TABLE 9.2 Itsy, Bitsy Spider Explained

Words	Description of Action
The itsy, bitsy spider went up the water spout.	Touch your thumb to the first finger on your other hand; then spin your hands up so the other thumb and forefinger touch. Keep moving your hands up.
Down came the rain and washed the spider out.	With your hands at shoulder height, face your palms down, spread your fingers, and move your arms down to your waist.
Up came the sun and dried up all the rain.	Let your arms dangle. Then touch your fingertips on one hand to the fingertips on your other hand, pull your arms apart, raise them over your head, and touch the fingertips of one hand to the fingertips of the other hand again.
The itsy, bitsy spider climbed up the spout again.	Touch your thumb to the first finger on your other hand; then spin your hands up so the other thumb and forefinger touch. Keep moving your hands up.

tinted purple so the child can see where the glue is. The color fades as it dries. Provide trays, placemats with raised edges, or box tops to define each child's work area. And make sure your demonstration relies as much on verbal description as visual. Choose crafts such as collage, weaving, and sculpture that do not rely on vision.

Sometimes it is the parent who is blind. Twin vision books are necessary for adults who read Braille to be able to read with their sighted child. When a parent who is blind attends a play program, try describing to the parent where the child is and what he is doing. Do this softly, so as not to attract the attention of the child. Juana, the mother with whom one librarian developed this strategy, was thrilled to know that her son was playing trains with another child. Eventually she became friendly with two of the other mothers in the program who began picking up where the librarian had to leave off.

Deaf Children and Children Who Are Hard of Hearing

A child with a hearing impairment may be difficult to identify unless an assistive hearing device, such as a hearing aid or cochlear implant, is visible. Often it is the child's speech or use of sign language that draws your attention. Because Deaf children are usually born into hearing families, parents and child may speak different languages: the adults speak English and the child American Sign Language. This divergence may slow the child's language development, as can hearing impairments that impede a child's exposure to spoken language. Most Deaf youth have some hearing.

If a child or parent at a parent/child program uses sign language, be prepared to engage the services of a certified sign language interpreter for storytimes and other children's programs. It is reasonable to request a week's advance notice for this service. To maintain the trust of the Deaf community, be sure that your interpreters are certified, even if they are volunteers. Check local schools for the deaf or local colleges that offer sign language classes for referral to sign language interpreters. Interpreter students under supervision who need experience for the practicum are also acceptable. If children are receiving services through EI or their local school district, a sign language interpreter for library-based programs may be provided as part of the child's Individualized Family Service Plan or Individualized Educational Program and should accompany the child to the library.

Position the child directly in front of the presenter during programs. Put the interpreter near the librarian holding the picture book so that the child can follow the activity more easily. Place flannel boards or other visuals between the librarians and the interpreter. The area should be well lit, with the staff and interpreter facing into the light.

Masks and puppets can be problematic because they can obscure nonverbal cues and interfere with sign language communication. Try the signing bear and other signing-enabled puppets. They are available from Deaf and hard of hearing service suppliers such as Harris Communication and ADCO Hearing Products.

Sensory Integration Disorder

Sensory integration disorder (SI) is sometimes grouped with sensory disabilities such as deafness and blindness and sometimes with autism. It also shares some characteristics with the learning disability dyspraxia. In order to understand SI, we need to expand our understanding of the perceptive senses. Most of us grew up learning about the five senses: sight, hearing, touch, taste, and smell. Those are the "far" senses. There are four additional senses, known as the "near" senses: vestibular, proprioception, interoception, and tactile. The vestibular sense refers to movement, gravity, and balance. Proprioception is the awareness of where one's body is in space. Interoception is the awareness of one's internal bodily functions: heart rate, breathing, hunger, sleepiness, and others. The tactile sense is the information received through the skin, often about the environment: is it humid or dry, hot or cold, still or breezy? It is distinct from touch.

People with sensory integration disorder experience the sensory world in extreme ways and have difficulty processing sensory input. They may be overwhelmed by average or even minimal input, such as the soft patter of a light rain or the sound of pen on paper. Or they may need greatly magnified input to experience the stimulus at all. The siren of a fire engine may barely register, and the loud ring of a phone may go unprocessed.

Because you do not know what is going on, these issues can be difficult to address in the library. Some very simple things can help. Have paper towels and hand wipes available for tactilely defensive children to wipe their hands on. Keep a weighted blanket or vest, which some people use to feel centered, on hand. Let families know about your quiet area. Allow program participants to move around as long as they do not interfere with the others. Have noise-blocking ear muffs available for youth overwhelmed by noise.

Physical Disabilities

Physical disabilities affect the skeletal/muscular system. People with physical disabilities do not have typical use of their bodies. It may be that gross or fine motor skills are affected, or it may be that limbs or digits are missing.

Gross Motor Skills

Gross motor skills are those that require the use of the large muscles. If they have gross motor impairments, the children may have paralysis of the legs, spinal abnormalities, low or high muscle tone, or central nervous system injuries, all of which affect how they balance, walk, jump, and play. Physical disabilities also encompass spinal cord injuries and missing limbs. These children may use a prosthesis, such as an electronic arm, a wheelchair, crutches, and standing boards, or other equipment to help them participate in activities.

When you use movement in your songs, circle times, or other program elements, use activities all the children can do. Do not shy away from movement but do be flexible; for example, be ready to substitute blowing or some other action in place of clapping or arm and hand movement in place of standing. A child in a wheelchair or crutches can participate in a line dance or a modified version of the Chicken Dance. Movement is important! We just need to be creative. Be sure materials are accessible and within reach of children in wheelchairs and pathways are free of clutter. All children need the opportunity to independently explore the environment. In play programs, provide tunnels, cushioned rams, and large balls to encourage movement and exploration.

Fine Motor Skills

Children with fine motor skill impairments have issues with the small muscles. They may experience difficulties in grasping objects, holding pencils or musical instruments, copying lines and circles, using table utensils, and manipulating clothing fasteners and door knobs. Cerebral palsy, muscular dystrophy, and low muscle tone are common causes. Children and teens with intellectual disabilities and autism spectrum disorder often have problems with fine motor skills too.

Make things easier to grasp by using beads or spools attached with glue, screws, or tape to puzzle pieces, cookie cutters, and other items the child may need to manipulate. Have large pencils, crayons, markers, and easy-to-use scissors available. Consider stamps and large foam cut-out shapes to apply paint. Adapt pencils and paintbrushes with foam and duct tape. An old glove with some Velcro strips can secure a pencil, crayon, marker, or paintbrush to substitute for a grip. Board books, now available at a variety of reading levels, are often useful for children who have trouble turning paper pages.

Speech and Language Delays and Other Communication Disorders

Children with speech or communication issues may have difficulty with one or more of the following:

- auditory comprehension—they hear but do not understand what is being said to them;
- expressive communication—they do not possess the vocabulary to converse, state their needs, or label objects;
- articulation—their speech lacks intelligibility because words are pronounced incorrectly because of things like hypernasality or profound stuttering; or
- a complete lack of expressive verbal language.

When working with children with speech issues we have one goal—to communicate effectively with them. First and foremost this means giving children the tools they need to communicate. Words are the essential tool. We know that children who are reading have significantly larger vocabularies than those who are not. So read to them, and, more important, encourage their families to read to them. Use self-talk. Describe your actions out loud as you do them, naming objects, giving visual cues, asking questions, and, in general, modeling and prompting communication whenever possible. Encourage families to do this at home.

Initiate conversation without pressuring the child or teen to talk. Ask questions and count silently to ten as you wait for a response. This pause gives the children ample opportunity to understand the question and formulate a response. This technique is borrowed from early childhood education and one that a professional used for many years without fully understanding it until she began studying Spanish.

Then she found it took her a long time to understand most questions and craft an answer as she translated the questions into English, formulated the responses, and finally translated them back into Spanish. Her frustration level was high, but the rewards made it well worth the effort.

Respond to all of the child's attempts at communication. Repeat and expand on these attempts as part of the conversational give and take. It is easy to rely on the parent to interpret what the child says, but this limits both the learning opportunity for the child and his independence.

If a child or teen uses an AAC (Augmentative and Alternative Communication) device or system, support her. Allow the child to express herself; do not jump in to finish a sentence that is being slowly articulated by a speech synthesizer. If the child has a pictorial communication system on paper, point to the appropriate pictograms as you speak

Increasingly, children with communication issues are using tablet computers with communication applications, or apps. These apps are game changers, moving the child who needs one from being the weird kid on the periphery who talks with that strange computer to being the cool kid with the latest technology that everyone else wants to use.

Finally, keep these two things in mind: One, it takes two to tango. Each person involved in a communication attempt must take responsibility for his part. Use "I" statements, such as "I'm sorry. I don't understand what you are saying," rather than "You are not speaking clearly" or "I'm having a hard time hearing you. Could you write it down?" Two, the ability to communicate is not the same as the ability to understand. If Stephen Hawking were judged solely on his ability to speak, the world would be a poorer place.

Learning Disabilities/Differences

Learning disability/difference (LD) is one of the largest special education categories. The definition refers to a difficulty processing information or language. These are some common learning disabilities:

- Dyslexia
- Dysgraphia
- Dyscalculia
- Nonverbal learning disability

Dyslexia affects a person's ability to process print and language: it is a receptive language issue. Dysgraphia, an expressive language issue, impacts a person's ability to express himself or herself through oral and written language. Dyscalculia interferes with mathematical processing, and nonverbal learning disabilities make it difficult for someone to interpret nonverbal social cues. Executive function, which mediates the ability to effectively make decisions and plans, is affected in most people with learning disabilities.

Because an LD is invisible, and very few people will self-identify, we need to consider the possibility that it may be contributing to a child's difficulty using the library, whether it is frustration, inappropriate behavior, or always choosing a book that appears to be too easy. If you listen carefully to your patron, you can usually meet his needs without having to know he has an LD.

Encourage teens with LDs to volunteer at the library. Perhaps a teen with an LD is a skilled artist or gamer or has great social skills and can contribute in that way. Libraries offer children and teens with disabilities the rare opportunity to be in an environment where they do not have to achieve some measurable objective or concentrate on skill remediation. Libraries offer children the chance for success and achievement in undervalued areas such as music, art, and movement. Working with an individual's strength will help you build a lifelong library supporter.

Intellectual Disabilities

Children with intellectual disabilities may be slower in several developmental areas, including motor coordination, hand/eye coordination, speech and language, and cognition. Down syndrome, Fragile X syndrome, and fetal alcohol syndrome are the most common causes of intellectual disabilities, accounting for one third of all cases of profound intellectual disabilities (Batshaw, Pellegrino, and Roizen, 2007: 250). Exposures to toxins such as lead and mercury and traumatic brain injury, often as a result of child abuse, are other common causes (Batshaw, Pellegrino, and Roizen, 2007: 251).

Offer a variety of alternative formats for youth with intellectual disabilities. Hi-lo books, audiobooks, abridged books, and digital books with read-along capacity may all be useful. Material with strong graphic cues such as graphic novels, comic books, and magazines often work well.

People with intellectual disabilities are often concrete learners: hands-on experience and repetition are useful tools. They may be friendly or withdrawn, impulsive or timid, easily overstimulated or difficult to engage. Often oblivious to cues from other children, social situations can be frustrating for them. Interaction with children and teens their own age stimulates social development and provides models of appropriate behavior.

Initiate activities with a child who is passive. Shy and withdrawn infants, children, and teens may need a great deal of gentle stimulation and coaxing to respond. The parents may also need extra encouragement and support from library staff as they try to elicit eye contact or a smile. Otherwise, the considerations discussed elsewhere, such as those relating to communication and behavior, apply.

Disabilities with Behavioral Implications

Behavior issues may occur as a side effect of another, primary disability. For example, children with communication issues may appear to be disinterested or distracted and can get frustrated if they do not get their needs met through attempted communication. During a middle-school class visit to the library, a student came up to a children's specialist shaking his fist in her face and stamping his foot. One of the classroom paraprofessionals quickly pulled him away from her and used a restraining hold. Neither the aide nor the teacher realized he was simply signing "toilet" and had stamped his foot because the librarian was the third person with whom he had attempted to communicate his need to use the bathroom.

On the other hand, behavior issues may be the primary manifestation of the condition. It is this type of disability that we will discuss here. These disabilities may be the most difficult to plan around. However, if you keep an open mind and work with the actual child in front of you, rather than your expectations for that child, you will rarely go wrong.

Attention Deficit Disorder with or without Hyperactivity

The Centers for Disease Control and Prevention (CDC) estimates that 9.5 percent of all children in the United States had been diagnosed with ADHD at one point in time (http://www.cdc.gov/ncbddd/adhd/data.html). There are three basic types of attention deficit disorder: inattentive, impulsive, and combined. They can occur with or without hyperactivity and generally present very differently in girls than in boys. Boys tend be very active, easily distracted, inattentive, disruptive, and impulsive. Girls tend to daydream more. While both boys and girls can become frustrated with their difficulty learning, boys tend to act out more whereas girls keep their feelings to themselves. Both have difficulty following directions and keeping track of time. Many children with attention deficit disorder draw a great deal of negative attention from staff, other parents, and children. It is one of the most common conditions with behavioral implications in childhood (Batshaw, Pellegrino, and Roizen, 2007: 345). Difficulty maintaining attention can also occur as a side effect to some medications, such as those that treat epilepsy, depressive disorders, and pain. Appropriate focus is also sometimes an issue in children with autism.

Emotional Disabilities

Children and teens have mental health issues too. Depression, bipolar disorder, schizophrenia, and many other types of emotional disabilities previously thought to be limited to adults have been found in children. Broadly speaking, these disorders are grouped as follows:

- Oppositional defiance and conduct disorders
- Impulse control disorders
- Anxiety disorders
- Mood disorders
- Psychotic disorders
- Eating disorders
- Adjustment disorders
- Maladaptive behavior disorders

As with adults, children with emotional disabilities are treated with medications and talk therapy.

Autism

Autism is a neurologically based condition that appears to involve a genetic predisposition that may or may not require an environmental trigger (Batshaw, Pellegrino, and Roizen, 2007: 325). In all its permutations, whether it is mild or profound, it manifests primarily in three areas: communication, behavior, and socialization.

COMMUNICATION

People with autism may have peculiarities in both verbal and nonverbal communication that are specific to autism. Some individuals with autism do not speak or are nonverbal. Some speak only to repeat what has already been said: echolalic speech. Labeling rather than grammatical speech is common. In the area of nonverbal communication, they may be unable to read facial expressions and body language. Irony that depends on facial expression or tone of voice may be totally inaccessible. AAC strategies described earlier for speech and language impairments are also useful here. And it is important to remember that expressive communication and receptive communication are distinct, though interdependent, skills.

BEHAVIOR

It used to be thought that the unusual behavior of people with autism was random. However, we are moving away from that view toward the understanding that the behaviors have meaning, even if we do not understand it. Generally speaking, people associate the following behaviors with autism:

- Ritual-like routines
- Repetitive motions such as flapping or spinning
- Self-injurious behaviors
- Rocking
- Catatonia
- Random vocalizations
- Tantrums
- Running
- Tactile defensiveness
- Lack of eye contact
- Unusual response to sensory input

So, how do we interpret these behaviors? Many of them may be communication attempts, responses to frustration, and/or attempts at self-regulation. For example, tantrums often occur at times of transition from one activity to another when frustration over the ending of one experience may be high or over the inability to communicate a desire to continue the first activity. Tantrums may also be a response to a negative sensory experience, such as the flickering of florescent lights or the high-pitched whine of a fan that others cannot hear. Repetitive motions such as flapping can help people regulate energy or anxiety.

SOCIAL INTERACTION

Several issues affect how many people with autism interact with others. Difficulties judging other people's responses or divining their emotional state from their affect impact the ability to effectively socialize. The tendency to take language literally can further complicate things.

An underdeveloped understanding of the theory of mind, or the concept that other people have a different point of view, is common in children and teens with autism. A teen with autism may entirely fail to understand that another youth is not as fascinated by the details of six-cylinder engines as she is.

The reactions of people without autism, or neurotypicals, to autism-related behaviors can amplify social problems. For example, inconstant or absent eye contact can be interpreted by a neurotypical person as disinterest, boredom, or disrespect. Other individuals have an intense eye gaze that neurotypicals often find to be scary. The grand, absent, or irrelevant body language, characteristic of some people with autism, can further confuse social interactions, especially when perceived as threatening. These misunderstandings can lead to a conversational quagmire.

In the library, social issues may present themselves in specific ways. A child with autism may seem to demand a book rather than ask for it. The child may just say the name of the book, a labeling behavior, and you may be in the dark as to whether the child is looking for the book, wants you to look for the book, is apologizing for returning it late, or asking you if you liked it. Some children may be ritualistically walking in circles during storytime, apparently not paying attention, but later able to recite the story word for word.

Library Service for Children with Disabilities with Behavioral Implications

Parents and teachers often speak of "behavior management" strategies. They may use systems such as Applied Behavioral Analysis (ABA) or behavior modification when interacting with students. When behavioral issues occur, schools implement the behavioral intervention plan developed as part of the IEP. However, librarians, who see the child only periodically, need different strategies.

We need to start from the understanding that managing behavior means managing needs and emotions. Within this framework, the techniques for working with children with disabilities with behavioral implications are similar to those we use with typically developing children. Many were discussed in previous sections. In addition, the following strategies are useful.

Let patrons know the reasons for the rules and when the rules change. With school-age children and teens, be specific and brief with directions, providing demonstrations to support the verbal instructions. Assume the child will comply, but have a "time-out" procedure available for a younger child and a "take a break from the library" procedure for a teen.

Try to distinguish social norms from required behavior. Remember that manners are culturally determined. Do not insist on eye contact, which can be difficult for some people and is considered rude in some cultures. Children with communication issues consistent with autism may have trouble with the traditional give-and-take of conversation, including "Please" and "Thank you."

Personal space is another culturally defined norm that may cause difficulty for some people. Be prepared for a child who enters your personal space. When he climbs into your lap, plays with your hair, or speaks to you nose to nose, gently disengage him and explain that you are uncomfortable with that behavior.

Catch the child doing something good. Acknowledge success when a child with a behavioral disability behaves appropriately. Offer frequent, positive verbal praise to reinforce appropriate behavior for all children. Clearly explain what to do instead of what not to do.

Help children make the connection between negative behavior and its consequences. Children may not understand that their pushing or grabbing causes other children to withdraw from then. Rather than just saying "Stop" or "Don't do that," explain how the other children feel and will probably react. Be prepared to intervene if necessary or encourage the parent to do so by using calm but firm language, maintaining eye contact (where possible), and reinforcing with a gentle hand on the shoulder to focus attention.

Some children are more comfortable during quieter, less crowded times in the children's room—early evening as opposed to directly after school in an urban area or before school in a school library media center. Introduce options for more calming, less active activities such as the use of earphones when listening to an audiobook or the computer. Have noise-blocking headphones available for children who need them. They can easily be cleaned with an alcohol or disinfectant wipe between uses.

Multiple Disabilities

Children and teens can have more than one disability. Children who have cerebral palsy often have articulation problems. Intellectual disabilities, obsessive compulsive disorder, and sensory integration issues are not uncommon in people with autism. Side effects of medication prescribed for some types of mental illness may mimic physical disabilities. Likewise, side effects of medication prescribed for epilepsy can impact a child's ability to learn. As always, it is essential to look at the whole child or teen and not to be sidetracked by or complacent about the obvious.

Examples of Inclusive Library Service

Environment

Sandra is three years old and has autism. She enjoys coming to the library with her mother but becomes easily overwhelmed with the noise and bustle of activity in the room. The staff talked with her mother and developed the following approaches: Mom chose a place in the room to sit with Sandra that is toward one of the corners of the room, out of the main traffic. Sandra, surrounded by some of the toys and puzzles she loves, is able to cope with the general excitement in this space of her own. The library has supplied a set of plug-in headphones so that she can listen to music when she wants to.

Information

After a parenting workshop, one mother took the librarian aside and said how much she enjoyed reading and had always loved the library. She wished that her fourth grade son could have the same enjoyment but, because of his LD, he did not read well. As they talked the librarian found out that the child loved comic books and subways. She explained that the library had graphic novels and could help him find nonfiction videos on subways. She mentioned audiobooks about trains. Mom had no idea that these formats were available and was looking forward to taking her son to the public library for the first time.

Programs

Inclusive Gardening

A one-hour gardening program built around Lois Elhert's (1996, 2009) *Growing Vegetable Soup* might look something like this:

1. Sing—Hello song
2. Read—*Growing Vegetable Soup*

3. Sing—"Beans in My Ears," traditional
4. Read—*The Curious Garden* by Peter Brown (2009)
5. Movement/music—"The Green Grass Grows All Around" by Pete Seeger (1967), with sign and movement
6. Read—*Vegetable Garden* by Douglas Florian (1994), big-book format
7. Craft—Tree collage or planting
8. Cleanup

Start by explaining the agenda on your picture schedule, and then follow it. Sing the hello song first, introducing yourself, the day's theme, and different kinds of gardens. While talking about the theme, ask children if they have gardened, if they like to garden, what type of soup they like, and so forth. Pass around some seeds, and then read *Growing Vegetable Soup*. As you read the book, hand children the vegetables mentioned. Mime cleaning and cutting them as that happens in the story, and encourage the children to join in. Take a pot around to each child, allowing the child to place the vegetables in and pretend to stir. Finally "ladle" the soup into their cupped hands, while the children blow on it and taste it. You can use plastic vegetables, but real ones are better because they add scent and texture to the experience.

Singing "Beans in My Ears" moves you from vegetables to fantasy. After that, read *The Curious Garden* and discuss different types of gardens. Next, introduce the song by demonstrating the signs for tree and bird. Sing "The Green Grass Grows All Around," incorporating the movement of the signs. Make sure you have the chorus programmed on the BIGmack, offering it to each child. *Garden Day* acts as a rhyming summary, closing the reading component and taking you to the art component.

The craft is a collage. Each child has a tray to work on. Provide tree silhouettes cut out to use or trace as a template and some blank paper. Children can choose to use a precut template, cut their own, or sketch and cut their own. Offer different types of scissors. Offer a variety of materials in different sizes and textures to glue onto the tree, as well as squeeze bottles of glue, glue sticks, and open pots of glue with popsicle sticks. The materials should be grouped together in the middle of the table where everyone can see them but cannot necessarily reach them so that they have to ask each other for help. Do the craft with them rather than having a premade model. This allows you to demonstrate the craft and the children to see you make mistakes. Give the children a warning about cleanup five minutes before. Finally, clean up, putting like materials together, capping the glue, picking up scraps of paper, and so forth. Anyone who has not finished can bag up their projects and the materials they need to finish at home. Alternatively, instead of doing the craft, plant some of the seeds used earlier in the program if you have a garden or even some pots.

Sensory Storytimes

Several libraries are using techniques from occupational therapy to create sensory storytimes. These programs incorporate sensory activities into multisensory storytimes. They may be just for children with sensory needs, or they may be inclusive. The techniques work well for all children, but many parents prefer the self-contained format. These programs have reading, singing, and movement components and may include art activities. So balance beams, bean bag games, blowing bubbles, and weighted vests may all be included. Stretching activities using resistance bands, a sensory walk like the one at the Ferguson Library (Stamford, CT), and allowing the children to move, even walk around, during the formal part of the program are some adaptations to consider. Part of the idea behind them is to give children the tools they need to self-regulate. You can find one example by Kiera Parrott (2011) online at http://libraryvoice.org/2011/02/28/steal-this-storytime-spectrum-storytime-edition/.

For librarians, creating the environment for children and teens is a familiar and comfortable strategy, regularly employed in our efforts to provide quality service. Additional consideration may or may not be necessary to create inclusive libraries. The basic requirements for successful inclusion are communication, observation, and a willingness to solve problems, experimenting until the barriers are overcome. When we have incorporated these considerations, inclusion works beautifully, as in the following story. Alexis unexpectedly attended a program one day that had a craft component. Alexis has cerebral palsy, which affects both her fine motor skills and her speech. The craft was making a collage to illustrate a part of the story they had read. Because she could not easily manipulate even the larger pieces, the librarian scribed for her, gluing things where she indicated, usually by pointing. After a few minutes, the child sitting next on the other side of the librarian, John, asked her if Alexis would "like some of these sequences." The librarian suggested to John that he ask Alexis, which he did. After another minute or two, John had taken over scribing for the librarian, much to his and Alexis's delight.

Resources

Akin, Lynn, and Donna MacKinney. 2004. "Autism, Literacy, and Libraries: The 3 Rs = Routine, Repetition, and Redundancy." *Children and Libraries* 2, no. 2: 35–43.

Alessio, Amy, and David G. Fassler. 2005. "How Can We Help? Counseling Connections for Teens through the Library." *VOYA* 28, no. 4: 284–287.

American Sign Language University. 2011. American Sign Language curriculum resource center. Lifeprint.com. http://lifeprint.com/.

Banks, Carrie. 2004. "All Kinds of Flowers Grow Here: The Child's Place for Children with Special Needs at the Brooklyn Public Library." *Children and Libraries*, 2, no. 1: 5–10.

D'Orazio, Antonette K. 2007. "Small Steps, Big Results." *Children and Libraries* 5, no. 3: 21–23.

Fienberg, Sandra, and James R. Keller, 2010. "Designing Space for Children and Teens." *American Libraries* 41, no. 4: 34–47. http://americanlibrariesmagazine.org/features/03142010/designing-space-children-and-teens.

Gray, Carol. 2010. *The New Social Story Book, Revised and Expanded 10th Anniversary Edition: Over 150 Social Stories That Teach Everyday Social Skills to Children with Autism or Asperger's Syndrome, and Their Peers.* Arlington, TX: Future Horizon.

Holmes, Paula. 2007. "A Parent's View: How Libraries Can Open the Door to the 20 Percent." *Children and Libraries* 5, no. 3: 24.

Kind, Viki. 2010. *The Caregiver's Path to Compassionate Decision Making: Making Choices for Those Who Can't.* Austin, TX: Greenleaf Book Group.

Kranowitz, Carol Stock. 2003. *The Out-of-Sync Child Has Fun: Activities for Kids with Sensory Processing Disorder.* New York: The Penguin Group.

Lushington, Nolan. 2008. *Libraries Designed for Kids.* New York: Neal-Schuman.

Perkins School for the Blind. 2011. "The Best Computer Games for Blind Kids." Perkins School for the Blind. http://www.wonderbaby.org/articles/best-accessible-computer-games-blind-kids.

Prendergast, Tess. 2011. "Beyond Storytime: Children's Librarians Collaborating in Communities." *Children and Libraries* 9, no. 1: 20–26, 40.

Rogovin, Anne. 1990. *Let Me Do It!* Revised ed. Nashville: Abingdon Press.

Schiller, Pam, and Pat Phipps. 2006. *Starting with Stories: Engaging Multiple Intelligences through Children's Books*. Illustrated by Kathy Ferrell and Debi Johnson. Beltsville, MD: Gryphon House.

Socol, Ira David. 2010. "The Unhappy Place: What Libraries Can Do to Welcome Kids Who Struggle with Print." *School Library Journal* 56, no. 5. http://www.schoollibraryjournal.com/article/CA6727276 .html.

Tots-n-Tech. 2010. "Using Assistive Technology to Support Socialization." *Tots-n-Tech E-Newsletter*, June. http://tnt.asu.edu/files/June2010.pdf.

Walling, Linda Lucas, and Marilyn H. Karrenbrock. 1993. *Disabilities, Children, and Libraries: Mainstreaming Services in Public Libraries and School Library Media Centers*. Englewood, CO: Libraries Unlimited.

Wemett, Lisa. 2007. "The Building Bridges Project." *Children and Libraries* 5, no. 3: 15–20.

Winson, Georgia, and Courtney Adams. 2010. "Collaboration at Its Best: Library and Autism Programs Combine to Serve Special Audiences." *Children and Libraries* 8, no. 2: 15–17.

Working Together Project. 2008. *Community-Led Libraries Toolkit*. Vancouver: Libraries in Communities. http://www .librariesincommunities.ca/resources/Community-Led_Libraries _Toolkit.pdf.

References

Batshaw, Mark L., Louis Pellegrino, and Nancy J. Roizen, eds. 2007. *Children with Disabilities*. 6th ed. Baltimore: Paul H. Brookes.

Brown, Peter. 2009. *The Curious Garden*. New York: Little, Brown.

Ehlert, Lois. 1996. *A Sembrar el Sope de Verduras/Growing Vegetable Soup*. Translated by Alma Flor Ada. New York: Houghton Mifflin.

———. 2009. *Growing Vegetable Soup*. Charlotte, NC: Paw Prints.

Florian, Douglas. 1994. *Vegetable Garden*. New York: Harcourt Children's Books.

Horning, Kathleen T. 2010. "Can Children's Books Save the World? Advocates for Diversity in Children's Books and Libraries: 2010 May Hill Arbuthnot Honor Lecture." *Children and Libraries* 8, no. 3: 8–17.

Kluth, Paula, and Kelly Chandler-Olcott. 2008. *A Land We Can Share: Teaching Literacy to Students with Autism*. Baltimore: Paul H. Brooks.

McGrath, Ben. 2004. "Chew On." *New Yorker*, February 2. http://www .newyorker.com/archive/2004/02/09/040209ta_talk_mcgrath.

Parrott, Kiera. 2011. "Steal This Storytime: Spectrum Edition." *Library Voice* (blog), February 28. http://libraryvoice.org/2011/02/28/steal-this-storytime-spectrum-storytime-edition/.

Seeger, Pete. 1967. *Abiyoyo and Other Story Songs for Kids*. CD. Rereleased 1992. Smithsonian Folkways Recordings.

Assistive and Adaptive Technology

10

Look Grandma, I can read.

—*Eight-year-old boy with LD after learning how to use BookFlix*

When we think of Assistive or Adaptive Technology, or AT for short, we tend to think in terms of complicated software such as speech output for computers and communication boards. In fact, most of us use some form of AT every day. Eyeglasses, pens with large, soft grips, adjustable desk chairs, and cars are all common forms of AT. When we conceive of it in these terms, it is not quite so scary. It is just an important tool for all of us.

Technology can assist with many areas of our lives: communication, such as listening, talking, reading, and writing; daily living tasks, such as working, cooking, and playing; and mobility and transportation. It can help us see, hear, learn, manipulate objects, get around, balance, eat, and perform any other function we need to perform. When it is simple, such as a handheld magnifier, it is called "low tech." When it is complex, such as a piece of software that enlarges print on a website, it is called "high tech."

AT can be used in any aspect of life. Occupational therapists generally divide it into 14 separate categories. Eight of those categories are useful in the library:

- Aids for daily living
- Communication
- Computer access
- Education
- Hearing

- Recreation and leisure
- Seating and positioning
- Vision

Aids for Daily Living

In the therapeutic world, the tools we use every day—forks, scissors, toothbrushes—are aids for daily living (ADL). ADL can also refer to items that provide disability-specific assistance, such as a grab bar on the bathtub, a bagel slicer, or a grabbing tool for reaching things too high or too low to comfortably reach otherwise. In the library we should be thinking about tools to help people write, toys that all children can use, appropriate craft materials, and nontraditional craft tools. Chapter 11 covers adaptive toys and includes suppliers.

Some children will need low-tech solutions to issues with crafts. Thick markers and crayons, pyramid-shaped crayons, pencils with padded grips, paintbrushes that can be strapped to a glove or directly onto a child's hand will all help a child with physical disabilities participate in a craft program. Foam or textured paint, paper that becomes three-dimensional when wet, or a drawing outlined with string or glue will help a child who is blind participate. A nonslip mat under the paper will keep it in place when the child with dysgraphia presses hard or erases over and over again. A tilt board will hold paper at different angles. High-tech options for crafts may include computers with graphic design and drawing programs, smart boards, or tablet computers with touch screen drawing programs or apps.

Writing presents a problem for many children. Foam and duct tape to build up grips, larger pens, commercial or special grips, signature guides, and many other adaptations are available. If the issue is a visual one, a slate and stylus for Brailling or a Brailler might work. Magnetic letters and words are another low-tech option. Special pens moved by open-handed gliding move us from low tech to high tech. High-tech solutions to writing include word processing on a computer, speech input software, and apps with letter or word manipulation capabilities. Game apps such as iWriteWords can help motivate students to practice writing.

A person with dysgraphia may not write by hand. Typewriters and computers can be the communication lifeline that allows a person

Suppliers of Low-Tech ADL Items

The types of low-tech items discussed in this section can be found in specialty catalogs from such suppliers as these:

- Abilitations/School Specialty
  PO Box 1579
  Appleton, WI 54912
  (888) 388-3224
  http://www.schoolspecialty
  .com/abilitations

- American Printing House for the Blind, Inc.
  1839 Frankfort Avenue
  Louisville, KY 40206
  (800) 223-1839
  http://www.aph.org/

- Flaghouse
  601 Flaghouse Dr.
  Hasbrouck Heights, NJ 07604-3116
  (800) 793-7900
  http://www.flaghouse.com/

- Patterson Medical
  1000 Remington Boulevard,
  Suite 210
  Bolingbrook, IL 60440
  (800) 228-3693
  http://www.pattersonmedical
  .com/app.aspx?cmd=go_home

with dysgraphia to function throughout school and to write a book. Word completion and spelling and grammar checking are great boons. Many people with this type of expressive language learning disability (LD) can now use voice input, speech-to-text devices to write. AT for computers is discussed later in the chapter.

Behavior is another daily living skill that comes into play in the library. Technology can assist here too. On the low-tech side, visual timers can help children with autism, LD, and attention deficit disorder better anticipate changes in activities, reducing frustration. There are apps for developing visual schedules and other social story–like tools for transitions and new experiences, such as iPrompts, Stories2Learn, and Strip Designer. Calendar and agenda apps can also help modulate behavior by planning for transitions in the same way that printed picture schedules help.

Communication

While the basics of Assistive and Augmentative Communication (AAC) were covered in Chapter 9, it is now time to look at specifics. Low-tech options here include pen and paper, instant messaging, and texting for people who do not speak. Even pantomime can work well. These are not perfect solutions. The former are limited to those people who can read and write, and the latter is not as exact a medium as may be required.

Printed communication boards with basic library concepts on it are a medium-tech choice. Here technology is used to produce the boards, but they are printed out and laminated to be portable and easy to use in programs. At the Brooklyn Public Library's The Child's Place for Children with Special Needs, staff use them for picture agendas of programs, isolated words needed for gardening, selecting books, and many other things.

High-tech options are the next step. Recordable switches such as BIGmacks can provide some communication options. By prerecording "yes" and "no" on the BIGmack, you allow children who do not speak or sign to answer questions by activating a switch. By prerecording the repetitive line in a book, you give them the opportunity to join in with the other children. These devises tend to be easy to program and the buttons large enough to be easily pressed by someone with visual or dexterity issues.

This type of basic communication device works well in both public libraries and schools. A BIGmack programmed with the chorus to the songs being sung could help children with disabilities, particularly those with profound and multiple disabilites, participate. To sing along, a child simply needs to press a large, very sensitive button. During one class visit, a child who cried more or less constantly during previous visits stopped crying when the librarian showed him how to sing along by using the BIGmack. Another child pointed to it, with increasing agitation, as the group sang the goodbye song, clearly wanting to participate. So the librarian reprogrammed the BIGmack with the goodbye song and he waved his hands in the air, the sign for clapping. It appeared that he was as proud of the librarian for understanding him as she was of him for asking for it.

Generally speaking, more complex AAC systems are purchased for people based on their individual needs and after extensive evaluation of their skills and abilities. They will often travel with their system and use it to communicate in the library. However, it is still useful for the library to have some AAC options for patrons. On the low-tech end of the spectrum, Picture Exchange Communication Systems (PECS) are versatile and easy to use and can work well for people who do not read. These pictograms, with or without the text, can be printed out on a sheet of paper and individually laminated or be part of an electronic or computer-based system. Traditional dedicated electronic speech boards are one way to go. These convert typing, pictogram selection, or other nonverbal input into speech. They tend to be bulky and very expensive.

Another option is an iOS device, which is any of the touch screen–based Apple products, including the iPhone, iPad, and iPod Touch. iOS devices can take the place of some the previously discussed items. They have several advantages: they run multipurpose apps that are relatively inexpensive, and they are perceived as cool, in sharp contrast to the bulky, stigmatizing technological devices of the previous generation. Apps such as TapSpeak Button can replace recordable switches. Picture- or symbol-to-speech apps can be used instead of a dedicated electronic speech board. Proloquo2Go was one of the first. Although it is not the easiest system to master, you can select basic communication sequences that work well in the library. Mayer-Johnson is currently developing apps to extend its Boardmaker software to the iOS platform. Sono Flex Lite is an exciting, free, and easy to use app that offers most of the communication concepts needed in the library. iOS devices are discussed in more detail later in this chapter.

Text-to-speech apps are useful. Some apps, such as iCommunicate, will translate English into sign language. In any case, new communication apps are being developed constantly, so it is worth monitoring them. Your local technology assistance center can help you experiment with various options before you buy.

Telecommunication also needs to be accessible. Traditionally, people who are Deaf or hard of hearing and those with speech disabilities have used TTYs (telecommunication devices for the Deaf). These devices work with a telephone or are attached to a telephone and allow text input instead of voice. If you do not have a TTY at you library, you can use a relay service in most states by dialing 711. The Federal Communications Commission maintains a list of relay services by state at http://transition.fcc.gov/cgb/dro/trs_by_state.html. While these still have a role, they are being supplemented by instant messaging, texting, tweeting, video, and web-based phones. Video relay services can also be use to communicate between American Sign Language users and non-ASL users in the library. Consider the Sorenson Video Relay Service, which is offered free to libraries and other nonprofit organizations.

Computer Access

From the very beginning, computers have been a boon for many people with disabilities, with the potential to be transformative for some. Naturalistic prosthetics controlled by computer chips, communication access for people who have been locked in by strokes, the ability to travel the world virtually for people who are homebound are all just the tip of the iceberg. However, there has also been a certain level of frustration with computers. Traditional desktop and laptop computers were designed for general use, with accessibility features added only later. The iOS devices—iPods, iPod Touches, and iPads—were designed with the needs of people with disabilities in mind and with their input.

Desktop Computers

For people with disabilities, there are many barriers to using personal computers. Computers require a fluid literacy to power up and log on and generally to operate. This can be a problem for people with

TTY and Video Relay Services

Video relay services supplement TTY relay services for phone calls between people who are Deaf, hard of hearing, or have expressive communication disabilities and people who do not have such disabilities. Most states have a relay service whereby a TTY user can, through a relay operator, speak to a non-TTY user on the phone. The TTY user types his message and the relay operator speaks it verbatim to the non-TTY user. Likewise, when the non-TTY user speaks, the relay operator types the message for the TTY user. Video relay allows analogous conversations between ASL speakers and non-ASL speakers. Here the video relay operator signs for the ASL user and speaks for the non-ASL user. Sorenson Video Relay Service offers such a service free to many users, including libraries. For more information, go to http://www.sorensonvrs.com/svrs?autoplay.

intellectual disabilities and dyslexia. Keyboarding requires one type of physical dexterity and using a mouse another. People with fine and gross motor skill disabilities are at a disadvantage here. Personal computers were designed for visual access, again posing problems for those with some learning disabilities and those who are blind or have low vision. Blinking cursors can be a distraction for people with attention deficit disorder or a trigger for someone with a seizure disorder. As a result, a certain amount of retrofitting, supplemental hardware and software, and even whole new devices may be required before someone with a disability can comfortably use a desktop.

The Windows and Mac operating systems both have built-in accessibility features. In Windows, these are available in the Control Panel with links to online guides. Microsoft has a nice article summarizing types of computer accessibility products at http://www.microsoft .com/enable/at/types.aspx. The Mac operating system also has integral accessibility options under "Preferences" in the Apple systems menu.

What follows is a brief overview of accessibility features available from the most popular operating systems, some supplemental hardware and software, and some purchasing and evaluation resources. For a more in-depth look at the issue, see *Assistive Technologies in the Library* by Barbara T. Mates and William R. Reed, published in 2011. For individually tailored help, contact your local AT resource center. You can use this book's appendix to locate the closest one in your state.

People with Physical Disabilities

Dexterity and strength issues can both create problems for computer usage. Wrist supports are one of the few low-tech solutions to the problem of computer access. They address the question of wrist and arm fatigue and are easy to find.

The most popular operating systems have many built-in keyboard accessibility features. For example, you can ignore repeated key strokes or slow down repeat times for people whose fingers move more slowly, like people with arthritis or cerebral palsy and young children. You can operate the mouse with keyboard controls or use sticky keys to allow you to operate the keyboard with one hand. Apple's options tend to be more extensive and seamless. Its on-screen keyboard offers adjustable designs. The basic mouse can be difficult for many people, including young typically developing children, to use. Left-handed people often switch the functionality of the buttons.

Desktops can accommodate variations on traditional keyboards and mice. There are a surprising variety of alternative keyboards. Keyboards can be smaller, larger, shaped differently, laid out differently, or part of a touch screen or have a flexible setup achieved by using overlays. Some of these keyboards have become mainstream because of the increased emphasis on ergonomics and can be purchased in office supply stores. Others must be purchased through specialty suppliers. Some are very specific in their use, such as an electronic pointer to manipulate an on-screen keyboard for people with low-incidence disabilities like quadriplegia. Others have broader applicability. Intellikeys is a popular, flexible keyboard alternative available only through disability product catalogs. Because it comes with many keyboard configurations and you can create your own, it can be helpful for young children and people with physical, learning, and intellectual disabilities.

Mice can be replaced by trackballs, joysticks, touch pads, and even switches. These types of tools can be found through office and computer supply sources, gaming sources, specialty catalogs, and your local technology resource center.

People Who Are Blind or Have Low Vision

There are multiple barriers to using desktop computers for people with visual disabilities: navigation, input, and output are the key issues.

NAVIGATING THE COMPUTER SCREEN

Making choices on a computer screen is daunting if you cannot see the screen well, or at all. Many appearance and accessibility options come with computers. You can change the desktop appearance by altering the background, resolution, contrast, and size of text and icons, adding a magnifier, or modifying the cursor. The Microsoft magnification settings have a limited range of sizes, and only one part of the screen is magnified. The standard Mac screen magnification program magnifies the entire screen.

Auditory cues and narration can be enabled. First included with Windows 7, the Microsoft Narrator has become a useful tool. To find out more about the Microsoft choices, go to http://www.microsoft.com/enable/. Mac's speech function, VoiceOver, is an extensive voice narration program that even helps navigate the web. VoiceOver is available for 22 languages, including Spanish, Cantonese, Arabic, and Russian. Nice touches such as a talking calculator and talking clock round out the picture for Macs. To find out more about Mac accessibility options, go to http://www.apple.com/accessibility/.

Moving from the options built into desktops to software and hardware add-ons, we find a variety of programs to assist in navigation. Start by purchasing a large-screen monitor. Other commercial options include screen enlargement and readers. ZoomText screen magnification is one of the most popular magnification programs. It can enlarge the entire screen, increase the size of one window on the screen, accommodate dual monitors, act as a scanner, and many other things. Magic Screen Magnification offers many of the same features but is limited to increasing text size by a factor of 16, compared to ZoomText's 36× capability. Neither is compatible with the Mac operating system, but many people feel that the built-in screen magnifier obviates the need for additional magnification software for Macs.

Screen reading software is another important navigation tool for people who are blind or with low vision. This type of software converts text to speech or Braille. JAWS has traditionally been a favorite. It provides both speech and Braille output. It is compatible with the Microsoft operating system, Internet Explorer, Foxfire, and Adobe Acrobat. Window-Eyes is similar software that is less expensive but works with Skype and PDF files. Many users find that the Mac built-in VoiceOver feature is more than adequate.

INPUTTING DATA

Inputting data and information can be another barrier to computer usage for people with vision issues. Alternative keyboards such as those with a large-print format can help. Braille overlays can be useful. However, straight typing is not always the best option for people with visual disabilities. Even proficient touch typists need feedback on what they are typing. Screen reading software can provide this feedback.

Voice recognition software and voice-to-text software allow the user to bypass typing and vision altogether. Windows also has a voice command function in the accessibility suite. Macs have a voice command recognition feature that is accessed through the "Systems Preferences" menu. Neither program is useful beyond commands, and both are imperfect, subject to failure with unusual or accented articulation.

Dragon Speak, which has products both for Macs and Windows, is the gold standard for speech-to-text inputting. It can be used throughout the computer system, including with word processing programs and the Internet. However, it needs to be configured for the individual, a long and detailed process that is not always feasible in a public library. In a school library media center, the librarian can work with the child to help him configure the program and learn how to use it. Dragon Speak products are available commercially (http://www.nuance.com/dragon/index.htm).

RECEIVING OUTPUT

Output is the final major barrier for people who are blind or with low vision. We have already discussed speech output. Braille is the other important output solution for people who are blind. Before something can be produced in Braille, it must be transcribed into Braille. In the Mac world, VoiceOver provides a similar function. In the Windows world, users must purchase additional software such as Duxbury Braille Translator, which works well for text files and HTML.

Once the material is in Braille format, it can be produced with Braille displays or Braille embossers. Refreshable Braille displays have pegs that move up and down to create Braille. Embossers are the equivalent of Braille printers. Embossers have a wide variety of options and price points. These are the features to consider before purchasing:

- Speed of embossing
- Noise
- Single or double sided
- Price

The National Federation for the Blind has useful descriptions of the Braille printers available and how to purchase them at http://www.afb.org/ProdBrowseCatResults.asp?CatID=45.

People with Learning Disabilities/Differences

Some of the adaptations discussed in previous sections can be helpful for people with LDs. Desktop appearance preferences such as size and color of font and the simplicity and color of backgrounds can be important. These changes can also assist some people with visual processing and perception disorders and are intrinsic to the operating systems discussed earlier. Screen readers and voice input can also be useful.

Other basic Windows and Mac features, such as word completion and spell check, are also useful. Mac's FaceTime face-to-face video calls and iChat are a nice supplement to e-mail for people with print disabilities. Mac's three-dimensional grapher, part of the calculator feature, can be helpful for people with some math disabilities. Finally, with the Mac Simple Finder you can limit the busyness of a page by displaying only certain features. Creating such visual shortcuts can help people with attention issues stay focused.

There are many software programs for people with LDs. Some of the adaptations, such as text-to-speech features and speech-to-text, discussed for people with impaired vision also work well for people with reading difficulties. Reading programs that highlight text and phonetic spelling programs are often helpful. Write:OutLoud makes writing easier for people with LD by reading aloud what is written as it is written. Some writing programs are bundled with screen readers, such as Read and Write Gold, that highlight text as it is read. What You Need Now (WYNN) goes a step further, allowing easy access for rereading a section, providing definitions when requested, and including an outline feature. Researchers are even working on a specific font, Dyslexie, to help people with dyslexia (Nalewicki, 2011), although the efficacy of the use of particular fonts has not yet been extensively researched.

People Who Are Deaf or Hard of Hearing

Audio cues are available in visual format through the accessibility features in both Windows and Mac systems. More problematic is the web. Audio in websites is a web design issue with no easy solution if the website has not provided one. Videos imbedded in websites and streaming videos are also problematic. While YouTube supports captioning, it is rarely used. Standard podcasts and webinars, both common tools in libraries, academia, and education, are also not helpful if you are Deaf. Podcasts accompanied by written transcripts are a better way to go, as are Webinars supported by captioning.

People with Intellectual Disabilities

Many of the adaptations described, such as screen readers, short cuts, and simplified keyboards, can help users with intellectual disabilities. Providing pathfinders, extra time on the computers, and training more than once are also useful.

Having accessible computer terminals expands your potential pool of volunteers. One of the staff computers at The Child's Place is configured for people who are blind. For three summers interns who are blind have worked at The Child's Place, doing everything from answering the phone and reading aloud in hospitals to creating a searchable database of our programming music and helping to create a life skills curriculum for elementary school students who are blind. Their participation would be neither as meaningful nor as productive if they did not have the proper equipment.

Laptops

Laptops pose their own accessibility problems. The smaller, less defined keys and touch pads may be problematic for some people with physical disabilities. To work around these barriers, supplemental keyboards and mice can be either plugged in or connected via Bluetooth. The size of the screen can be difficult for people with visual disabilities. The Windows operating system is configured slightly differently on laptops than on computers but provides many of the same features. The accessibility options do not change with the Mac operating system.

Patrons who need a particular software adaptation for a desktop or laptop computer, such as a screen reader, may bring it with them in the form of a thumb drive. Many libraries will not allow patrons' programs to be run on library computers. In some places, firewalls will prevent them from opening. These policies and procedures may be problematic if their implementation prevents someone with a disability from using a library computer.

iOS Devices

The needs of people with disabilities were incorporated into the initial design phases of iOS devices, including iPods, iPod Touches, and iPads. Consequently, they are some of the most flexible and accessible technologies currently available. They are intuitive and well designed for use by people with a wide range of abilities. The ease of designing apps and their proliferation has only broadened their appeal and usability. Apps take the iOS devices' uses outside the world of computers into the worlds of communication, education, reading, personal organizing, recreation, and many others.

iOS systems have the same accessibility options as a Mac operating system. VoiceOver and ZoomText, previously discussed, are the nexus of access for people who are blind. VoiceOver turns the touch keyboard into an audio keyboard, where the names of the letter are voiced before selection. You can also use it to hear what you have typed. One difference between VoiceOver for the Mac and VoiceOver for the iPad is that the iPad has 36 languages available. There are also apps for voice input. Dragon Speak even has a well-regarded free app. For Braille input, the iPad can be connected to a Braille keyboard or run an app that allows the user to type in Braille on the screen, with the screen finding the user's fingers.

For users who are Deaf or hard of hearing, sound cues can be made visual and audio output can be directed to one ear or the other; the latter is compatible with a variety of earphones and headphones. The direct, intuitive nature of iPads makes them easier for people with LDs, intellectual disabilities, and some information processing issues to use. Young children also find them easier to successfully manipulate. No longer does the individual have to learn remote cause and effect. Moving a mouse is not intuitive. Connecting the movement of the mouse with what happens on the screen can be difficult for someone with an intellectual disability. With an iPad you simply touch the screen and it works.

Accessible Websites

The best AT will not help if websites are designed poorly or use programming languages not compatible with screen reading software. Mates and Reed (2011: 17–20) suggest some basic design considerations:

- Images should have a text equivalent.
- Icons should have a text equivalent.
- Multimedia should be supplemental and not essential to the messages.
- The site should work in black and white.
- Users should be able to change the settings.
- Tables should be text based and accessible to screen readers.
- Frames must be labeled.
- Blinking and flickering need to avoid the 2 to 55 Hz range.
- Text-only parallel sites should be available for non-ADA complaint sites.
- Streaming, animated features need text labels or be able to be disabled.
- Supplemental programs and plug-ins need to have their accessibility features easily available.
- Online forms must be in an accessible format.
- The ability to skip repetitive navigational links is a boon to people who use screen readers.

- The ability to extend the amount of time before a page automatically times out makes them usable for many readers.
- The Help page must be accessible.

More information is available from the World Wide Web Consortium (http://www.w3.org/) and on the U.S. government's official Section 508 website (http://www.section508.gov/#).

When linking to resources, make sure that they are also accessible. Hyperlinks should take users to accessible websites. Uploaded documents need to be in formats that work with screen readers. Keep these guidelines in mind both when selecting websites to link to and when creating your own.

One last note: it is important to test the final configuration of a website to see if it really works. WAVE (http://wave.webaim.org/) and NCAM Accessibility QA Favelet (http://ncam.wgbh.org/invent_build/web_multimedia/tools-guidelines/favelet) are two tools that help you evaluate your websites. It is also important to have live users test it (Mates and Reed, 2011: 22–23). Reach out to your users and community partners and ask for their help in testing your product and correcting any issues that arise. It is likely that they have more expertise in this area than you. And, as discussed in Chapter 8, involving community members can help them feel welcome and could even lead to the formation of a user group or advisory board.

Evaluating, Selecting, and Finding AT for Computers

Several sources can help you evaluate and select AT for computers. *Assistive Technologies in the Library* (Mates and Reed, 2011), previously mentioned, is a good print overview. Periodicals such as Closing the Gap's *Solutions* (http://www.closingthegap.com/solutions/) can help. Websites such as Tots-n-Tech (http://tnt.asu.edu/), a joint project of Arizona State University and Thomas Jefferson University, the American Foundation for the Blind (http://www.afb.org/default.asp), and the Center for Assistive Technology and Environmental Access (CATEA) (http://assistivetech.net/) are good resources. These resources and others generally provide ordering information as well. Your state or local technology resource center can often both make recommendations and allow you to try the technology before purchasing it.

Sites That Evaluate and Recommend Apps

- Apps for Children with Special Needs
  http://a4cwsn.com/
- Autism APPs
  http://www.autismspeaks.org/family-services/autism-apps
- 40 Amazing iPad Apps for the Learning Disabled
  http://www.matchacollege.com/blog/2011/40-amazing-ipad-apps-for-the-learning-disabled/
- SNApps4Kids.com: Special Needs Apps for Kids
  http://www.snapps4kids.com/
- For Spanish: iAutism
  http://www.iautism.info/

Types of Accessible Instructional Materials

- Audiobooks
- Braille books
- Large-print books
- Digital text

Sorting through the multitude of apps can be a daunting task. *School Library Journal* (http://slj.com/) periodically recommends apps. *Apps for Autism* by Lois Jean Brady (2011) was one of the first to evaluate and recommend apps specifically for people with autism. See the sidebar for other evaluation and recommendation sources.

There are also disability networks that blog about computer accessibility. These have the advantage of easily being able to keep up with new releases and changes in the systems. The go-to Windows blog is sponsored by Microsoft and can be found at http://blogs.msdn.com/b/robmar/archive/2011/01/28/windows-accessibility.aspx. There are several long-standing, independent, and enthusiastic Mac and iOS blogs. Mac-cessibility Network (http://maccessibility.net/?contrast=standardcontrast) provides one such blog. ATMAC: Empowering Disabled Apple Users (http://atmac.org/) is an exciting, independent, and well-organized site that looks at all aspects of Apple accessibility, including apps.

In particular it is the role of the school librarian to provide "leadership in the use of information technologies and instruction for both students and staff. . . . [T]he school librarian offers expertise in accessing and evaluating information [and] using information technologies. . . ." (American Association of School Librarians, 2012: 1). Krueger and Stefanich (2011: 45) take this idea a step further and see the school library media specialist as the nexus for information on AT across the curriculum: "The school librarian can serve as a collaborator to ensure accessibility of an array of material that correlates with the units in the science curriculum." They also suggest that it is the job of the school librarian to keep abreast of developments in AT and Accessible Instructional Materials (AIM) and disseminate that knowledge through the school to students, faculty, and parents (Krueger and Stefanich, 2011: 44).

Education

Assistive Technology in the area of education can refer to several different areas, including reading, writing, doing math, and accessing content. AIM are at the core of educational AT. They are of particular importance in school library media centers.

Reading and AIM

As librarians, we are familiar with the traditional "alternative formats." Digital text is new to many of us. Digital text can appear similar to what you see on e-readers such as Kindle. However, it is more flexible and can be downloaded to a variety of platforms. First, it can easily be reformatted with font, color, and size options. Second, it can allow the text to be spoken and highlighted at the same time. This feature makes a program such as BookFlix appeal to young children as well. It is precisely its flexibility that makes digital text useful for children with print disabilities. While digital text can be accessed from any computer, the computer must be accessible to the person using it. Muhammad, a fifth-grader with a print disability, loved biographies and the idea of reading but just couldn't understand the words. He was thrilled when the librarian showed him how to download audiobooks. As the librarian walked back toward him after speaking with his grandmother, she heard him saying, "I can't believe it. I really wanted to read this book. And it's here!"

E-readers have both pluses and minuses for children and teens with disabilities. Advantages include the fact that they are smaller and lighter than many books. Their adjustable text size, even though limited by the relatively small screen, their overall size, and the simplicity of page turns are all welcome by many readers with visual and physical disabilities. The text-to-speech feature is another point in their favor: even after the copyright litigation-imposed three-month wait, they are generally available sooner than commercially produced audio version. The drawbacks to many e-readers include small buttons, difficulty in being able to see the buttons, and the often poor quality of the audio renditions. Again, these are best purchased with a view to the individual child's ability to use them and may be more practical for children in the school library media center.

Some technology may be necessary to support AIM. With the exception of Playaways, a device to play audio formats, such as a computer, MP3 player, or CD player, is needed for audiobooks and digital text requires accessible computers. In 2009 and 2010, the Brooklyn Public Library helped the Reading Is Fundamental organization pilot an audiobook program. We gave the students at a middle school inexpensive MP3 players and coupons for free audiobooks and showed them how to download the library's audiobooks. The program was a huge success. The students loved it. One young man was initially dismissive, saying, "I don't like books." But even he started reading his new book as soon as the download finished. Two students shared ear buds, one fighting with an air saber as he listened to *Star Wars* and the other staring open-mouthed into space completely enthralled.

Scanners turn print books into AIM and are an important tool for children with vision issues or learning disabilities. They allow print such as a book, a magazine, a letter, a bill, or a receipt to be scanned and read out loud or magnified. Scanners that function as AT are different from commercial scanners in two essential ways. First, they must be accessible to the people who need them; for example, a scanner with instructions printed on the device will not work for a person who is blind. Second, they need to scan the text as a text file, not a graphic file, so it can be read by screen reading software.

The actual scanner can be part of a computer or a stand-alone unit. Either way, a flatbed reader is what makes scanners work. Kurzweil was the gold standard for stand-alone scanners for many years and now makes a scanner/software system for computers. OpenBook is another scanning and reading program. Stand-alone scanners that read aloud include ScannaR and Scanning and Reading Appliance (SARA). School library media specialists should be aware of Learning Ally, formerly known as Recordings for the Blind and Dyslexic. This organization records textbooks for students with visual and learning disabilities. Many school districts are members. Individual students can become members with fees based on a sliding scale. More information can be found at http://www.learningally.org/. Bookshare is another popular resource that uses DAISY technology to produce digital books in a variety of formats. It is free to eligible students. Find out more at http://www.bookshare.org/. Both systems are compatible with a variety of e-readers and iOS devices.

Writing

Writing takes on more importance in the school library media center than in the public library. There are a number of helpful writing programs available to assist students with LD and other writing disabilities. Organizing is as important as putting words down, and programs that do both are great. Inspiration and Kidspiration help users visually organize ideas for writing. Read&Write GOLD has a phonetic-based spell checker, highlighting, and online fact checking. Kurzweil 3000 has templates for idea generation, writing, graphic writing templates, and other features. Co:Writer and Write:OutLoud are also useful programs (O'Cummings, 2011: 71).

Educational Media

Media accessibility is an important factor in education in general and in school library media centers in particular. Are videos described for students with visual impairments? Is open- or closed-captioning available for Deaf and hard of hearing students? Instructional computer programs and DVDs must also be evaluated. PowerPoint presentations can be problematic for students with visual, learning, and attention issues. The National Center for Accessible Media has an excellent overview of these issues at http://aim.cast.org/learn/accessiblemedia.

The importance of alternate formats and media accessibility cannot be overstated. AIM gives the student with a disability the same access to text as the general education student. By extension, it gives her the same access to the curriculum as her peers. These two areas are key to full inclusion for children with print disabilities in school and the broader society of children.

Hearing

Hearing disabilities come into play in two areas in the library: communication and programming. The Assistive Technology discussed in the communication section will cover most of the issues that arise with children who are Deaf or hard of hearing. Two systems exist that can help such children in programs: FM systems and induction loop systems, also called hearing loops. Captioning, or having a print display of the speaker's words, is not an ideal system for young children who do not read and for older children who do not read fluidly.

FM systems use a microphone, transmitter, and earphones to amplify the volume for individual listeners. Multiple microphones can be used, and the more sophisticated systems have more than one channel. This is a useful feature if you are using the FM system to translate into a different language. With more than one channel, the same device can be use for more than one language. Several vendors sell them, including ADCO Hearing Products (http://www.adcohearing.com/ald_fm_sys.html) and Barinas (http://www.barinas.com/index.htm).

Induction loop systems work differently. Cables or telecoils are laid around a given area and transmit the sound directly to a person's hearing aide. Theaters, concert halls, and many other venues use them to make performances more accessible. Schools and libraries would benefit as well. A list of suppliers can be found at http://www.hearingloop.org/vendors.htm.

Recreation and Leisure

AT is central to a child's ability to participate in recreation and leisure activities. Adaptive sports equipment, barrier-free theaters and stages, sensory-aware museums, and universally designed playgrounds and gardens are just some of the tools that help children participate. We need to make sure that the library's recreational programs and materials are also available to all children.

Of course, reading is also a recreational activity and an important part of our missions. In their "Position Statement on the School Librarian's Role in Reading," the American Association of School Librarians (2011) states:

> Library media centers provide students, staff, and families with open, non-restricted access to a varied high quality collection of reading materials in multiple formats that reflect academic needs and personal interests . . . including traditional and alternative materials.

The full statement can be found at http://www.ala.org/aasl/aaslissues/positionstatements/roleinreading. Some other recreational areas to consider in the library are gaming, performances, and book clubs.

Gaming

Gaming is a fixture in many libraries. Not much is required to make it universally accessible. Low-tech solutions work well for low-tech games. Let's take checkers, for example. Outline the grid on the board with glue and string, or even just a thick glue, and add texture and a high-contrast color to either the red or black pieces. Voilà—you have a game that is accessible to children with vision issues and to those with dexterity issues.

Gaming is a multimedia activity: mobility, dexterity, vision, hearing, learning, and cognitive issues all come into play. Electronic games require high-tech solutions. Sometimes the issue is with the interface between the game and the user. If this is the case, and they are computer-based games, some of the AT described earlier under computers will be helpful. Sometimes the barrier is within the design of the game itself. To avoid this problem, check out reviews of the games on websites listed in the sidebar or reach out to the gaming community itself.

When purchasing a stand-alone gaming system, check out the accessibility features. The Wii system is widely held to be accessible to youth with physical disabilities and autism. Many of its games work well for players with low vision and with attention issues. The direct control makes it easier for youth with intellectual disabilities, and the sports games in particular are very popular. A self-advocate colleague of one librarian loves the bowling game and regularly tries to get her to play. Nevertheless, Wii is a very visual system with limited access for people with many visual disabilities.

Individual PlayStation games can work well for people with physical disabilities. Adaptive switches and other input devices are available, although they do tend to be expensive. Likewise, Xbox presents many barriers to gamers with disabilities. Initially, Microsoft listed only five Kinect games as accessible to seated gamers. However, many games do work well for children with dexterity problems who have good gross motor control, children with autism, and some children with intellectual disabilities.

PC gaming tends to be more flexible in terms of vision, hearing, learning, and intellectual disabilities. You may already have the AT you need for your desktop computers, and it does transfer over to gaming. There are many accessible gaming apps for iOS devices. They tend to be flexible and easy and have the advantage of not needing additional equipment.

There are many online guides to help you sort through the world of accessible gaming. The British site GameBase (http://www.gamebase. info/home.html), sponsored by SpecialEffect, is a great place to start. Reviews of games, discussion groups, forums, and video tutorials are all part of the package here. AbleGamers (http://www.ablegamers. com/) is another helpful guide to the world of universally designed gaming. Its blog is a particularly helpful resource.

Performances

Technology can help make performances in the library fully accessible. Induction loop and FM systems, mentioned earlier, can help

---

Sources of Accessible Electronic Game Reviews

- AbleGamers
  http://www.ablegamers.com/
- Blind Accessible iPhone and iPad Games
  http://www.pcsgames.net/
  iPhoneGames.htm
- e-Bility
  http://www.e-bility.com/links/
  games.php
- GameBase
  http://www.gamebase.info/
  home.html
- Perkins School for the Blind:
  "The Best Computer Games for Blind Kids"
  http://www.wonderbaby
  .org/articles/best-accessible
  -computer-games-blind-kids

make live performances accessible for people who are hard of hearing. Descriptive videos, another example of AIM, help moviegoers who are blind follow the action.

Book Clubs and Recreational Reading

Alternative formats and AIM are the keys to universally designed book clubs. Sighted and blind readers can read the same books. So can readers with and without learning disabilities or intellectual disabilities. Weigh whether or not books are available in audio, Braille, large print, and digital formats for inclusion when deciding on book lists such as a summer reading list. Indicate those titles on the final list.

Seating and Positioning

Seating is an important part of any library design, and it is something we are used to thinking about. People are tall or short, wide or thin. They have legs or do not have legs. They balance well or do not. In all cases we hope to make them comfortable in the library.

Many low-tech adjustments can help with seating and positioning. Cushions are the most obvious one. Large soft blocks can be used for supporting a child on the floor and as building blocks during playtime. Foot rests are also a simple fix for some seating issues. Wedges for use on chair seats or on the floor aid in balance. Bean bag chairs are a type of seating that works well for some children with physical and sensory issues. However, they should be removed or closely supervised when very young children are present. Cube chairs with different levels of support on every side are another flexible variety of seating. Ball chairs are a specialty item that can support people with autism, sensory issues, and attention issues. They are essentially large therapy/exercise balls with rigid sides to keep the ball that the individual sits on stable and backs and armrests for support.

On the high-tech end are adjustable chairs. We already use them in many libraries, particularly in staff areas at desks. Some libraries also use them in public areas.

Tables are also a consideration. Tilt boards act like tabletop easels with more range of settings. They are placed on a table and adjusted so that a piece of writing or drawing paper lays at an angle rather than flat. Their tacky surface prevents slippage. They can also define a child's personal space. Adjustable desks can put the computer in reach for a short child or a child who uses a large wheelchair or prone stander. These desks can be adjusted manually or electronically.

Vision

AT for vision starts with glasses and contacts. Children with visual disabilities will have their own. There are many additional tools the library can provide to make reading and navigating the library easier for them. Handheld and tabletop magnifiers are a good, low-tech place to start. They can be simple magnifying lenses or have light built into them and can be used for reading, looking at pictures, working on a craft, or signing a library card. They are the low-tech equivalent of CC TV, which captures and projects the image that is then magnified on the screen in real time. Signature guides and felt tip pens can help with signing library cards. Strong lighting with minimal glare and the odd, movable desk lamp can go a long way toward making the library work well for children with low vision as well as their grandparents.

When thinking about AT at your library, look for a broad variety of versatile products. These are your basic tools to meet the needs of children and teens with and without disabilities. However, in and of themselves, they are useless. It is the knowledgeable staff who are comfortable with VoiceOver and ZoomText, who know to offer a pillow to a child struggling to stay seated, and who advertise the FM system that make the library truly barrier free and welcoming to youth with disabilities and their families.

Resources

American Academy of Audiology. 2011. "Get More from Hearing Aids or Cochlear Implants with Hearing Loops." American Academy of Audiology. http://www.audiology.org/resources/consumer/Documents/20110225_FactSheet.pdf.

American Speech-Language-Hearing Association. 2012. "Hearing Assistive Technology." American Speech-Language-Hearing Association. http://www.asha.org/public/hearing/treatment/assist_tech.htm.

Association of Specialized and Cooperative Library Agencies. 2010. "Library Accessibility: What You Need to Know." American Library Association. http://www.ala.org/ascla/asclaprotools/ accessibilitytipsheets/.

Apple, Inc. 2012. "Accessibility." Apple, Inc. http://www.apple .com/accessibility/.

Copeland, Clayton A. 2011. "School Librarians of the 21st Century: Using Resources and Assistive Technologies to Support Students' Differences and Abilities." *Knowledge Quest* 39, no. 3: 64–69.

Jendron, Janet. 2012. "AT and Learning Disabilities." South Carolina Assistive Technology Program. Last updated October 9. http://www .sc.edu/scatp/ld.htm.

Microsoft. 2012. "Microsoft Accessibility: Technology for Everyone." Microsoft. http://www.microsoft.com/enable/default.aspx.

PACER Center. 2011. *There's an APP for That: iPOD/iPAD 101.* Minneapolis, MN: PACER Center. http://www.pacer.org/webinars/ stc/iPod_iPad_Resources_Handout050511.pdf.

PACER Center and National Center of Accessible Instructional Materials at CAST. 2011. *Accessible Instructional Materials (AIM): A Technical Guide for Families and Advocates.* Minneapolis, MN: PACER Center. http://www.pacer.org/stc/pubs/STC-22.pdf.

PACER Center and Tots-n-Tech. 2011. *EZ AT 2: Simple Assistive Technology Ideas for Children Ages Birth to 3.* Minneapolis, MN: PACER Center. http://www.pacer.org/stc/pubs/EZ-AT-book-2011 -final.pdf.

Pugliese, Madalaine, and Current Students from the Simmons College Assistive Technology Graduate Program. 2011. "APPsolute Fit: Selecting the Right Mobile Device Apps." *Closing the Gap*, October/ November. http://www.closingthegap.com/media/solutions/ articles/2011/10/1872/1872.pdf.

Scheeren, William O. 2010. *Technology for the School Librarian: Theory and Practice.* Santa Barbara, CA: Libraries Unlimited.

Stanberry, Kristin, and Marshall Raskind. 2012. "Assistive Technology Tools: Reading." Great Schools. http://www.greatschools.org/special -education/assistive-technology/948-reading-tools.gs?page=1.

Tech-Ease. 2011. "4All." Tech-Ease: For All Your Classroom Technology Needs. http://etc.usf.edu/techease/4all/.

Vandenbard, R. Todd. 2010. "Tending a Wild Garden: Library Web Design for Persons with Disabilities." *Information, Technology and Libraries* 29, no. 1: 23–29.

Welsch, Mary, and Jean Baily. 2010. *Potential and Possibilities: Model for Providing Children with Disabilities Access to Benefits of Play Experiences.* Chicago: National Lekotek Center. http://www.lekotek .org/general-info/resources/lekotek-white-paper.

Wong, Peggy, and Allen McGinley. 2010. "Rated E for Everyone: Expanding Services to Children with Special Needs." *School Library Journal* 56, no. 12: 22–23.

References

American Association of School Librarians. 2011. "Position Statement on the School Librarian's Role in Reading." American Library Association. http://www.ala.org/aasl/aaslissues/positionstatements/ roleinreading.

———. 2012. "Position Statement on the Role of the School Library Program." American Library Association. http://www.ala.org/aasl/ aaslissues/positionstatements/roleslp.

Brady, Lois Jean. 2011. *APPS for Autism: An Essential Guide to over 200 Effective Apps for Improving Communication, Behavior, Social Skills, and More.* Arlington, TX: Future Horizons.

Krueger, Karla S., and Greg P. Stefanich. 2011. "The School Librarian as an Agent of Scientific Inquiry for Students with Disabilities." *Knowledge Quest* 39, no. 3: 40–47.

Mates, Barbara T., and William R. Reed. 2011. *Assistive Technologies in the Library.* Chicago: ALA Editions.

Nalewicki, Jennifer. 2011. "Bold Strokes: New Font Helps Dyslexics Read." *Scientific American*, October 26. http://www.scientificamerican.com/ article.cfm?id=new-font-helps-dyslexics-read.

O'Cummings, Edward O. 2011. "Assistive and Adaptive Technology Resources." *Knowledge Quest* 39, no. 3: 70–73.

3

PART 3
Developing Collections and Services

Playing and Learning— in the Library and at Home

11

She's never played with a toy before.

—*Teacher commenting while watching a 12-year-old child in a self-contained classroom play with a switch-toy giraffe at the library*

Play is important and universal. Existing across cultures, time, and species, it is essential to all areas of our lives, including literacy. "Play is how we are made, how we develop and adjust to change. It can foster innovations. . . . But in the end the most significant aspect of play is that it allows us to express our feelings and connect most deeply with the best in ourselves, and in others" (Brown, 2009: 218). It is so important that even the United Nations recognizes the right to play in Article 31 of the UN Convention on the Rights of the Child (United Nations Children's Fund, 1990).

The Association for Library Service to Children and the Public Library Association have included play, along with singing, talking, reading, and writing, as one of the five early literacy practices. These activities help children learn the six early literacy skills discussed in Chapter 2 (Association for Library Service to Children and Public Library Association, 2011: Section 1-5, p. 5). These principles are as true for children with disabilities as for typically developing children.

Increasingly, barriers to play affect all children. The focus on academic skills and testing has led to more direct instruction and less free play in formal educational settings. Even in Head Start and preschool programs, play has been relegated to a less important activity. Busy schedules for children also impede play. For children with disabilities this is compounded by the need for multiple medical appointments, which often supercede playtime rather than school time. Children with disabilities face one more additional roadblock: the lack of appropriate, affordable toys.

Establishing a toy collection at the library encourages families to appreciate the central importance of play in a child's development. Allowing the collection to circulate provides appropriate toys for use at home. Providing a toy collection tells all families that libraries are fun and welcoming places. For a child with a significant disability that limits his or her ability to move or communicate or manipulate a toy, the availability of toys is more than delightful. It is the difference between whether the child can independently experience the pleasure and learning afforded by play or not.

Play

It is through play that children learn about the world around them. Children develop emotionally, physically, socially, and cognitively by playing. They learn new skills and practice them during play. They can experiment with different ways of handling social situations and emotions. Inclusive play allows children to do so in a natural environment.

The Types and Stages of Play

Play itself develops and has three stages: solitary play, parallel play, and social play. Each stage involves different skills, has a different focus, and utilizes different types of play. There are seven basic types of play:

- gross motor skills,
- fine motor skills,
- sensory and exploratory,
- construction,
- imaginative/fantasy,
- cooperative, and
- organized.

When we understand how they come together, we can better facilitate children's play.

In the first stage, solitary play, children play alone. This play is primarily gross and fine motor play and sensory/exploratory play. Here a child is reaching for things, moving around, and putting things in his mouth. This stage gradually evolves into parallel play. During parallel play, the first three skills are used, and construction play is added. At this point, children are watching and mirroring each other but not engaging each other. Parallel play is supplanted by social play. Social play includes all the basic types of play. Here the child is finally interacting with other children. Social play itself evolves as children grow, with structure and rules becoming more important (Elkind, 2007: 146).

Inclusive Play

As we have seen, play in general has many developmental benefits. Inclusive play in particular has its own rewards. For children with disabilities, it promotes physical and psychological health and the development of new skills. It creates connections within the community (Schleien, Ray, and Green, 1997: 73). It is a great way for children with disabilities to practice social and communication skills in a natural way. Children both with and without disabilities develop a sense of well-being, expand and hone their emotional responses, and enhance their interpersonal skills (Casey, 2005: 6). They also form friendships, develop an appreciation for diversity, increase their acceptance of individual differences, and experience an increase in empathy and social cognition (Hobbs et al., 2001: 47).

Some benefits of inclusive play are unique to typically developing children. Their attitudes toward people with disabilities often become more positive. Young children without disabilities learn how to share attention, relate to others, read emotional and social signals, solve problems, and think creatively in facilitated inclusive play (Kordt-Thomas and Lee, 2006: 86).

Enabling inclusive play has an important and beneficial side effect for those children who are not diagnosed with a disability but have trouble playing nonetheless. "It's often noticeable that there are children who flit around on the margins and are rarely engaged in play or play with others. These children often gain enormously from changes within the environment" (Casey, 2005: 7). In other words, Universal Design works well for everyone.

Play in the Library

Many libraries already incorporate play. It can be structured or unstructured. It can be for babies, first graders, or teens. Library programs often incorporate play components such as fingerplays and puppets. Many of us have actual play programs, with or without a book component. The Farmers Branch (TX) Library (https://www.farmersbranch.info/play/manske-library/library-programs-and-events/personal-growth) advertises "Baby Bounce . . . Learn games to play with your newest family member." The Brooklyn Public Library offers "Read, Play, Grow," which includes tips for playing with babies and toddlers and preschoolers, on its website (http://www.bklynpubliclibrary.org/first-5-years). November 12 is National Gaming Day at libraries throughout the country, attracting tweens and teens. Many libraries have toys available in the children's rooms and games in the teen sections. The main branch of the Houston (TX) Public Library circulates electronic games internally for use on its many gaming systems. Ensuring that play is inclusive and fun for all is the next step.

Facilitating Play

While play is natural, it must sometimes be facilitated to go smoothly. A library program may be the first group interaction experience for a child. Or the children may be new to each other. Or, if it is inclusive play, they may have questions, voiced and unvoiced, about each others' abilities. Facilitating the play also lets us model appropriate play for parents in the same way we model appropriate literacy activities in our reading and storytelling programs. The type of support necessary will vary with the type of play.

Facilitating play is different from correcting play. Adults often feel the need to correct play. At one play program, the father of a regular participant in a play program told his son that the toy stove was just for girls. While the librarian felt constrained by the differences in their cultures not to intervene, she did later in that program join two other children, a boy and a girl, in that area and support their play. Parents will often insist on the right use of a toy, placing the engine in the front of a train or telling a child not to roll the bells meant to be instruments. These sorts of interventions stifle the child's creativity. That being said, there are many ways to constructively facilitate play.

Solitary Play

When a child is playing alone we need to:

- provide appropriate materials that the child can reach;
- use parallel talk, a form of language enrichment that involves responding to the baby, naming things the baby is using, and describing the baby's play;

- model play;
- follow the child's lead; and
- include books.

Modeling play is an indirect teaching method but a very effective one at this stage. It is also a lot of fun.

Following a child's lead can be hard. Children may want to play with those two blocks for an extended period of time even though it is obvious to you that they can never be balanced. Letting the play continue long after you are bored allows the children to develop perseverance and focus.

Parallel Play

In terms of facilitation, parallel play differs very little from solitary play. We still need to provide accessible materials, follow the child's lead, use parallel talk, and avoid overwhelming him. In addition, we need to provide potential playmates, creating the opportunity for observing interaction but not forcing it.

Social Play

Social play is the most complex type of play; facilitating it is correspondingly complex. Preparing the play becomes more important. Select activities and toys that lead to interactions. For example, blocks, balls, trucks, and bean bags are all toys that facilitate social play. Materials that support social pretend play might include toy phones and toy food. Activities such as dancing and singing encourage interactions.

Provide an appropriate environment and some scenarios. For example, have some train tracks and train cars on the floor and ask two children where it can go. Ask the children questions, including leading ones, about what and how they intend to play. Sometimes it is appropriate to encourage them to plan their play, and sometimes we need to demonstrate imaginative play, such as what a stethoscope is for or using something for an unintended purpose. You may have to help them define and negotiate their roles, particularly if everyone wants to be the teacher and no one wants to be the student or principal. Finally, you also need to know when to back off and let them play together.

In addition to helping children plan their play, talk to them about it. Again, it is important to follow the child's lead. Some children will need to practice pretending. You may be able to help them move from a toy drum set to pretending a pencil is a drumstick.

Sometimes it will be necessary to intervene directly. The children may be having difficulty getting started or getting along or even be in danger of hurting each other. When it is necessary to intervene, it is best to enter the play naturally. If they are role-playing, adopt an appropriate role for the scenario and try facilitating from that position. For example, if two children are arguing about who should be the teacher and who should be the student, enter as the principal and assign them alternating class periods. Or if other children are having trouble working on the puzzle together, sit down with them and demonstrate turn taking and sharing the pieces. Once the conflict has been resolved, disengage as quickly and smoothly as you can, no matter how much fun you are having.

Children with and without disabilities do not necessarily have a lot of experience playing together and may need some help. As much as adults like to pretend they do not exist, children's differences can be obvious to each other. When questions arise, involve the child in the discussion when possible. If a child asks, "Why does John have that thing on his leg?," refer the question to John. If he does not want to answer it, ask John if you can answer it. If he again says no, respect his wishes and say something like, "John wants his privacy right now." It is helpful in situations like these to have toys that reflect all the children. Perhaps the curious child can find a doll and a brace to play with. Model appropriate behavior such as supporting a child with disabilities without taking over and asking whether help is wanted before helping.

Older children need to play too. As children become teens and young adults, the balance between studying, working, and playing becomes harder to manage. Keeping play that they choose because they enjoy it in their lives gives them a sense of perspective. It also helps them develop a constructive peer group (Brown, 2009: 113). All types of games, including computer games and pick-up sports, are central to play for older children and teens. Indoor sports, cooperative building programs, loosely structured crafts, miniature railroad clubs, and many other activities can encourage tweens and teens to play in your library. And encouraging them to play in the library sends the message to parents that play is important for tweens and teens too.

The Lekotek Program Model

Acknowledging the importance of play, the Lekotek program offers adaptive toy lending libraries and play programs. The underlying principles that Lekotek Centers use when designing programs can serve as one model for librarians who wish to offer inclusive play programs for children. Though developed with young children in mind, the principles apply to playing children of all ages.

- *Every child deserves to have fun.* Recognizing the extraordinary stress that children with disabilities and their families often experience, fun is at the center of the Lekotek model. While the services provided by Lekotek Centers do foster skill development, it is the one visit or appointment a family may have in the mosaic of services that is designed specifically for fun.
- *Play should focus on what a child can do, not on what he or she can't do.* This strength-based practice is a key component of mental health services for children and teens. Mastery of skills learned through play with toys and games and on computers helps foster feelings of satisfaction and adequacy. Play leaders select toys for children that challenge them to create successes for themselves.
- *Play sessions are family centered.* Multigenerational families and friends are integral to helping a child with a disability reach her potential. These sessions provide opportunities for play leaders to give special attention to siblings as well as to the individual with the disability.
- *Play sessions are opportunities to provide family support services.* Play leaders help parents understand the importance of play in much the same way as children's librarians have traditionally helped parents understand the role of reading aloud. In addition, play leaders help parents build the set of skills they need to navigate through the maze of information, support systems, and available services.
- *Play sessions promote the inclusion of children with disabilities into family and community activities.* Play leaders find creative ways to enable children with disabilities to play with the same materials as their peers without disabilities. Toys are adapted and games are played in ways that enable everyone to participate. And of course, adaptive toys are available to typically developing children too.

The National Lekotek Center: Play Leaders

Lekotek play leaders are trained professionals with backgrounds in the various child development fields. They receive additional training from the National Lekotek Center in therapeutic play and the paradigm that play helps children understand and relate to the world around them. The center and its play leaders offer training to people interested in starting programs as well as free advice on toy selection. They can be reached at http://www.lekotek.org/ or 773-528-5766.

Floortime

Developed by Stanley Greenspan, the Floortime model of autism treatment seeks to "follow the child's lead to enter his emotional world, then create a series of opportunities and challenges to help him move to higher levels of relating, communicating and thinking" (Greenspan and Wieder, 2009: 181). It is a process with two goals: to follow the child's lead and to entice the child into a shared world.

Following the child's lead starts with the understanding that a child's actions have purposes. Copying the child's activities or becoming a character in his pretend play allows us to enter the child's world and create shared attention. Using that shared attention, we can create playful challenges and barriers to extend her skills and draw her into the shared world.

While Floortime is a therapeutic process traditionally done one-on-one, group Floortime involves siblings and peers and is applicable to the library setting. Here we can structure the play by giving each child the chance to be the leader and encouraging the children to follow the leader, joining in her play. Our role is to actively bring the children into the leader's play without taking over. Floortime is a proven method of helping some children with disabilities, especially those with autism, engage in inclusive play.

Greenspan views social and emotional development as a lifelong process. As children grow up, Floortime is replaced by the learning community model. These communities provide an "interpersonal context" in which people can continue to develop emotional, communicative, and social skills (Greenspan and Wieder, 2009: 230). Learning communities should be natural environments, with meaningful activities that facilitate social interaction and ideally can provide the opportunity for meaningful work. The performing and visual arts, gardening, and gaming can all be parts of learning communities (Greenspan and Wieder, 2009: 231–232). Our libraries are ideally placed to provide the setting for inclusive learning communities for teens and young adults with disabilities.

Sensory Storytime

Sensory storytimes bring techniques from occupational therapy to library play sessions. Carol Kranowitz's (2006: 10–12) SAFE framework is a simple way to look at sensory play:

- *S is for sensorimotor.* Sensorimotor activities develop the coordination between sensation and movement. The connection between these two areas aids in sensory processing.
- *A is for appropriate.* The sensorimotor activities you incorporate in library programs should be appropriate to the environment and the skill and developmental levels of the children.
- *F is for fun.* Fun is both a motivation for doing the activity and a result of mastering a challenge.
- *E is for easy.* The activities are easy to set up, easy enough for the child to enjoy, easy on the budget, and easy on the environment.

For example, create a path with different textured squares to walk on. Make a game of guessing scents with bottles of basil, coffee, pencil shavings, and other strong aromas. Create a fishing game with cardboard fish, safety pins, and magnets attached to string. Kranowitz's (2006) book *The Out-of-Sync Child Has Fun: Activities with Sensory Processing Disorder* is full of exciting and SAFE ideas.

Play at Home

However you combine the models for play in the library, helping parents understand the importance of play and encouraging them to take play home with them is part of the goal. Modeling play is a good start. Teaching them about play and giving them the tools they need to play at home is the next step.

Helping Parents Play

Parents need to understand the importance of play. How many times have we heard "He's just playing"? Just as we have become adept at incorporating early literacy hints into our programs for young children, we need to include play hints. Describing a child's play in developmental terms is a great place to start. Having handouts and starting informal discussions is another. Offering more formal workshops on play, early learning, and literacy is another way to go. Circulating literacy kits that include toys will help parents get the idea. The Every

Child Ready to Read @ your library program has many more concrete suggestions to help parents embrace play. Making toys available is another way we can support play at home.

Toy Collections and Toy Lending Libraries

Julie is the "she" in the quotation at the beginning of this chapter. She came to the library once a month with her class. Julie is deaf/blind and has physical and intellectual disabilities. During her first visit with her class, after hearing two stories about animals and singing "At the Zoo" the children were selecting and playing with toys. Julie did not have one so the librarian took her a mechanical giraffe that walked and brayed when you pressed a switch. She chose the giraffe because of the strong contrast between the spots and the background and for its auditory and tactile appeal. Because Julie had very little vision or hearing, the librarian and Julie's aid snuggled the long neck of the giraffe against her neck and guided her hand to the switch. Julie caught on after the first couple of tries and laughed out loud with pleasure. Her teacher explained that her parents had no means to provide the expensive adapted toys she needed and neither did the school. It really was likely that this was this first time she had a toy that she had been able to play with independently.

The lack of availability of appropriate toys creates obstacles to learning through play for children with disabilities. Establishing a toy lending collection in the library not only provides appropriate toys for use at home but also encourages families to appreciate the central importance of play in a young child's development. A toy collection that integrates commercial toys—and ideas for adapting them—with specifically designed adaptive toys entices children with a wide range of disabilities and their families to come to the library.

To promote inclusion, libraries that circulate toys often include toys for children with and without disabilities. An inclusive collection recognizes the value of toys for all children and avoids the possibility that children with disabilities will be labeled "special" when they approach the circulation desk. What follows are guidelines and suggestions on developing a toy collection for all children.

If you cannot develop a toy lending collection, be aware of any toy lending libraries in your area. Even though the library Julie used did not lend toys, the librarian was able to refer Julie and her family to the SHARE Library, an adaptive toy lending library run by United

Cerebral Palsy (https://www.sharelibraries.info/index.htm). The USA Toy Library Association lists its members on its website (http://www.usatla.org/). In the best-case scenario, you can partner with them, sharing resources, patrons, and referrals. One librarian conducts class visits at the SHARE Library and offers programs for parents on the United Cerebral Palsy campus where it is located. They publicize her library's programs and allow her to register the students for library cards and summer reading.

Building a Toy Collection

Building a toy collection is a lot like building a book collection. It involves selecting and buying the toys and can be a lot of fun.

Selection Guidelines

Unfortunately, librarians do not learn how to select toys in graduate school. Fortunately, other people do. The National Lekotek Center is a treasure trove of information on toys for children with disabilities. They publish evaluations of toys and buying information on one of their two sites at http://www.ableplay.org/. If you need a more personalized consultation on how to select appropriate play materials and activities for children with disabilities, you can call the Lekotek Toy Resource Helpline at 1-800-366-PLAY. If you are lucky enough to have a Lekotek Center in your area, you have a wonderful resource and exciting potential partner. Lacking a nearby Lekotek Center, you can reach out to your state's Assistive Technology resource center.

Local Early Intervention and preschool special education professionals can play an important role in toy selection. Museum educators, particularly those who work in children's museums and science museums, are a wealth of knowledge about toys for elementary school-age students, tweens, and teens. Consult teachers, including math and science teachers, child life specialists in hospitals, and after-school program providers. Many will be happy to share their expertise, especially if the library's collection can be used by their families. And remember, each conversation has the potential to develop into a mutually beneficial partnership.

In addition to working with these providers when selecting toys, librarians need to consider the following guidelines.

Versatility

Functional versatility is the ability of a toy to be used in a number of different ways to fit a child's moods, personality, and capabilities. Toys with a high degree of functional versatility are part of the core collections. Examples of such toys include balls, dolls, blocks, and stacking/nesting toys. This is in contrast to a toy that can be used only in highly rigidly defined ways (e.g., a jack-in-the-box). Toys that have a high level of functional versatility allow children to use their imaginations to fill in the details and expand their use.

While it is not necessary to select only toys with a limited number of pieces, it is important to choose toys that are versatile enough to function even if a few pieces are damaged or lost, such as DUPLO blocks or a set of dishes. If each piece of a multiple-item toy is essential to the operation of that toy, it is not an advisable purchase. Try keeping a lost toy basket with the toys and put the pieces in there when they are separated from their toys, games, or puzzles. Usually within a week or two they are happily reunited.

Adaptability

A toy collection targeted to children with disabilities needs to include capability switches, specially designed adaptive toys, and commercial toys that can be used by children with a range of abilities and interests. They must also reflect the backgrounds and abilities of the children who use them. These toys and materials promote physical and cognitive growth and empower the child to control his environment.

Toys with switches are an essential learning tool for children with physical disabilities. Children learn the cause and effect by doing something and observing the consequences. If you are limited in the way you can affect the world, your ability to understand this basic concept is also limited. Julie's story illustrates the way in which this fundamental learning can intersect with fun and why it is important for children to have access to appropriate toys.

CAPABILITY SWITCHES

The giraffe Julie played with was activated by a capability switch. These devices permit children to activate toys with minimal pressure, sound, or movement. Having a variety of switches available anticipates the needs of individual children and enables them to play with adapted toys. Plate switches of various sizes utilize the slightest pressure from individual body parts, whereas other switches may rely on a puff of air or a tilt of the head to activate the toy. Capability switches include a lighted sensory plate switch, grip switch, vibrating plate switch, joystick, pillow switch, pull switch, signal switch, and puff switch.

ADAPTIVE TOYS

Adaptive toys are modified, battery-operated toys than can accommodate any capability switch. There are also adaptive toys, such as multisensory activity boxes, bead chains, and stacking towers, that do not require an external switch to be operational. Adaptive toys include toys for sensory play (texture boards, rhythm instruments, etc.); manipulation toys (tracking boards, lacing sets, etc.); toys that emphasize sensorimotor exploration (multisensory activity boxes, somatosensory bead chains, etc.); toys that stimulate cause–effect or visual tracking (switch-activated toys); and infant sensory stimulation toys (crib mobiles, music boxes/mirrors, floor rollers).

COMMERCIAL TOYS

Toys need not be specially designed adaptive devices to be appropriate for children with special needs. Choose well-designed toys that are easy to manipulate, are stimulating to multiple senses, show cause and effect, and have potential to be used by children with a wide range of ages and abilities.

Many commercial toys are appropriate for the child with sensory, developmental, or physical needs. Some features, such as easy-grip puzzle pieces or blocks that connect with magnets or bristles, may help make toys more suitable for children with physical disabilities. Purchasing soft foam instead of hard plastic blocks is safer for all young children. Plastic and wood blocks have their place too, especially in sensory play.

Provide materials that stimulate or rely on senses other than, or in addition to, vision. Commercially available items include musical instruments, plush toys with sound effects, shape sorters, pegboards, blocks, balls with internal bells, and puzzles with textures. Consider creating texture boats using tubs of tactile-rich materials like oatmeal, rice, or commercially available sand/water tables. Use universally designed toys such as magnetic letters or alphabet blocks with Braille on them.

Many commercial toys can be easily adapted for use by children with disabilities. You can create your own switch toys using battery interrupters. Attach Velcro to stacking blocks, adding texture and making them easier to build with, especially by children who lack fine muscle control. Have some dolls' clothes that fasten with Velcro as well

Toy Guides and Reviews

There are many sources of toy guides and toy reviews. It is just as important to evaluate the source as it is the toy. Some sources are commercial entities, and you need to think about the motive for listing a toy. Others are not for profit and have no stake in selling the toys.

- Abledata (http://abledata .com/abledata.cfm) lists and reviews AT, including toys, for the federal Department of Education. The site includes detailed product descriptions as well as manufacturer and ordering information.

- Oppenheimer Toy Portfolio (http://www.toyportfolio.com/) is an independent commercial source for toy evaluations and suggestions. They have a separate section for "Special Needs Adaptable Products."

- AblePlay (http://www.ableplay .org/), maintained by the National Lekotek Center, is devoted to toys for children with disabilities and has an amazing search engine.

Continued on p. 205

as with the more difficult buttons and snaps. Use curly shoelaces on some lacing toys. Use battery interrupter switches to make a motorized or electronic toy accessible. The Tots-n-Tech website (http://tnt .asu.edu/) and its free newsletter offer simple, inexpensive solutions to common concerns, such as gripping issues and recapping markers.

Include toys that work well for children with fine motor skill issues in your toy collections. These toys, all developed for commercial use by typically developing children, include magnetic or bristle blocks, large-knobbed puzzles, DUPLO blocks, toys designed to be used with remote switches, and toys that respond to voice commands.

Increase tactile stimulation by adding sand or other textures such as rice to finger paint. Have clay and play dough on hand. Include texture in gluing activities by incorporating cloth, sandpaper, corrugated cardboard, and twigs with traditional construction paper.

Because some children may be reluctant to touch unfamiliar materials or are tactilely sensitive, always describe the material and never force the situation. Imagine Bertie Bott's Every Flavour Beans (boxes of jelly beans with flavors ranging from banana to rotten eggs, featured in the Harry Potter series) to understand tactile defensiveness. You never know if you will get one that tastes like butterscotch or ear wax. Describing texture will both enrich language and provide information about the new experience for which they have no visual cues to prepare them. Try substituting a different texture that may be more pleasing if one creates a problem. Making the materials available to the entire group will prevent any stigma.

A selection of commercial toys that fall into the following categories should be considered for a core collection:

- Construction toys (alphabet blocks, magnetic blocks, bristle blocks, DUPLO, LEGO, and K'NEX, etc.)
- Nesting/stacking toys (stacking cups, ring tower, nesting dolls, etc.)
- Balls of varying sizes and textures
- Dolls and puppets
- Puzzles (easy grip, wooden, foam, cardboard, floor, and jigsaws of various sizes and complexity)
- Imaginary play toys (animal sets, dolls, dishes, doctor kits, toy cars and trucks, role-playing games, costumes, tools)
- Shape/sorting toys
- Push/pull toys

- Sensory toys (Thera-Bands, medicine balls, weighted blankets, balance beams, textured balls, etc.)
- Games

NICHE TOYS

Universal Design was clearly used in the design of some toys. Alphabet blocks with print, carved, Braille, or manual alphabet letters on them is one such example. Other toys have also crossed over from the therapeutic field into general play, such as large medicine balls. These types of toys are available from specialty suppliers.

GAMES

The games category is a large one that encompasses board games, computer and video games, and sports. Many board games work well for some children with disabilities. Electronic monopoly has the potential to be accessible to people with physical and visual disabilities.

Games and puzzles are even easier to adapt than toys. Add Velcro or heavy-duty tape, and use Hi Mark tactile pens, textured paint, or glue to define borders, dots, and lines of board games. This will also help children with fine motor skill issues. Add texture to differentiate the pieces. Checkers requires only the addition of white felt on the red pieces to make it accessible to youth who are blind or color blind.

Ensure that electronic games and gaming systems meet ADA standards for accessibility. The Perkins School for the Blind has a great website that includes sources for accessible games at http://www.wonderbaby.org/articles/best-accessible-computer-games-blind-kids. Think about each game's usefulness, adaptability, and fun factor when purchasing it. The same groups that evaluate toys tend to evaluate these games as well.

Computer and video games have their place in our collections and program offerings. There are many benefits to playing computer games. They engage active thinking and problem solving and help develop computer literacy. Games in which students assume alternate identities can help foster understanding of others and help develop the theory of mind, or the idea that other people have a different point of view than we do (Elklind, 2007: 58–59). That understanding is the basis for all successful social interactions. The right game can have therapeutic benefits in pain management, help promote fitness, and even help manage post-traumatic stress disorder (Streisand,

Continued from p. 204

The suggested products are accompanied by a detailed description, including how the products can be used, ratings for each of the categories, large photographs, and ordering information.

- Consumer Reports (http://www.consumerreports.org/cro/toys/buying-guide.htm), a not-for-profit organization, offers a general introduction to developmentally appropriate toys as well as reviews of specific toys.
- Toys"R"Us Toy Guide for Differently-Abled Kids (http://www.toysrus.com/shop/index.jsp?categoryId=3261680) is a hybrid source, a partnership between the company and the National Lekotek Center.
- Autism Speaks: Toys and Games (http://www.autismspeaks.org/family-services/resource-library/toys-games) is another type of hybrid; they recommend specific products, reviewed by parents, and include links to them on their website for financial consideration.

2006: 48). And, more to the point, they bring tweens and teens into the library.

When considering computer-based gaming, remember that the underlying technology must be accessible in order for the games to be accessible. Large monitors, speech synthesis and output software, a good magnification program, trackballs, and other mouse alternatives are all important. The Association for Specialized and Cooperative Library Agencies has guidelines on accessible technology at http://www.ala.org/ascla/sites/ala.org.ascla/files/content/asclaprotools/accessibilitytipsheets/tipsheets/11-Assistive_Technol.pdf. For more information on accessible games and gaming, see Chapter 10.

Quality and Safety

Certain toy companies have established reputations as providers of quality products for children. Be cautious of discount toy catalogs that offer "clones" of popular toys at reduced prices. Products made with inferior materials may not be as durable or safe as their better-known counterparts. For example, one toy discount supplier offer low-priced "easy grip" puzzles from which the "grip" can be easily dislodged from the puzzle piece. This creates a potential choking hazard.

Limit selection to toys that are durable and safe. The better toys are constructed of materials such as shatterproof, durable plastic, safety mirrors, and solid wood rather than flimsy wood laminates. There should be no small piece that could easily break or fall off.

Passed in 2008, the Consumer Product Safety Improvement Act significantly decreased the amount of lead and phthalates allowed in products for children under the age of 12. It also requires agencies (such as schools and libraries) that make these products available to children be able to provide documentation as to the levels of these substances in the products children use. The toys in your library must comply with this law.

Bypass toys with hard-to-clean surfaces. Children with disabilities may mouth toys beyond the toddler years. Some programs have a basket in which adults can place toys that have been exposed to saliva and other bodily fluids to be cleaned before their next use. Toys that are circulated require a cleaning procedure. Consider purchasing a small, portable dishwasher. It will save you a lot of time with the LEGOS. To prevent corrosion, store batteries outside of the toys they power. Consider using tweens and teens to clean the toys. Many of them appreciate the opportunity to "play" with toys they consider too young for them.

Age Appropriateness

At the outset, establish the age level to which the collection is geared and divide the toys by developmental levels. Toys for eight-year-olds are not necessarily safe for six-month-olds to play with. Be clear with the parents that some toys in your collection are not appropriate for children under the age of three. Because we must have adaptive toys, some with batteries, we need to be vigilant about supervising the children as they play.

While it is essential that the age appropriateness of a toy be considered, do not be bound by suggested age levels printed on the package. Many conventional toys geared for younger children may be ideal for older children with special needs. For example, DUPLOS are usually suggested for preschool-age children. However, they may be an ideal building toy for a ten-year-old with fine motor skill issues.

Cost

Parents are less likely to buy some toys because of their cost. This is particularly true for adaptive toys, which are often very expensive. When a library purchases and circulates toys, as well as other materials, the cost is a shared expense. The library's toy collection, especially one that includes adaptive toys, gives all children a wider range of choices than any individual family's budget may allow. In addition to sharing expensive resources, the library's toy collection offers an opportunity for parents and children to experience playing with a toy prior to purchasing it.

In addition to sharing expensive resources, the library must determine whether it can afford to provide batteries on an ongoing basis. Providing batteries can be a costly proposition. One option is to make the families borrowing the toys responsible for providing batteries for their own use. If you choose this option, make sure that your patrons understand their responsibilities or it can lead to frustration.

Another option is for the library to provide the batteries. If this is the case, be sure to include an ongoing supply of them in any grant budget. When selecting toys, it is a good idea to keep track of the number and size of batteries each toy requires, estimate how many times the toy can circulate on one set of batteries, and purchase them in bulk. Invest in good quality batteries and rechargers. The expense of batteries is a particularly important consideration when purchasing adaptive and assistive toys and switches, many of which are battery operated.

Sources for Toys

There are many reputable toy suppliers. The following list includes some popular vendors of traditional, commercial toys and games as well as suppliers of adaptive toys, switches, and games.

Popular Toy and Game Vendors

- Constructive Playthings
  13201 Arrington Road
  Grandview, MO 64030
  (800) 448-1412
  http://www.constructiveplaythings.com/cgi-bin/s.sh/2.0/index.html
- Discovery Toys
  (800) 341-TOYS (8697)
  http://www.discoverytoyslink.com/esuite/control/ecommerceMain?MARKET=US (United States)
  http://www.discoverytoyslink.com/esuite/control/ecommerceMain?MARKET=CA (Canada)
- Folkmanis and Folkmanis Puppets
  1219 Park Avenue
  Emeryville, CA 94608
  (800) 654-8922
  http://www.folkmanis.com/ (United States)
  http://www.firetheimagination.ca/ (Canada)
- Kaplan Early Learning Company
  1310 Lewisville Clemmons Road
  Lewisville, NC 27023
  (800) 334-2014
  http://www.kaplanco.com/
- Lakeshore Learning Materials
  2695 East Dominguez Street
  Carson, CA 90895
  (800) 778-4456
  http://www.lakeshorelearning.com/
- School Specialty
  PO Box 1579
  Appleton, WI 54912-1579
  (888) 388-3224
  http://www.schoolspecialty.com/

Suppliers of Adaptive Toys, Switches, and Games

- AbleNet, Inc.
  2808 Farview Avenue North
  Roseville, MN 55113
  (800) 322-0956
  http://www.ablenetinc.com/
- AblePlay
  National Lekotek Center
  2001 North Clybourn Avenue
  Chicago, IL 60614
  (773) 528-5766 x401
  http://www.ableplay.org/
- Achievement Products for Special Needs
  PO Box 6013
  Carol Stream, IL 60197-6013
  (800) 373-4699
  http://www.achievement-products.com/
- American Printing House for the Blind, Inc.
  1839 Frankfort Avenue
  Louisville, KY 40206
  (800) 223-1839
  http://www.aph.org/
- Dragonfly Toy Company
  291 Yale Avenue
  Winnipeg, MB Canada R3M OL4
  (866) 559-1086
  http://www.dragonflytoys.com/
- Enablemart
  Manufacturers Resource Network, Inc.
  5353 South 960 East, Suite 200
  Salt Lake City, UT 84117
  (888) 640-1999
  http://www.enablemart.com/
- Enabling Devices
  50 Broadway
  Hawthorne, NY 10552
  (914) 747-3070
  (800) 832-8697
  http://enablingdevices.com/catalog

- Flaghouse
  601 Flaghouse Drive
  Hasbrouck Heights, NJ 07604-3116
  (800) 793-7900
  http://www.flaghouse.com/
- Kids on the Block, Inc.
  9385 Gerwig Lane
  Columbia, MD 21046
  (800) 368-5437
  http://www.kotb.com/
- Learning Resources
  380 North Fairway Drive
  Vernon Hills, IL 60061
  (800) 333-8281
  http://www.learningresources.com/category/special+needs/
  disorder-disability/cognitive/autism.do?code=CAT-HSH11
- SensoryEdge
  8469 Canoga Avenue
  Canoga Park, CA 91304
  (800) 734-8019
  http://www.sensoryedge.com/
- TFA Special Needs Toys
  4537 Gibsonia Road
  Gibsonia, PA 15044
  (800) 467-6222
  http://www.specialneedstoys.com/usa/

Operating a Toy Lending Library

Cataloging

If you are going to circulate the toys, they will need to be cataloged. Toy circulation works best when toys are processed like other items in the library's collection. Then they are easily accessed by staff and patrons. *Anglo-American Cataloguing Rules: 2002 Revision, 2005 Update* (American Library Association, 2005) covers guidelines for cataloging toys, games, and other realia. MARC records are available on OCLC for many toys. If a record for a particular toy is not available, use a similar toy to create a template and modify it. If the collection is housed out of sight of the patrons, be sure to include pictures in the catalog record.

Processing

Here are some additional processing tips after a toy has been cataloged:

- Mark each piece of the toy with indelible, nontoxic ink, using a unique identifying number.
- Mark each piece with a property stamp of some kind.
- Package toys in bags for storage and circulation. Mesh bags are flexible for use with toys of varying shapes, come in an assortment of sizes, can be seen through, and are durable and washable. Plastic bags, a common alternative, are more difficult to wash, tend to rip, and are an asphyxiation hazard.

Attach a laminated identification tag to the bag. This tag should include the following information: toy title, classification number, identifying number, number of pieces, and recommended age range as assigned by the manufacturer. Including the age range is helpful in identifying the developmental level for which the toy was designed (see Figure 11.1). If the toy has many pieces, and the loss of a few of them will not keep it from being useful, do not include the exact number of pieces on the tag. Instead, substitute a generic description such as "multiple pieces." This will prevent the necessity of producing a new tag each time a piece is lost or destroyed. It will also prevent the frustration of families looking for pieces that no longer exist.

FIGURE 11.1 Sample Tags

Call No.: Toy Collection J793.7 Dome
Title: Dome Alone with Switch
Content: 1 self-contained dome   4 rechargeable C batteries
Library Barcode Here

This item is not renewable.
Do not remove this tag.
Please check contents for missing pieces.
Library Barcode Here

Storage

Where you house the toy collection depends on its use. If it is a circulating collection, a nonpublic area is advisable. Maintaining the collection for circulating purposes is difficult if the toys are left out in the open for public use. Establishing a separate in-house collection is recommended.

The storage space needs to be easily accessible to staff members responsible for retrieving the toys. Retrieving toys takes time. Placing the storage area near the children's room yet out of the young patron's "reach" is ideal, although this can lead to frustration. Of course, if you are using a self-check system, you want it to be accessible to their parents.

One efficient and flexible storage system for a toy collection is a wall-grid system, complete with detachable brackets and hooks of various sizes and shapes. Hooks may be used for small toys, while larger/heavier toys require the extra support of a basket. This type of storage system provides for collection expansion because additional grid pieces and accessories can be purchased at a later date. Where you place such a system depends on whether library staff are checking the items out or you are using a self-check system.

Toys are often arranged on the grid by call number, similar to the shelving of traditional library materials. Another option is to arrange the toys according to type. A portion of the grid system can be designated for each type, with a color assigned to each section. A label of the same color is then part of the laminated tag.

Budget

The initial costs for developing a toy collection include toy purchases, cleaning and storage supplies, publicity materials, a battery charger, and replacement batteries. How and where the toys are housed can also add to the initial budget. Remember, your initial budget is simply a wish list, and like all wishes, you may find that you get less than you ask for. Figure 11.2 provides a budget template that you can adapt for your own use.

Once the toy collection is in place, it becomes less expensive and can be maintained on a smaller budget. Consider establishing an "endowment" for maintenance. The endowment should be large enough to earn enough money to pay for cleaning supplies, batteries, and replacement toys each year and will depend on the size of your collection. It should also cover the expenses of having a digital camera to take pictures of the toys for a binder or the catalog.

FIGURE 11.2   Sample Budget

Storage system   _____

Toys (total)   _____

        Adaptive toys   _____

        Capability switches   _____

        Commercial toys   _____

        Batteries   _____

Processing, storage, cleaning supplies (total)   _____

        Mesh bags   _____

        Ties for bags   _____

        Batteries   _____

        Battery charger   _____

        Laminator   _____

        Laminator sleeves   _____

        Portable dishwasher   _____

        Cleaning supplies:

           Bleach   _____

           Bleach wipes   _____

           Cloths   _____

           Spray bottles   _____

           Dishwasher detergent   _____

           Markers   _____

           Plastic basket   _____

           Laundry bag   _____

           Laundry detergent   _____

           Laundry mat reimbursements   _____

        Digital camera   _____

Publicity (brochures, flyers, posters, etc.)   _____

Staff (total)   _____

    __ % of librarian salary   _____

    __ % of clerical salary   _____

Policies and Procedures

Each toy collection is unique in purpose, scope, organization, policies, and procedures. If possible, visit an established toy lending or play library to observe and learn what works best for them. The USA Toy Library Association (http://www.usatla.org/USA_Toy_Library_Association/Welcome.html) has a public directory of members. There are over 200 libraries listed, including 22 Lekotek programs and at least 13 public libraries or library systems.

Policies

Here are some of the questions to consider when establishing policies:

- Is it a circulating collection or for in-house use?
- Who can borrow the toys (parents only, each child in the family, grandparents, Early Intervention providers, etc.)?
- What is the length of the loan period?
- Can toys be reserved or renewed?
- What is the patron responsibility and liability regarding damaged toys or missing pieces?

The size of the collection will be a determining factor in many of these policies. If patrons are limited in the number of toys they can borrow, remember that certain adaptive toys require the loan of a capability switch in order to be activated.

Because the toy collection is part of the larger public library, many lending policies would exclude out-of-district residents from borrowing their items; however, if the size of the collection permits, consideration may be given to Early Intervention professionals and other educators working with families within the library district. Consideration may also be given to local early childhood centers or agencies that would like to borrow toys for use at their site. By expanding the loan of toys and games to educators and therapists, the library reaches children and families who may not be regular library users. The issue of out-of-district borrowing can be avoided by sharing resources, and therefore toy borrowing privileges, with other library districts.

Procedures

Necessary to any well-maintained toy collection are clearly stated procedures regarding use of and access to the toy collection and circulation, if it is a circulating collection. Maximizing access with minimal inconvenience to staff and patrons should be of primary importance.

ACCESSING THE COLLECTION

If it is a circulating collection, there must be easy ways for patrons to discover what toys are in the collection and whether a certain toy is available for circulation. A catalog entry that is integrated into your general catalog is ideal as long as it includes a picture of the toy. Databases or spreadsheets are other options as long as there is a visual representation of the toy. Finally, a document that can be accessed online or at the desk in either a word processing or PDF format can also work.

CHECKOUT PROCEDURES

What happens after a patron has chosen a particular toy will depend on whether circulation staff check out your material or you have a self-check system. Checkouts should be handled in the same way you handle other checkouts. The difference is that with staff checkout, staff may need to retrieve the item, whereas with self-check the item should be available to the patron. Consider using your circulating DVD or Blu-ray collection as a model.

CHECK-IN PROCEDURE

When toys are returned, again use your standard check-in procedure. Extra steps will, however, be necessary just as they are with DVD and Blu-ray returns:

- Check the toy or game for damage or missing pieces.
- If the toy has batteries, remove them first to prevent corrosion. Replace weak or dead batteries, and put the used ones in the recharger. Batteries stored outside of a toy will have a longer life, and so will the toy.
- Clean hard plastic surfaces with a fresh bleach and water solution or a bleach wipe.
- Check the identification number or bar code on the toy and rewrite the information if necessary. Ensure that the bar code numbers match the tag.
- Make sure that the laminated tag is still firmly attached.
- Examine the bag, and replace it if necessary.
- Reshelve the toy or game.

If there are any problems when the toy is returned, describe them and place the toy aside to be dealt with. Some toy manufacturers will replace parts free of charge or for a nominal fee. An alternative idea is to purchase extra copies of toys to keep for replacement parts.

Marketing and Promotion

"If you build it, they will come!" is not necessarily true in the case of a new circulating toy collection or services to children with disabilities in general. Patrons, community agencies, professionals working with families, and the entire library staff must be made aware of this special collection. Remember, toy collections are not typical. The public rarely thinks of getting toys through the library. To promote the toy lending collection, librarians may adopt specific strategies, including publicity, collaboration, and programming.

Publicity

Publicity needs to begin even before the toys are ready to circulate and continue after the collection is developed. Because the toy collection can be beneficial to a wide variety of people, (grandparents and others appreciate being able to borrow toys when young children come to visit), publicity needs to target the entire community.

PUBLICIZE AS YOU GO

Publicity for the collection starts when you approach your partners and community members for their thoughts on the types of toys and games you should purchase. Put up a toy suggestion box in the library. Have children vote for their favorite toys. Be sure to reach out to children receiving special education services and at your local rehabilitation programs. Once the collection is in place other types of publicity will kick in.

FLYERS AND BROCHURES

In-house flyers and brochures can be helpful in letting people who already use the library know about the collection. Share this material with doctor's offices and medical and rehabilitation centers. Child life specialists in hospitals and Early Intervention and special education providers will all be interested. Ask schools to send flyers and announcements home with their students. Post the flyers in supermarkets, at local businesses, and in family-friendly restaurants.

Develop mailing and e-mailing lists and use them. While many of us are trying to go paperless for economic and environmental reasons, remember your audience. Parents of children with disabilities do not necessarily expect the library to have anything for them or their child beyond a book. Therefore, they will not check your website to see what is going on for their child. A judicious use of printed flyers and brochures can go a long way to promote a program.

POSTERS

Posters are good for promotion both in the library and in the community. Small posters can be put up in shop windows, on the bulletin boards of community centers, in speech therapists' offices, in schools, in the offices of elected officials, through social media, and many other places.

PRESS RELEASES

Press releases, always with accompanying photographs, can be sent to a variety of places:

- Local newspapers
- Local TV news
- Community cable stations
- Community and parenting blogs
- Elected officials' offices
- Newsletters of PTAs, advocacy and support groups, and other organizations

PERSONAL PROMOTION

Library staff know their patrons and can publicize the collection to them. They can also promote it in their own neighborhoods, play groups, and schools. Have a 30-second elevator speech that staff can spout automatically when an opportunity presents itself. Because she could summarize her needs quickly and eloquently, one parent got the services her daughter needed when she ran into the New York City Schools Chancellor while waiting for the elevator. Ask patrons to use their resources to promote the program. Word of mouth is still one of the most effective ways to get the word out.

UNIVERSAL DESIGN AND PUBLICITY

When you are designing your publicity campaign, remember Universal Design. Make printed materials adhere to large-print guidelines. The most critical aspects of this are:

- 14 point or larger type,
- serif-free or sans serif typeface,
- a high degree of contrast between the color of the print and its background, and
- text that is not superimposed on a graphic.

Using these guidelines will allow people with low vision, including grandparents, to read your flyers and will provide a good literacy model for the children with and without disabilities. Have alternate formats such as audio and Braille available. Also, remember that Microsoft Word documents are accessible to screen readers, while some other formats, like PDF, particularly in their older versions, are not.

Distribution and Programming through Collaboration

Use the contacts you developed while assessing the library and designing inclusive services to publicize the toy collection. Any agency that works directly with families and children is a potential publicity outlet. Identifying and working cooperatively with these agencies maximizes the benefits of the toy collection.

Librarians can visit these agencies to demonstrate some of the toys and explain how the collection can be used. Special arrangements can be made to circulate these toys to agency staff members. Make sure they have the link to your online material. Have a printed list available, with pictures, if they want one. Invite parent organizations to the library for an orientation. Have a big launch-day play date and let the press know.

Targeted programs for adults can be developed in collaboration with these agencies to promote awareness and demonstrate appropriate ways of using the toys and games in the collection. Occupational and physical therapists, special education teachers, and other professionals are invaluable facilitators for such programs. Evening programs might be offered to give parents an opportunity to learn how to use the toys or even how to adapt commercially produced toys. Have a simultaneous children's program where they actually use the toys. Parent/child programs in the library also give families the opportunity to become familiar with the toys in the collection. The inclusion of Early Intervention personnel and special educators in such programs provides a personal resource to answer specific questions parents may have.

Toy collections and play sessions often bring families into the library for the very first time. This is particularly the case for parents and children with disabilities and may very well be the key to changing a family's perception of public libraries. In addition to enabling the child or teen with a disability to participate in library services and develop literacy skills, toys provide a wonderful opportunity for librarians to attract new patrons and serve as a bridge to other services and programs available to them. And remember Julie's smile? Play is also fun.

Resources

Biel, Lindsey, and Nancy Peske. 2005. *Raising a Sensory Smart Child: The Definitive Handbook to Helping Your Child with Sensory Integration Issues*. New York: Penguin Books.

Bodrova, Elena, and Deborah Leong. 2003. "Building Language and Literacy through Play." Scholastic Early Childhood Today. http://www.scholastic.com/teachers/article/building-language-literacy-through-play.

Greenspan, Stanley. 2013. "Floortime: What It Really Is, and What It Isn't." Interdisciplinary Council on Developmental and Learning Disorders. Accessed February 13. http://www.icdl.com/dirFloortime/documents/WhatFloortimeisandisnot.pdf.

L'Abate, Luciano. 2009. *Praeger Handbook of Play across the Life Cycle: Fun from Infancy to Old Age*. Santa Barbara, CA: Praeger, ABC-CLIO.

Kranowitz, Carol Stock. 1998. *The Out-of-Sync Child: Recognizing and Coping with Sensory Integration Dysfunction*. New York: Skylight Press.

Powers, Laurie E., George Singer, and Jo-Ann Sowers. 1996. *On the Road to Autonomy: Promoting Self-Competence in Children and Youth with Disabilities*. Baltimore: Paul H. Brookes.

Schwartz, Sue. 2004. *The New Language of Toys: Teaching Communication Skills to Children with Special Needs*. Bethesda, MD: Woodbine House.

Welsch, Mary, and Jean Baily. 2010. *Potential and Possibilities: Model for Providing Children with Disabilities Access to Benefits of Play Experiences*. Chicago: National Lekotek Center. http://www.lekotek.org/general-info/resources/lekotek-white-paper.

Western Australia Association of Toy Libraries. 2010. *A Guide to Starting and Running a Toy Library*. Kalamunda, Australia: Western Australia Association of Toy Libraries. http://www.toylibrary.asn.au/downloads/Manual-setting-up-and-running-a-toy-library.pdf.

References

American Library Association. 2005. *Anglo-American Cataloguing Rules: 2002 Revision, 2005 Update*. Chicago: American Library Association.

Association for Library Service to Children and Public Library Association. 2011. *Every Child Ready to Read @ your library*. 2nd ed. Developed by Susan B. Neuman and Donna Celano. Chicago: American Library Association.

Brown, Stuart. 2009. *Play: How It Shapes the Brain, Opens the Imagination, and Invigorates the Soul*. New York: Avery.

Casey, Theresa. 2005. *Inclusive Play: Practical Strategies for Children from Birth to Eight*. 2nd ed. Washington, DC: Sage.

Elkind, David. 2007. *The Power of Play: How Spontaneous, Imaginative Activities Lead to Happier, Healthier Children*. Jackson, TN: Da Capo Press.

Greenspan, Stanley, and Serena Wieder. 2009. *Engaging Autism: Using the Floortime Approach to Help Children Relate, Communicate, and Think*. Jackson, TN: Da Capo Press.

Hobbs, Tim, Lori Burch, John Sanki, and Cheryl Astolfi. 2001. "Friendship on the Inclusive Electronic Playground." *Teaching Exceptional Children* 33, no. 6: 46–51.

Kordt-Thomas, Chad and Ilene M. Lee. 2006. "Floortime: Rethinking Play in the Classroom." *YC: Journal of the National Association for the Education of Young Children* 61, no. 3: 86–90.

Kranowitz, Carol Stock. 2006. *The Out-of-Sync Child Has Fun: Activities for Kids with Sensory Processing Disorder*. New York: Penguin Group.

Schleien, Stuart J., M. Tipton Ray, and Frederick P. Green. 1997. *Community Recreation and People with Disabilities: Strategies for Inclusion*. 2nd ed. Baltimore: Paul H. Brookes.

Streisand, Betsy. 2006. "Not Just Child's Play." *U.S. News and World Report*, August 14: 48.

United Nations Children's Fund. 1990. "The Convention on the Rights of the Child." UNICEF. http://www.unicef.org/crc/files/Survival _Development.pdf.

Resource Centers for Children, Families, and Other Professionals

> After parents Google things and get overwhelmed, they go to the library.
>
> *—Overheard at the 2010 Learning Disability Association Conference in the Exhibit Hall*

> My daughter has Down syndrome and is meeting her young cousins for the first time. I need something to explain it to them.
>
> *—Reference question at The Child's Place for Children with Special Needs*

Including children with disabilities in libraries means including their families. Stanley Greenspan, the developer of the DIR (Developmental, Individual difference, Relationship-based)/Floortime model for treating autism, puts it this way:

> Rather than talking about a child with special needs, we should talk about families with special needs—whether the cause is ASD or a severe language, motor, or other problem—the entire family has a challenge. (Greenspan and Wieder, 2009: 163)

A family resource center is the library's invitation to exceptional families.

What Is a Family Resource Center?

Family resource centers go hand-in-hand with inclusive library services. They provide important information to all family members:

parents, children, aunts, uncles, grandparents, and even cousins. They help families identify developmental needs in children, cope with these needs, and find community resources available to address them. They facilitate information and resource sharing among community agencies regarding parenting and developmental disability issues, providing a range of parenting services to families, caregivers, and professionals in their communities. These services can include:

- core collections of resources;
- information and referral services;
- group educational programs;
- collaboration with organizations and advocacy groups; and
- outreach.

Services for children and teens are similar, with some unique aspects, including:

- collections with age and developmentally appropriate nonfiction, including sibling issues, and fiction with positive portrayals of people with disabilities;
- information about community-based resources for them;
- role models;
- outreach activities geared to their groups, such as after-school groups and support groups; and
- a place to feel comfortable and be themselves.

The services of family centers within institutions are both defined and enriched by the setting. For example, family centers located in school library media centers have the additional role of supporting teachers and the curriculum and the additional input of the educational professionals who work there. Hospital-based family centers may be part of a child life program or the hospital's library. They necessarily have a medical focus as well as access to the rich informational resources of the hospital. Those centers located in public libraries tend to have a more general focus.

This chapter identifies resources and strategies to assist librarians in building library services that meet the needs of children with disabilities and their families and of those working to support them. It also provides guidelines on developing a parent/professional collection and a collection for children and teens.

Developing the Plan

The development of a family resource center requires time to plan and implement the following strategies:

- identifying existing resources and potential partners;
- preparing a budget and securing ongoing funding;
- identifying staff;
- establishing an advisory committee;
- developing collaborative arrangements;
- preparing space;
- acquiring materials and equipment;
- developing educational programs;
- building information and referral capacity;
- conducting outreach, public education, and awareness efforts; and
- designing initial and ongoing evaluation activities.

Linking the Family Resource Center to the Library's Mission

Family resource centers can advance a library's goals, such as reaching underserved members of the community, responding to the needs of families, or increasing circulation. If the program is seen as helping the library achieve its goals, it is more likely to obtain the internal and external support necessary to initiate and maintain a parent collection and activities and to minimize staff resistance to changes in library routines or reallocation of resources. It is particularly important that those individuals who make decisions regarding the ongoing activities of the program understand how the efforts of the family resource venter can influence the library mission. The boards of trustees, friends groups, library director, and department heads are among those who need to be kept informed of the benefits to the library resulting from the center's activities. Sharing great stories when they happen in person or by e-mail can help keep you on the radar and reinforce your support within the library.

Once the center is under way, it may be necessary to address barriers that emerge and to reexamine library policies and practices prompted by staff experiences. Policy changes might include instituting amnesty policies for outstanding library fines that some families are unable to pay or adjusting the number of days that parenting materials can be borrowed or number of times they can be renewed to accommodate limited transportation access or periods of hospitalizations or recovery. Critical to the long-term success of a center is the administrative commitment of ongoing resources through outside funding or internal operating funds.

Building a Network

Early and ongoing collaboration is essential for establishing family resource centers so that they are responsive to community needs. Networks that library staff build with providers and advocacy and support groups facilitate community awareness and use of library programs. Network members identify and recruit participants who may need parenting information but are not familiar with libraries, assist in resource identification for the parent collection, and sensitize staff to issues such as scheduling, transportation, and child care that may affect program attendance. Additionally, collaboration can result in resource sharing that enables libraries to increase the breadth and quality of the services they offer.

Plugging into existing networks is a good place to start. The National Library of Medicine has a network of member libraries that share resources and training. Membership is free. Find out more at http://nnlm.gov/. The ALLIANCE National Parent Technical Assistance Center is another valuable network. Affiliated centers provide support and advocacy for parents throughout the country. To find the center in your area go to http://www.parentcenternetwork.org/national/aboutus.html. Your regional Parent Training and Information Center (PTI), part of the federally financed network, can also be a good initial partner.

Community input can be gained through focus groups, personal contacts with local service provider organizations and families, or establishing a formal advisory committee. For more information on working with parents and community resource professionals, see Chapter 8.

When meeting with key leaders, ask for help in identifying network members, recommending materials for the collection that would be useful to the parents they serve, and suggesting speakers for parenting programs and workshops. Potential contacts include:

- disability-specific support organizations;
- cooperative extension associations;

- county departments of health and social services;
- Early Intervention providers;
- early childhood direction centers;
- Head Start centers;
- local and regional education agencies;
- school districts;
- special education service providers;
- maternal and child health clinics;
- WIC programs;
- county developmental disabilities councils;
- mental health associations;
- pediatric rehabilitation centers;
- parent/teacher organizations; and
- youth bureaus.

Providing Reference, Information, and Referral Services

The librarian's skill and sensitivity in helping parents to define the nature and extent of the information they want is critical in order to proffer useful information without overwhelming them. Provide access to appropriate information in a respectful, supportive way, clarifying that a librarian is not a health specialist. Never attempt to assist individuals or family members in interpreting medical information. Suggest that they raise specific questions or concerns with their health-care provider, hoping that their dialog can be more productive if the individuals and family members are armed with information about the issues. The kind of information they are looking for, their readiness for increasing levels of information, and their ability to absorb this information will probably change over time. Patrons need to be the guide for the kind and extent of information they require.

Family resource centers provide information and referral services to connect youth with disabilities and their family members to resources and organizations that offer additional assistance on specific issues. Familiarity with community resources and an ability to organize this information and make it readily available can make a tremendous difference in the lives of families. Access to these people resources and services is a critical piece of the family support collection, augmenting the materials and resources and elevating the librarian's role to community information specialist.

Librarians need to have a mechanism for helping families locate local community resources and services. Being familiar with respected consumer health databases such as MedlinePlus and the National Dissemination Center for Children with Disabilities (NICHCY) is important. So is paying attention to local agencies and being able to refer parents to the blogs and websites that evaluate them. Informed access to these community resources is critical for all families and especially for families of children with multiple needs. Google provides lists of entities, but we need to help families evaluate and select individual resources. Chapter 8 provides detailed information on how to provide information and referral in the library setting. Chapter 12 discusses the evaluation of online resources.

Providing reference and information and referral sources has traditionally depended on being asked for them. Sometimes, however, it is necessary to be proactive. Amy Alessio and David G. Fassler's (2005) excellent article "How Can We Help? Counseling Connections for Teens through the Library" identifies situations in which librarians should feel compelled to reach out to struggling teens and suggests resources to offer them. Talk about suicide, extreme changes in behavior, or unexplained bruises may be signs that a young person needs help (Alessio and Fassler, 2005). Have the numbers of mental health and crisis intervention hotlines on hand, in a format such as a business card that can unobtrusively be shared. Know the procedures for reporting suspected child abuse in your community. Being a family resource center means being a resource for the entire family, including the children.

Programming for Parents, Siblings, Caregivers, and Educators

Parents of children with disabilities often feel a tremendous sense of isolation. Full community involvement in programs at the local library, place of worship, or neighborhood center helps families to connect with one another. Programs can range from highly interactive parent and child workshops to seminars on topics of interest that parents attend individually or in a series. The library is in a unique position to offer neutral ground for controversial topics that other agencies might be constrained from presenting. At a workshop on behavior management and youth with developmental disabilities, a custodial grandparent asked how to help her grandson control his masturbation. She was told by the presenter from a local education authority that they were not permitted to answer questions about sex and sexuality. The librarian immediately offered to sponsor a workshop on sexuality and youth with developmental disabilities. This workshop proved so popular that they now offer it annually.

Parents of children with special needs have also noted the importance of parent support groups as forums for developing friendships, establishing mutual sources of respite, and sharing transportation and information. Parent support groups generally fall into three categories: informal gatherings of parents facilitated by members themselves; parent-led advocacy organizations; and formal groups facilitated by professionals, usually social workers, and often affiliated with medical agencies or service providers. The former may develop from parents who meet at library-sponsored workshops and choose to develop a parent support group that continues to meet after the program ends. If possible, it is nice to be able to offer the library as a meeting place. Community bulletin boards, whether physical or virtual, are great ways to help family members connect.

Brothers and sisters of people with disabilities have their own information and support needs that should be addressed by any family resource center. The Sibling Support Project (http://www.siblingsupport.org/) has taken the lead on this nationally; there are also local groups and blogs. Support groups should be facilitated by someone trained to work with children and teens, often adult or young adult siblings. Sibshops (http://www.siblingsupport.org/sibshops) is an effective model for these types of programs. Over 100 people attended a two-day training offered at the Brooklyn Public Library in 2009. It was the first time the workshop had been offered in a library, for free, and translated into Mandarin. The workshop led to the library's continuing involvement in the sibling community.

Promoting Awareness and Use of the Family Resource Center

The community at large needs to be informed of family resource centers' collections and services if they are to be well used. Some strategies include:

- making formal presentations to community groups, including fraternal organizations, town and city council meetings, community board and school board meetings;

- distributing bookmarks, flyers, and brochures;
- having a formal opening or open house and inviting elected officials;
- placing articles and announcements in library newsletters and local newspapers and magazines;
- doing radio and cable interviews;
- making announcements through local cable stations;
- having informal conversations with community members (in the library and other community locations) to promote programs and services;
- sending out mailings and e-mail blasts;
- using prominent touts on your website;
- announcing events on your library's Facebook page and through tweets and other social networking sources;
- announcing at community and school board meetings; and
- asking other organizations to announce library activities at meetings, on their calendars, and on their bulletin boards and websites.

Outreach Strategies

- Presentations to community groups
- Distributing promotional material
- Open house
- Newspaper coverage
- Media interviews
- Public Service Announcements
- Networking with community members
- Mailings and e-mail blasts
- Website touts
- Social media
- Calendar listings

Remember to go outside your comfort zone to agencies and communities you have not traditionally worked with, such as your local hospital's community affairs departments, the county's developmental disabilities council, special education parent groups, and others. When a librarian first started attending her county's Children's Mental Health Committee meetings, she felt out of place. All of the other participants were practicing mental health professions, most with PhDs or MDs. There were clinical presentations at each meeting, including individual cases. While she was learning a lot about mental health services, she was not sure what she was contributing. That changed the day a parent came up to her after the meeting to thank her for the referral to an advocacy agency that the librarian had made for her son. The agency had made two phone calls on his behalf and solved a long-standing problem. The librarian continues to go to the meetings on an irregular basis. The library has hosted events, compiled resources, and cosponsored events. It has been a fruitful area of outreach and collaboration over the years.

Exploring new territory can be challenging. When The Child's Place librarian was first asked to be part of an advisory board to Brooklyn's Community-Based Sickle Cell Outreach Project, she felt uncomfortable. The other members of the board were medical professionals, mostly doctors from three local hospitals. Furthermore, sickle cell disease is not a condition that generally affected her demographic, and she knew very little about it. Nevertheless, she surveyed the literature of sickle cell disease and agreed to join the board. Over the years they developed a fruitful partnership. The librarian helped them with outreach and publicity and supported their early literacy efforts through workshop and Reading Is Fundamental distributions. The other members of the committee helped her decide which books to purchase. She brought new books to their attention. They jointly developed a pathfinder for families of children newly diagnosed with sickle cell or the sickle cell trait. Project staff regularly conducted workshops on sickle cell at many Brooklyn Public Library branches. At the height of the partnership, The Child's Place was serving 60 percent of the children diagnosed with sickle cell or the trait in Brooklyn on an annual basis.

Generating publicity should be a continuous activity to promote visibility and good feelings about the resource center and the library, as well as lead families to the resource center when they need parenting information. Be sure that publicity reflects the library's commitment to serving all families with young children in the community even if some activities are targeted to specific populations.

Reaching Out to New Audiences

When reaching out to populations that are not regular library users, issues to consider include scheduling programs in the evening or on weekends, providing babysitting or programming for siblings, and arranging for transportation.

Libraries can benefit from programs organized by outside community groups. Library meeting space for parenting classes may be sought by outside groups because it is free or low cost, centrally located, and considered neutral. Seminars organized by community-based agencies may help the library meet its goals and provide the added benefit of attracting members of the community who have not been regular library users. Flexibility and a willingness to become familiar with the culture, needs, and interests of these new constituencies are necessary. It takes time to build awareness and trust and to develop the collaborative relationships with other community agencies that can help you reach new audiences. The following are some effective strategies.

Identify and Enlist the Help of Gatekeepers

Gatekeepers are key individuals who can introduce the library's programs to community members, bring people to the library, or cosponsor programs. They may include parents, staff from a community agency whom your target audience trusts, respected members of some local support groups, or community leaders such as members of the clergy, the PTA president, or political leaders. Gatekeepers can become our ambassadors.

Sometimes the gatekeeper is simply the person who knows everyone and to whom everyone turns. For several years The Child's Place for Children with Special Needs had difficulty reaching people in Brooklyn's Cantonese-speaking community. Then the librarian met Jennifer, whose teenage son, Harry, had autism. Harry started volunteering at the library, helping with craft programs. His mother accompanied him. She was constantly on her phone answering questions about the immigration process, where to shop for dried squid, and how to find doctors who spoke Cantonese. Jennifer was clearly a nexus in her community, and she was so impressed with the craft program that she invited her friends. Pretty soon Harry was interpreting programs from English into Cantonese as well as passing out crayons, and the librarian was making presentations on emergent literacy and children with disabilities to groups of parents originally from Guangzhou. That contact led to others, and even though Jennifer has moved on, The Child's Place is still included in her community.

Make Personal Contacts with Potential Participants

Personal contacts are important for attracting new library users. Personal invitations and reminder calls may be needed for new patrons who sign up for workshops and seminars. Parents of children with disabilities are used to experiencing rejection in public places. We have a lot to overcome. However, once people find that they really are welcome, they often bring in others.

Hire Staff Already Connected to the Target Audience

People who are unfamiliar with the library will be more willing to come to programs that involve people they already know. Consider hiring the part-time counselor in a local therapeutic child-care program to serve as a part-time bilingual outreach worker for the library; a Head Start assistant as a part-time library programming assistant;

or respite workers to provide child care at library programs. People with personal connections to people with a disability can be highly skilled too. A sibling or parent of someone with a disability might have some great programming skills or be adept at modifying toys. Or, hire someone with a disability with connections in the community.

Making People Feel Welcome

Conducting programs or displaying collections in ways that are affirming, inclusive, and not stigmatizing and having equipment and resources that accommodate special needs promote the use of collections and services. Anticipating what will make it difficult for people to participate in is important. Child care and transportation are two support services frequently identified as critical to promoting use of parent programs. Offering child care or simultaneous programs for children facilitates parent participation in educational workshops. Providing these services through collaboration with other agencies should be explored.

Funding

Family resource centers will involve cost outlays: how much depends on your plans for the center. A simple streamlined model in which a small collection is purchased for an existing space is less expensive than a full collection in a new or remodeled space with a dedicated staff. Many libraries seek outside funding to begin these programs, recognizing that they will ultimately incorporate the project's operating costs into their annual budgets; however, a committed library can establish and maintain a family resource center without outside funding. Despite some anxiety over funding, all of the 15 libraries participating in the New York State Developmental Disabilities Planning Council family center demonstration project are still offering some materials and services 14 years later. All offer books on a variety of developmental disabilities. At least two have Adaptive Technology centers, several have links to exceptional parenting resources, and at least one has a book club for young adults with developmental disabilities. The Child's Place for Children with Special Needs is one of the original 15 projects.

There are four general sources of funding for establishing a parent resource center: governments, private foundations, local groups and individuals, and the library itself. Of course, it is also possible to combine these funding streams. You may find other sources, often less lucrative but just as important.

Government Sources

Federal, state, and local government agencies may be a source of funding specifically for the family resource center or for the program as a whole. Contacting agencies involved with the target audiences is recommended for learning about current funding opportunities. These include government agencies that oversee education and library services, developmental disabilities services, and youth, health, and social services. Many libraries have joined with other community groups to develop a broad response to community needs for which the library-based family resource center is one aspect of a larger grant-funded project.

Private Foundations

Private foundations are potential supporters of family resource centers. It is important to identify those foundations interested in the youth you wish to serve. Regional and local foundations, in particular, are interested in funding local programs. It may help to look outside the realm of traditional library supporters to foundations that support disability or other related issues. The Child's Place has received funding from Colgate Palmolive and the National Gardening Association. Information about foundations' priorities and procedures can be obtained through the Foundation Center (http://foundationcenter .org/). Its library and other free and relatively low-cost resources are a boon to novice fundraisers.

Once you have identified potential funders, research their funding priorities, guidelines for proposals, and application process. Make sure your project meets their specifications and guidelines. These can be very detailed. It is a waste of your time and theirs to submit a proposal outside their funding area. And it will predispose them to look askance at your next application. Deadlines are also critical. They will get plenty of applications within their time frame and will usually not even look at ones that come to them outside of it.

For first-time grant writers, it may be good to think about recruiting a community volunteer to help. Volunteer organizations such as Retired Seniors Volunteer Program (RSVP) may even have professionals available to help. Consider college and university students. They often have excellent writing skills and some experience with grant writing for school groups. Perhaps a library staff member could take a grantsmanship course. Is your regional library system, cooperative library agency, or state consultant able to help develop a proposal or review a draft of one you have developed? There are many options that can and should be explored.

Local Groups, Individuals, and In-Kind Support

Community groups were important contributors to family resource center programs in all of the Developmental Disability Planning Council (DDPC)–funded sites in the New York State program. In some cases, groups like the Kiwanis and Lions Clubs raised hundreds of dollars for the general support of a center. Others, such as library friends groups, designated their donations for building renovations or for the purchase of specific resource books or materials for workshop participants.

Community agencies, associations, and individuals found various ways to support the programs. Their contributions included parenting videos, materials on specific disabilities, and subscriptions to magazines. Individuals contributed their expertise to the program by leading seminars, speaking on panels, or being resources at workshops, as well as by assisting with collection development.

In-kind support can also be less formal. Local merchants may be open to sharing their products or at least posting your flyers. There is a garden supply stand that is part of a prisoner reentry project at a farmer's market a librarian frequents. Every time she buys plants there and mentions how well they will work with children who are blind (or deaf, or have autism, it doesn't really matter) she finds extra plants in her bag when she opens it.

Ongoing Library Support

While outside funding may support the early phases of a project, maintaining a library-based family resource center depends on the people who make decisions about local library budgets and programs: town supervisors and boards, city councils, library trustees, and the library director. Keeping them informed about the strengths and successes of the program can help maintain their support. Bringing positive publicity to the library is another tool you can use.

It is important to establish internal procedures that ensure that the needs of the family resource center are incorporated into annual planning and resource allocation. This is critical whether you are creating a specific budget line for the family resource center or drawing on funds from existing lines to maintain services. Family resource center duties need to be incorporated into staff job descriptions to ensure that these tasks are continued.

You need to think about ongoing support when applying for funding and establishing your center. Consider establishing an endowment specifically for the program. Even a small one generating $100.00 a year in income can help offset the unusual expenses associated with a parent center and toy library. Once you have secured financing, you can turn your attention to the collection and building that family center.

Guidelines for Developing a Family Resource Center Collection

All parents need access to information, and parents of children with disabilities will benefit from the information found in a general parenting collection. For this reason, information for parents of children with disabilities should be integrated into general, inclusive collections for parents, enabling families with special needs to find these materials easily and, if desired, anonymously. Likewise, materials for children and youth should be integrated into their respective nonfiction sections. Integrated collections enable the individual with the disability and her family members to browse for resources without feeling embarrassed, uncomfortable, or different.

Special collections devoted to parenting concerns and family issues are very effective in promoting awareness of these resources and are particularly well located in a children's room, where parents are regular and frequent visitors. Experience has demonstrated benefits to putting the collection next to or within the children's section so that parents can keep an eye on youngsters while browsing for the information they need. Children's librarians come into direct contact with parents when they use the children's room and the resulting familiarity can lessen the parent's intimidation at seeking assistance. Toys available near the parenting collection keep young children occupied while parents browse.

When planning for a family center, you must consider who will order the books. If your library has a centralized ordering system, you will need to decide who has the subject knowledge to order the specialized collection. Wherever the responsibility lies, it is important to have input from subject experts and the exceptional parenting, special education, and medical and service provider communities.

Target Audience

The first step in building the collection is to determine the target audience. Will the resources be selected to meet the needs of parents only? If not, you also need to decide how much of the collection will be for children and teens with disabilities and their siblings and peers. Will the collection also be useful for professionals? The Child's Place has served family day-care providers who include children with disabilities in their homes and centers, classroom teachers and paraprofessionals, Early Intervention service providers, and preschool special education providers. Health-care workers (e.g., nurses, speech therapists, and physical therapists) who provide services to children in their homes, schools, and the community as well as in residential facilities also use that collection.

Even if it is determined that parents will be the primary focus of the collection, there will be decisions to be made about the level of materials to be included. Many parents, regardless of their general educational level, know very little about the disability their child has and may not have even heard of it before. Making the referral that gets the father the information he needs to feed his newborn daughter with a rare condition is at the core of a parent center's mission. Providing this type of basic information can be transformational for children with disabilities and their families.

On the other hand, some parents have a very sophisticated understanding of their child's disablity. Their questions may require access to reference material written primarily for professionals, at the nursing level and above. Libraries must decide if they are able, or feel it is within their role, to provide access to this level of specialized material. It is a quandary often faced by consumer health librarians.

In any case it must be a diverse collection. Materials need to appeal to a multicultural audience in the languages they speak. Finding sufficient information that coincides with educational and medical practice in North America can be difficult. Meeting the needs of people with low literacy skills is another challenge. MedlinePlus has written materials for new adult readers and videos designed to be accessible to adult emergent readers.

Scope

There are many options to assist in determining the scope of a collection. Will any form of needs assessments, user survey, or focus group be conducted to solicit input on either the subject or the scope of the collection? Will you ask parents or professionals working with families of children with disabilities to recommend or assess materials for the collection? User input is particularly helpful in selecting video material, given the considerable expense involved, and provides the added benefit of group viewings as a networking and community coalition–building activity. Be aware of your licenses and fair use guidelines when showing a CD, DVD, or video in a group setting.

Most of your collection will be concentrated in a few Dewey decimal numbers. Collections for parents of children with disabilities and the professionals who work with them should include information on:

- pregnancy and general child development;
- specific disabilities and health conditions;
- legal rights;
- financial and insurance concerns;
- public benefits and programs;
- advocacy techniques and strategies for educational, medical, legal, and financial challenges;
- hospitalization;
- emotional and social aspects of exceptional parenting;
- sibling issues;
- coping with chronic illness;
- dealing with death;
- discipline and behavior management;
- Assistive and Adaptive Communication;
- play and activities for children;
- Universal Design;
- educational rights and issues;
- inclusion;
- communication between home and school and between parents and professionals;
- speech and language development;

- nutrition and feeding concerns;
- health and safety issues, especially as related to specific disabilities;
- person-centered planning;
- sexuality, reproduction, and gender identity;
- being a parent with a disability;
- child abuse prevention and reporting;
- Adaptive and Assistive Technology;
- transition planning;
- travel training;
- secondary education;
- adult services;
- self-advocacy;
- biographies and memoirs written by parents and siblings; and
- biographies and memoirs written by individuals with disabilities.

Formats

Materials should be available in a wide variety of formats, such as Braille, large print, tactile, and twin vision books; audiobooks configured for a variety of players; e-books; books for dedicated readers such as Nook and Kindle; DVDs; books for beginning adult readers; and captioned and descriptive videos. Parents with print issues need just as much information as parents who are fluid print readers. Many types of disabilities, such as learning disabilities (LDs), attention deficit disorder, and various types of blindness, have a strong hereditary component, reinforcing the argument for multiple formats.

For children with print disabilities, such as LDs, provide information in multiple formats, audiobooks, book/audio sets, large-print books, Braille books, Blu-ray discs, CDs, DVDs, educational software, and computer programs that expand technology. Children and teens with LD may register with the National Library Service for the Blind and Physically Handicapped (NLS), often locally known as the Regional Braille and Talking Book Library. However, this service is not a substitute for public, school, and academic libraries. Furthermore, the NLS does not have an early literacy component. Have a supply of tactile and scratch-and-sniff books, audio children's books, and Braille and large-print books. Work with your Regional Braille and Talking Book Library to develop and share collections. Encourage parents to bring their child to storytimes and to read aloud regularly at home. Especially when the technical process of reading or learning to read is challenging, parents and librarians need to provide many opportunities to nurture a love of stories and literature and the language enrichment provided by them.

Health Literacy

Health literacy is a major concern among medical providers. It refers to the ability to understand medical information, appointment slips, and consent forms and to follow instructions and navigate the medical and insurance systems. While print literacy is an important component of health literacy, so is the ability to process the information received. Context and setting are as important to health literacy as education. Receiving technical, detailed, worst-case scenario information during a rushed medical appointment would be difficult for anyone. Reading a book or viewing a video in one's first language at home or in the library might be all it takes to achieve health literacy. We must take the goals of health literacy into account when planning our family resource centers.

Selection Considerations

Not all material published on a given topic is reliable. It is important to read review sources and to make your own evaluation of a book or other item before purchasing it. Using reliable publishers and authors can also help. See the sidebar for evaluation criteria for health information.

Accuracy is important. To the extent that you can rely on subject experts, including parents, to review and suggest material, do so. Make sure that you have materials that rely on evidence-based medicine. Alternative and experimental therapies also have a place, but their points of view should be clearly stated.

Medical information is generally considered out of date after five years and often sooner. Laws change more often than that. Supplementing print information with web-based sources can help you keep the collection current. And weed regularly. Out-of-date information can be more harmful than no information.

Relevance of a treatment modality is a concern for materials published outside of North America. Mental health treatment, in particular, varies from county to county and culture to culture. Source reliability is critical. Many consumer health materials advocate a specific agenda or treatment modality. It is best if this is done in a

Health Information Evaluation Criteria

- Accuracy
- Timeliness
- Relevance of treatment modalities
- Bias
- Reliability of source

balanced way. At the very least, have materials representing both sides of a controversial issue.

Points of view that reflect those of a sponsoring entity are an issue in medical publications, from books to websites and journal articles to pamphlets. For example, pharmaceutical companies often underwrite publications on topics such as asthma and diabetes, and many not-for-profit organizations accept advertising on their websites. Evaluating websites is discussed in more detail in Chapter 13.

Nonfiction material for children can be particularly problematic. It tends to be updated even less frequently than adult material. It is often written by experienced writers rather than subject experts, and in recasting complex concepts for children, crucial bits of information can get lost. In the late 1980s, a children's services librarian reviewed a book for middle schools on AIDS that stated if you were heterosexually, monogamously married you could not get AIDS. Maternal transmission, medical transmission, transmission through IV drug use, and the possibility of a partner's infidelity, all risk factors that were well known at the time, were completely ignored. There is a fine line between making things understandable to children and oversimplifying. The tone of the book can be important too, especially when its targeted audience is teens. Anything that is condescending will be rejected outright.

When ordering material in languages other than English there are some additional considerations. If it is a translation of an English book, you need to assess the quality of the translation and the timeliness of the work. Translated books are often published a year or two after their English versions. If the book was originally written in another country, the treatment modalities and protocols may be different from what is available here. Social situations may be different enough that the effectiveness of the book is diminished. A Spanish-language book about mental health treatment options in the Philippines may only serve to complicate things for a family in Milwaukee. You must also provide information on treatments options in Milwaukee. Finally, the book must be culturally aware and competent. It is best to have a native speaker look at the world language material before purchasing it.

Review Sources

Standard review sources that are traditionally utilized for general public and school library ordering feature reviews of popular trade books that are of interest to parents, including materials of special interest to parents of children with disabilities. These include *Booklist*, *Library Journal*, and *Publishers Weekly* for adult material and *School Library Journal*, *Kirkus*, and *Cooperative Children's Book Center* for children's and YA material. *Audiofile* reviews audio formats. Look for exceptional parenting books primarily under the "Psychology," "Education," and "Health and Medicine" headings. The newest titles by well-known authors and the largest publishing houses will be reviewed in these standard review sources.

However, much of what is needed for a parent center collection is overlooked by traditional library review sources: you may need to look at nontraditional sources for recommendations. Magazines and newsletters aimed especially at parents of children with disabilities, for example, *Autism Asperger's Digest*, are excellent sources of reviews of new material. Many of these special publications feature review sections, bibliographies, or book lists attached to feature articles. Because these publications appeal to a targeted audience, they are among the best sources of the latest and most highly recommended titles in a specific disability- and health-related subject area. If at all possible, have someone on staff assigned to review specific periodicals on a regular basis, noting new and recommended items for purchase as well as the things to stay away from. A list of newsletters and periodicals specifically directed at parents and professionals around health and disability issues appears later in this chapter.

Reference Materials

For Adults

Many of the specialized resources containing health and medical information sought after by parents and other professionals have traditionally been for in-library reference use only. Although this strategy is useful for libraries, it is not as useful for parents. Parents may be distracted by their child's needs while in the library. Or their time in the library may be limited. Even though it may be financially difficult, it is important to make these materials available for circulation.

The core reference materials listed in the sidebar anticipate many of the reference questions asked by parents of children with disabilities. Because several topics lend themselves to coverage through databases and online sources, a mix of print and electronic resources are necessary. Some materials are printed in limited runs or updated more frequently online. Government publications increasingly fall into the former category and children's medications and guides fall into the latter.

Much of the reference material you need is offered by the publishing sources listed later. However, several publishers carry only one or two essential books. These books include the following:

- *The Mayo Clinic Family Health Book*. 2009. New York: Little, Brown. Available in English and Spanish and revised every six years, although the Spanish edition lags behind.
- *The Merck Manual Home Health Handbook*. 2011. Hoboken, NJ: John Wiley and Sons. Updated every other year and available in Spanish.
- *The PDR Consumer Guide to Prescription Drugs*. 2011. Jackson, TN: Physician's Desk Reference, Inc. Covers pediatric as well as adult medications.
- Turnbull, Rud, Nancy Huerta, and Matthew Stowe. 2008. *The Individuals with Disabilities Education Act as Amended in 2004*. 2nd ed. Upper Saddle River, NJ: Pearson. Updated after each reauthorization of IDEA.
- Wright, Peter W. D. 2007. *Wrightslaw: Special Education Law*. Hartfield, VA: Harbor House Law Press. Updated when laws are changed.

For Children and Teens

When building your reference collections, set aside a portion for the reference needs of children and teens. Although seminal works are harder to come by for these audiences, several publishers, such as Omnigraphics, offer materials that can be included in a children's or teen reference collection. Omnigraphics publishes a series for teens titled *Health Information for Teens*. These are useful overviews of specific conditions such as suicide and eating disorders and are revised every three to five years. Rosen has some useful titles as well as their Teen Health Database at http://www.teenhealthandwellness.com/.

Ordering Sources

For Parenting and Professional Materials

Many organizations and small presses specialize in information on specific health, disability, or related topics of interest to parents and

---

Core Reference Materials

- Medical encyclopedias and dictionaries
- References on childhood disabilities, illnesses, and syndromes
- Guides to school facilities, organizations, and equipment for children with disabilities
- Children's literature guides
- Medical and educational testing guides
- Children's medications guides
- Legal references
- Guides to camps, recreation facilities, and family activities
- Government publications

professionals. It is a good idea to peruse their catalogs and lists periodically. Likewise, some publishers specialize in health and disabilities issues and are worth monitoring. The Special Needs Collection of the publisher Woodbine House is a great source for professionally published material on low-incidence disabilities. The following publishers have a proven track record in the field:

- A.D.D. WareHouse
  300 Northwest 70th Avenue, Suite 102
  Plantation, FL 33317
  (800) 233-9273
  http://www.addwarehouse.com/
  A clearinghouse for material on learning and behavioral disabilities and autism. Books and DVDs are available for adults, teens, and children in English and Spanish.
- American Academy of Pediatrics
  141 Northwest Point Blvd.
  Elk Grove Village, IL 60007
  (847) 434-4000
  http://www.aap.org/
  Many resources on general parenting and health related issues as well as chronic illness and disability concerns.
- American Foundation for the Blind
  11 Penn Plaza, Suite 300
  New York, NY 10001
  (212) 502-7600
  http://www.afb.org/
  Books and other materials relating to blindness.
- American Printing House for the Blind, Inc.
  1839 Frankfort Avenue
  Louisville, KY 40206
  (800) 223-1839
  http://www.aph.org/
  Braille, print/Braille, and large-print books as well as supplies for people who are blind.
- Blind Children's Center
  4120 Marathon Street
  Los Angeles, CA 90029-3584
  (323) 664-2153
  http://www.blindchildrenscenter.org/index.htm

Books and videos on low-incidence conditions relating to blindness and vision.

- The Caption Center, Descriptive Video Services
  Media Access Group at WGBH
  1 Guest Street
  Boston, MA 02135
  (617) 300-3400
  http://www.access.wgbh.org/
  Descriptive videos.
- Charles C Thomas Publisher
  2600 South First Street
  Springfield, IL 62704
  (217) 789-8980
  http://www.ccthomas.com/
  Books on special education topics for education professionals.
- Child Development Media, Inc.
  5632 Van Nuys Blvd., Suite 286
  Van Nuys, CA 91401
  (800) 405-8942
  http://www.childdevelopmentmedia.com/
  Books, CDs, and DVDs on a variety of child development issues for parents and other professionals.
- Corwin
  2455 Teller Road
  Thousand Oaks, CA 91320
  (800) 233-9936
  http://www.corwin.com/
  Inclusion and autism education for education professionals and parents.
- Council for Exceptional Children
  2900 Crystal Drive, Suite 1000
  Arlington, VA 22202-3557
  (888) 232-7733
  http://www.cec.sped.org/
  Professional educators are the primary audience for these special education resources, many of which are accessible to knowledgeable parents. Most are print-only, although several are published as print/CD or print/DVD kits.
- Elsevier
  3251 Riverport Lane

Maryland Heights, MO 63043
(800) 545-2522
http://www.elsevier.com/wps/find/homepage.cws_home
A large publisher of medical and scientific works mostly for professionals, including works on specific conditions at the nursing level.

- Fanlight Productions
  Icarus Films
  32 Court Street
  Brooklyn, NY 11201
  (800) 876-1710
  http://www.fanlight.com/
  Film and video productions on a variety of health issues, including exceptional parenting, health and disability issues, and parenting with a disability.

- Future Horizons
  721 West Abram Street
  Arlington, TX 76103
  (800) 489-0727
  http://fhautism.com/Default.aspx
  Books, CDs, and DVDs on autism and Asperger's syndrome.

- Gale Cengage Learning
  27500 Drake Road
  Farmington Hills, MI 48331
  (800) 877-4253
  http://www.gale.cengage.com/
  Publishes several encyclopedias, one on general medicine, one on genetic disorders, and one on mental health issues, that are revised regularly.

- Gallaudet University Press
  Gallaudet University Book Store
  800 Florida Avenue, NE
  Washington, DC 20002-3695
  (202) 651-5488
  http://gupress.gallaudet.edu/
  Material in many formats on deafness, Deaf culture, American Sign Language, and hard of hearing issues.

- Gryphon House, Inc.
  PO Box 10
  6848 Leon's Way

Lewisville, NC 27023

(800) 638-0928

http://www.gryphonhouse.com/

Resources for early childhood educators and parents about education focusing on inclusion. Some material available in Spanish.

- James Stanfield Co., Inc.

  Drawer: WEB

  PO Box 41058

  Santa Barbara, CA 93140

  (800) 421-6534

  http://www.stanfield.com/

  Videos that concentrate on the skills needed for the transition to adult life, medical advocacy, and social skills and are meant to be shared with youth with developmental disabilities.

- Jessica Kingsley Publishers

  400 Market Street, Suite 400

  Philadelphia, PA 19106

  (866) 416-1078

  http://www.jkp.com/

  Based in Great Britain, Jessica Kingsley books and DVDs cover many types of disabilities but focus on autism.

- New Harbinger Publishing

  674 Shattuck Avenue

  Oakland, CA 94609

  (800) 748-6273

  http://www.newharbinger.com/

  Self-help and professional books, some available as audio, primarily on mental health issues and autism with a cognitive behavioral therapy point of view.

- Nolo

  950 Parker Street

  Berkeley, CA 94710

  (855) 802-8230

  http://www.nolo.com/

  Legal issues are Nolo's purview, and it offers several relevant guides, including how to get SSI, how to write an IEP, and family law. Some digital and software formats.

- Omnigraphics, Inc.

  PO Box 8002

Aston, PA 19014-8002

(800) 234-1340

http://www.omnigraphics.com/cservice.php

Publishes a respected health reference series and a teen health series in print and e-book formats.

- O'Reilly Media, Inc.
  1005 Gravenstein Highway North
  Sebastopol, CA 95472
  (800) 998-9938
  http://oreilly.com/contact.html
  Publishes the Patient-Centered Guides to several rare childhood conditions. Materials available in a variety of formats.

- Paul H. Brookes Publishing
  PO Box 10624
  Baltimore, MD 21285-0624
  (800) 638-3775
  http://www.brookespublishing.com/
  A major publisher of books and videos on developmental and learning disabilities, including the *Dictionary of Developmental Disabilities Terminologies* and Batshaw's *Children with Disabilities*, 6th ed.

- PRO-ED, Inc.
  8700 Shoal Creek Boulevard
  Austin, TX 78757-6897
  (800) 897-3202
  http://www.proedinc.com/Customer/default.aspx
  Materials, including CD-ROM formats, for special education and mental health professionals covering a range of cognitive, emotional, developmental, and behavioral disabilities.

- Prufrock Press
  PO Box 8813
  Waco, TX 76714-8813
  (800) 998-2208
  http://www.prufrock.com/
  Focuses on autism, LD, and ADD in the classroom and covers Assistive Technology.

- Sign Media, Inc.
  4020 Blackburn Lane
  Burtonsville, MD 20866-1167

(800) 475-4756

http://www.signmedia.com/

ASL products in print and DVD formats.

- Teaching Strategies, Inc.

  7101 Wisconsin Avenue, Suite 700

  Bethesda, MD 20814

  (800) 637-3652

  http://www.teachingstrategies.com/

  Focuses on curriculum material kits and child development. Some materials available for parents. Books, CDs, and DVDs.

- Thorndike Press

  10 Water Street, Suite 310

  Waterville, ME 04901

  (800) 233-1244

  http://thorndike.gale.com/

  Thorndike, a part of Cengage Learning, is one of the largest publishers of large-print material, and a significant publisher of children's and YA large print.

- WGBH

  PBS Distribution

  PO Box 609

  Melbourne, FL 32902

  (800) 531-4727

  http://www.shoppbs.org/

  DVDs on learning disabilities, autism, general health, and mental health from PBS TV shows.

- YAI Network

  460 West 34th Street

  New York, NY 10001

  (212) 273-6517

  http://www.yai.org/resources/trainingstore/

  A collection of nonprint materials focusing on daily living and decision-making skills for individuals with developmental disabilities, their parents, and the other professionals who work with them.

For Children's and Teens' Material

Although there are not as many consistent publishers of material for children and teens, the following are worth consulting.

- Enslow Publishers, Inc.
  Box 398
  40 Industrial Road, Dept. F61
  Berkeley Heights, NJ 07922-0398
  (800) 398-2504
  http://www.enslow.com/
  Carries two series for middle and high school students with a few useful titles: Diseases Update and Investigating Diseases.
- Free Spirit Publishing
  217 Fifth Avenue North, Suite 200
  Minneapolis, MN 55401-1299
  (800) 735-7323
  http://www.freespirit.com/
  Books, some with CD-ROMS, on social and emotional issues, bullying, learning disabilities, and autism for children and teens.
- Gareth Stevens Publishing
  111 East 14th Street, Suite 349
  New York, NY 10003
  (800) 542-2595
  http://www.garethstevens.com/
  The Taking Care of Myself series, written at the third to fifth grade levels, and Cutting Edge Medicine, written at a sixth grade level, work well for new teen and adult readers.
- Magination Press
  American Psychological Association
  750 First Street, NE
  Washington, DC 20002-4242
  (800) 374-2721
  http://www.apa.org/pubs/magination/index.aspx
  Books for children and youth on a wide variety of emotions and learning, attention and behavioral disabilities.
- National Braille Press
  88 St. Stephen Street
  Boston, MA 02115
  (888) 965-8965
  http://www.nbp.org/
  Original Braille and twin vision books, some with tactile illustrations, and literacy products.

- Rosen Publishing Group
  29 East 21st Street
  New York, NY 10010
  (800) 237-9932
  http://www.rosenpublishing.com/index.php
  Several series for teens, including graphic novel style
  nonfiction, a hi-lo series, and the Coping with . . . series,
  a long-standing, well-regarded series covering many
  disability-related issues. Supplemented by its Teen Health
  website at http://www.teenhealthandwellness.com/.
- Seedlings
  PO Box 51924
  Livonia, MI 48151-5924
  (800) 777-8552
  http://www.seedlings.org/
  Inexpensive, commercially available books with added
  Braille transcriptions, some with tactile illustrations, and
  some learning materials.
- Sibling Support Project
  Don Meyer, Director
  6512 23rd Avenue, NW, #213
  Seattle, WA 98117
  (206) 297-6368
  http://www.siblingsupport.org/
  A Kindering Center program. Books for adults, teens,
  and children on the issues facing siblings of people with
  disabilities.

Some distributors, such as the following, are worth paying attention to because they preselect material on a given topic and are often
affiliated with a group that works in the disability community:

- CHADD
  8181 Professional Place, Suite 150
  Landover, MD 20785
  (301) 306-7070
  http://www.chadd.org/
  All things ADD for all audiences: adults, teens, children,
  and Spanish speakers.
- Epilepsy Foundation of America
  8301 Professional Place

Landover, MD 20785

(800) 332-1000

http://www.epilepsyfoundation.org/

A good source of material in a variety of formats for adults, teens, and children in English and Spanish.

- Harris Communications, Inc.
15155 Technology Drive
Eden Prairie, MN 55344
(800) 825-6758
http://www.harriscommunications.com/
Distributes assistive products, including books and videos for deaf and hard of hearing people.

Finally, the Louis Database is the seminal source for material available in Braille and large-print formats. It indexes all U.S. Braille and large-print publishers as well as Braille and large-print transcribers, who range from inmates at federal facilities to senior citizens at a kitchen table. It can be found at http://louis.aph.org/catalog/CategoryInfo.aspx?cid=152.

Periodicals

Specialized newsletters and periodicals written specifically for parents of children with specific disabilities and health conditions abound and can be excellent sources of the most up-to-date theories and research, new technologies, treatments, legal and entitlement information, and so forth. They often include parent-to-parent and new publications sections and are important additions to any collection aimed at parents of children with special needs. See the following list for some suggested periodicals. Many are available online and in print editions. Paid, online-only subscriptions are not included as they can be problematic for library access. Free online periodicals are in included in Chapter 13, "Electronic Resources." An asterisk (*) denotes those of particular interest to professionals and those with a more academic, research, or practitioner orientation.

- *ADDitude Magazine*
New Hope Media
39 West 37th Street, 15th Floor
New York, NY 10018

(646) 366-0830

http://www.additudemag.com/

Covering ADD and learning disabilities as they occur with ADD, *ADDitude* is published quarterly. The focus is on children and parenting, but adult issues are also discussed.

- *ADHD Report*
Guildford Press
72 Spring Street
New York, NY 10012
(800) 365-7006
http://www.guilford.com/cgi-bin/cartscript.cgi?page=pr/
jnad.htm&dir=periodicals/per_psych&cart
_id=55512.10100
Edited by Russell A. Barkley, this newsletter is published six times a year and covers the latest developments in ADHD research.

- *Allergies and Asthma Today*
Allergies and Asthma Network/Mothers of Asthmatics
8201 Greensboro Drive, Suite 300
McLean, VA 22102
(800) 878-4403
http://www.aanma.org/
Published by the four times a year, this magazine discusses advocacy and managing asthma in a variety of environments.

- *Arthritis Today*
Arthritis Foundation
PO Box 433082-3082
Palm Coast, FL 32143
(800) 283-7800
http://www.arthritistoday.org/
Published six times a year, *Arthritis Today* comes with an Arthritis Foundation membership and covers juvenile as well as adult arthritis.

- *Autism Asperger's Digest*
Future Horizons, Inc.
PO Box 2257
Burlington, NC 27216
(336) 222-0442
http://www.autismdigest.com/
From work to home to school, bimonthly *Autism Asperger's*

Digest covers a broad swath of issues for people of all ages with autism.

- *Early Childhood Report**
  LRP Publications
  PO Box 24668
  West Palm Beach, FL 33416
  (800) 342-7874
  http://www.shoplrp.com/product/p-300003.html
  The focus of this monthly newsletter is the educational and legal issues of Early Intervention, with an emphasis on behavioral disabilities.

- *Endeavor*
  American Society for Deaf Children
  #2047, 800 Florida Avenue, NE
  Washington, DC 20002-3695
  (800) 942-2732
  http://www.deafchildren.org/
  This quarterly newsletter of the American Society for Deaf Children concentrates on family life with deaf children and addresses education, feelings, and fun.

- *Families of Children with Disabilities Newsletter*
  Support for Families of Children with Disabilities
  1663 Mission Street, 7th Floor
  San Francisco, CA 94103
  (415) 282-7494
  http://www.supportforfamilies.org/index.html
  Published in English, Spanish, and Chinese versions, this quarterly newsletter is a source of information for families whose local focus is outweighed by its multilingual access.

- *LDA Newsbriefs*
  Learning Disabilities Association of America
  4156 Library Road
  Pittsburgh, PA 15234-1349
  (412) 341-1515
  http://www.ldanatl.org/
  This quarterly journal reports on research and multidisciplinary advocacy for people with learning disabilities.

- *Military Parent*
  Costal Carolina Parent

Tidewater Parent

150 West Brambleton Avenue

Norfolk, VA 23510

(757) 222-3905

http://mytidewatermoms.com/content/military-parent
-magazine-our-military-families

This periodic publication is a partnership between
Tidewater Parent and the Camp Lejeune *Globe*, which is
regional in focus but has articles relevant to all military
families.

- *New Mobility*

  United Spinal Association

  75-20 Astoria Blvd.

  East Elmhurst, NY 11370

  (800) 404-2898

  http://www.newmobility.com/

  This monthly magazine addresses the many aspects of using
  a wheelchair, from advocacy to repair and sports to access
  and peer support. While most of its coverage is of adult
  issues, it does occasionally address issues specific to children.

- *Odyssey Magazine*

  Gallaudet University

  800 Florida Avenue, NE

  Washington, DC 20002

  (800) 621-2736

  http://www.gallaudet.edu/clerc_center/information_and
  _resources/products_and_publications/odyssey.html

  The free, quarterly magazine focuses on deaf education and
  showcases best practices and current research.

- *Pediatrics**

  University of Vermont College of Medicine

  Given Building S261

  89 Beaumont Avenue

  Burlington, Vermont 05405-0068

  (802) 656-2505

  http://pediatrics.aappublications.org/

  This peer-reviewed journal of the American Academy of
  Pediatrics is published monthly and translated into Chinese,
  Italian, Polish, Portuguese, and Spanish. A technical journal
  covering research-based medicine for children, it is often
  surprising in its scope and readability; recent articles have

covered best practices in promoting literacy by doctors and addressed bullying.

- *Quest*
  Muscular Dystrophy Association
  3300 East Sunrise Drive
  Tucson, AZ 85718
  (800) 572-1717
  http://quest.mda.org/
  Published quarterly the online version of this periodical is updated more regularly. It is an invaluable source of information, although it is somewhat controversial because of its affiliation with the Telethon.

- *Roundtable*
  National Resource Center for Adoption
  Spaulding for Children
  16250 Northland Drive, Suite 120
  Southfield, MI 48075
  (248) 443-0306
  http://www.nrcadoption.org/newsletter/roundtable/
  Published twice a year, *Roundtable* covers extraordinary adoptions issues such as adopting children with disabilities, sibling groups, support groups for parents, and postadoption counseling. Back issues are available free online.

- *TASH Connections*
  TASH: Equity, Opportunity and Inclusion for People with Disabilities
  1001 Connecticut Avenue, NW, Suite 235
  Washington, DC 20036
  (202) 540-9020
  http://tash.org/
  This newsletter for health-care consumers comes out four times a year. It addresses family issues, best practices, and advocacy for people, including children, with multiple and profound disabilities.

- *Teaching Exceptional Children**
  Council for Exceptional Children
  1110 North Glebe Road, Suite 300
  Arlington, VA 22201
  (703) 264-9427
  http://journals.cec.sped.org/tec/

Published six times a year, TEC covers research-based practices for special educators.

Kits

There are various ways of packaging, presenting, and guiding people to the information in the family support collection in order to increase access, awareness, and utilization of materials. Kits provide an opportunity to assemble a variety of materials on a specific theme or with a specific focus and package them together so they are attractive and easy to use. Particular audiences can be targeted, and the time-consuming task of material selection, often when the patron is in a rush with children in tow, can be avoided. Kits can be developed to welcome new babies, provide pregnant moms with prenatal and early infant care information, help parents occupy sick-at-home children, provide early literacy support for family day-care providers, or assist grandparents with visiting grandchildren. The possibilities are endless.

Libraries can design kits to circulate, packaged in plastic or cardboard containers, plastic, cloth, or mesh bags, or even see-through backpacks. Kits can also be used as giveaways, to be kept by the patrons, packaged in large paper envelopes and printed with colorful logos, illustrations, and decorative boarders for eye-catching appeal. Either type can be developed especially to meet the needs of parents of children with disabilities. Kits should be age appropriate and contain information reflecting current practices. Some examples follow.

Hospital Kit

A circulating hospital kit, targeted to children entering the hospital and their families, might contain:

- a picture book with a hospital theme for a parent to read aloud to younger children, such as *Maisy Goes to the Hospital* by Lucy Cousins (2009), or a simple informational book for an older child to read herself, such as Victoria Parker's (2011) *Going to the Hospital*;
- a video on the hospital experience for children: a CD, DVD, or online video that you have personally reviewed;
- a toy doctor's kit or other toy to encourage play about hospitals;

- a toy or game not related to the hospital to pass the time while there;
- information designed for parents to help them prepare their child to cope with the experiences, such as the KidsHealth for Parents site (http://kidshealth.org/parent/system/surgery/hosp_surgery.html), which is available in print and audio and in English and Spanish; and
- a bibliography of material available in the library for adults, children, and teens.

Special Education Services Resource Kit

A special education services family resource kit can be provided as a giveaway to parents who are concerned that their child might have a disability and need special education services. The kit could include:

- your school system's guide to special education services and the child's rights;
- a Developmental Milestones Checklist that provides information on the stages of development and typical ages for arriving at certain milestones, such as the one in Table 3.2 (pp. 33–35);
- a list of resources for the most common special education classifications and disabilities;
- information on parent support groups, your local parent-to-parent network, advocacy training opportunities, the local family consumer council, your local parent training center, and so forth;
- bibliographies of library materials of interest to parents of children with disabilities;
- a listing of the parenting and children's programs available at the library; and
- library card applications.

The sidebar lists some additional topics that lend themselves well to kits.

Topics for Kits

- Assistive and Adaptive Technology
- Braille literacy
- Brothers and sisters of children with disabilities
- Bullying
- Death
- Early literacy and children with disabilities
- Feelings
- iPads and early literacy
- Specific disabilities and medical conditions
- Universal Design for Gardening

Kits and Partnerships

Developing and distributing kits can be a great opportunity to partner with community agencies. The Child's Place for Children with Special Needs has partnered with a sickle cell treatment program to develop a kit for parents of children newly diagnosed with sickle cell or the sickle cell trait, who are usually identified and located in the first months of life through newborn screening. The kit includes a bibliography of the library's sickle cell resources for adults, children, and teens (developed with the clinic), a library card application, information on early literacy, usually a commercially available brochure, an age-appropriate gift book, and a library promotional item such as a bib that says "Read to me" and has the library's logo on it. These kits are given to families by the clinic at the first visit.

Model Programs

Family resource centers come in many guises. They can be part of public libraries, school libraries, or even hospital libraries. Currey Ingram Academy (Brentwood, TN), a private day school for children who learn differently, has a family resource center in the center of its commons area. The Grace Rea Garrett Children's Library and the Mr. and Mrs. G. Lloyd Bunting Sr. Family Resource Center at Johns Hopkins Children's Center (Baltimore, MD) are located centrally in the children's hospital. The Children's Library provides a calm place for children in the hospital to read and borrow books for use while they are in the hospital. The Family Resource Center is a 3,000-volume library that provides information and support for the parents. It also provides bibliographies on topics such as books about hospitalization for children.

In a unique public library partnership, Camp Lejeune, a training camp for Marines, works with the Onslow County Public Library (Jacksonville, NC). The resulting Military Family Resource Collection addresses the unique needs of military families, including those dealing with disabilities issues. A small section is set aside in one of their libraries, and there is a designated liaison between the public library and the military base. What all these library-based family resource centers and programs have in common is their commitment to serving children with disabilities and their families.

Resources

Arnold, Renea, and Nell Colburn. 2005. "Don't Delay: Help Parents Find Language Development Resources." *School Library Journal* 51, no. 6: 31.

Batshaw, Mark L., Louis Pellegrino, and Nancy J. Roizen. eds. 2007. *Children with Disabilities.* 6th ed. Baltimore: Paul H. Brookes.

Diamant-Cohen, Betsy, ed. 2010. *Children's Services: Partnerships for Success.* Chicago: ALA Editions.

Dunn, Diane Weaver. 2006. "Middle School Helps Parents with Resource Center." Education World. http://www.educationworld.com/a_admin/admin/admin147.shtml.

Durani, Yamani. 2011. "Preparing Your Child for Surgery." KidsHealth from Nemours. http://kidshealth.org/parent/system/surgery/hosp _surgery.html#.

Gallagher, Peggy A., Thomas H. Powell, and Cheryl A. Rhodes. 2006. *Brothers and Sisters: A Special Part of Exceptional Families.* 3rd ed. Baltimore: Paul H. Brookes.

Kepler, Ann. 2011. *The ALA Book of Library Grant Money.* 8th ed. Chicago: ALA Editions.

Sullivan, Michael. 2012. "Never a Dull Moment: Body Piercing? Extreme Sports? Teen Pregnancy? Welcome to the Action-Packed World of Hi/Lo Books." *School Library Journal* 58, no. 2: 31–34.

Winetrip, Michael. 2011. "Lessons in Coping for Children of Deployed." *The New York Times,* December 5: 12, 19.

References

Alessio, Amy, and David G. Fassler. 2005. "How Can We Help? Counseling Connections for Teens through the Library." *VOYA,* October: 284–287.

Cousins, Lucy. 2009. *Maisy Goes to the Hospital.* Somerville, MA: Candlewick Press.

Greenspan, Stanley, and Serena Wieder. 2009. *Engaging Autism: Using the Floortime Approach to Help Children Relate, Communicate, and Think.* Jackson, TN: Da Capo Press.

Parker, Victoria. 2011. *Going to the Hospital.* Chicago: Heinemann Library.

Electronic Resources

I feel like it's all on me. I need to connect to someone.

—*Parent of a child with phenylketonuria, a rare disorder*

The Internet has become a major source of information for librarians as well as for parents. It is a convenient way to find information both for medical professionals and for people without a medical background. Different treatment modalities can be readily compared. Parents of children with disabilities who once felt isolated can connect with other parents like them. Information about rare medical conditions and low-incidence disabilities, once impossible to find, is now easily accessible. Specific points of disability law are no longer the provenance of lawyers and education professionals alone. In short, the Internet has profoundly changed the experience of parents of children with disabilities.

However, there are drawbacks to relying on the Internet. Not everyone has easy access to computers or the Internet. The quality and reliability of information varies widely from one site to the next. The amount of information can be overwhelming, especially when some of it is contradictory. Finding the right fit between the complexity of what is presented and the searcher's ability to understand can be a challenge. Librarians can help patrons get past the worst of these limitations and successfully navigate the Internet.

Navigating the Internet

Knowing how to evaluate a website is a crucial skill when searching for reliable information. For websites with medical information, consider the source, accuracy, and timeliness of the material. To evaluate the source, start with the domain name. It is a .gov, .org, or .com domain? Federal, state, and local governments all use the .gov domain name. If it is a .gov, is the particular governmental source a reliable one? Is the information balanced? Does it reflect the political agenda of the current officeholders? Is it acceptable to the intended user? Many people from a variety of political backgrounds are suspicious of U.S. governmental sources. Verifying such information by using a second source, perhaps even another governmental source such as one from Canada, Great Britain, or Australia can be useful. It is worth keeping in mind that different countries often use different medical protocols.

Domain names ending in .org are not-for-profit organizations and charities. They may present a variety of points of view or present only the view of the organization. For example, The Autism Speaks website (http://www.autismspeaks.org/) strongly reflects the organization's belief that autism can be cured. The Autism Society of America's website (http://www.autism-society.org/) has a very different point of view, focusing on coping with autism and presenting a range of perspectives. Similar rifts exist in other disability communities over cochlear implants, a cure for spinal cord injuries, and blindness. Digging further into the background of the site by looking at the About Us sections and mission statements can be useful. Websites lacking those or equivalent sections should be examined with caution.

Websites ending in .com are commercial enterprises, which have something to sell. This often colors the content on the site. A website ending in .mil belongs to the military and reflects that point of view. Those sites are also important sources of information for military families. Less obvious are the points of views in the .edu, .lib, and .info sites. Many universities do research into one or more aspects of a disability. That research is often supported by an outside agency, or they partner with an outside agency such as a pharmaceutical company. The information on their websites may be friendlier to their research sponsors or anticipate the expected results of the research. Libraries may be directly or indirectly affiliated with those universities or have supported special collections that they feature. Again, a second opinion is always valuable.

Ease of use and comprehension are also important. Very technical, detailed information is not likely to be useful to someone who has not finished high school. Likewise, medical or legal information presented in English may not be easily understood by someone whose first language is not English, even if they have a good grasp of English in general. Each field has its own jargon.

Likewise, it is important to teach website users how to evaluate sites for themselves. The 5 Cs model (Roberts, 2010), developed for nurses in Great Britain, directs users to look at:

- credibility,
- currency,
- content,
- construction, and
- clarity.

Children and teens also need to know how to evaluate websites. One research-based method is WWWDOT. In this system, students are taught to examine:

1. Who wrote this and what credentials do they have?
2. Why was it written?
3. When was it written?
4. Does it help meet my needs?
5. Organization of the site?
6. To-do list for the future? (Zhang, Duke, and Jiménez, 2011: 152)

People with some disabilities such as mental illness have additional issues when using the Internet. Here, research indicates that providing guidance and support are helpful (Kuosmanen et al., 2010). This scaffolding may also be useful for individuals with intellectual disabilities and people in stressful situations. Suggesting accurate resources that are comprehensible to the individuals requesting information is a good way to start. Checking back with the individuals to see if their needs are getting met is the next step. At this point, you may have to reassess their competencies and adjust your recommendations. This is an ongoing process that ends when your patrons are satisfied.

Disability-Related Electronic Resources

There are thousands of disability-related sites on the Internet. The following list of sites is just a sampling of what is available. Librarians are encouraged to explore these sites and follow the links offered.

Developing a comprehensive inventory of Internet sources for information can help meet the needs of their patrons who are looking for information related to disabilities, support, health, educational, and legal issues.

For Adults

- AbleData: The National Database of Assistive Technology Information
  http://www.abledata.com/
  This extensive database lists information on Assistive Technology available both commercially and noncommercially from domestic and international manufacturers and distributors. It is a comprehensive resource for practitioners, researchers, engineers, advocates, and consumers of Rehabilitative and Assistive Technology.
- American Academy of Child and Adolescent Psychiatry
  http://www.aacap.org/
  This site is for both professionals and parents, offering resources for families, medical students and residents, and Academy members and information about primary care, meetings, and online continuing medical education opportunities.
- American Academy of Pediatrics
  http://www.healthychildren.org/
  This website offers basic health and developmental information from the medical model point of view. The Safety and Prevention and Health Issues sections cover specific disabilities and issues such as vaccine safety.
- American Diabetes Association
  http://www.diabetes.org/
  This site covers information, advocacy, recent research and legislation, local resources, and *Diabetes Forecast* magazine. The magazine has recipes.
- American Foundation for the Blind
  http://afb.org/
  Here is a wealth of information on low vision and blindness as they affect people of all ages. It includes an online community just for parents.
- American Society for Deaf Children
  http://www.deafchildren.org/

Parents and other advocates for the full inclusion of children who are deaf or hard of hearing in education and the community are responsible for this website. It offers membership information, resource materials, position papers, *Endeavor* magazine, and much more.

- The Arc
  http://thearc.org/
  The Arc supports people with intellectual and developmental disabilities and their families, educators, and caregivers. The website is rich in information on policy and legislative issues. Some basic information on conditions is available to nonmembers, with sections focusing on people with various relationships to the individual with the disability.

- Beach Center on Disability
  http://www.supportforfamilies.org/index.html
  Research-based support and information for families of people with disabilities can be found here. The resource section is strong and includes information in Spanish and Chinese.

- CAST: Center for Applied Special Technology
  http://www.cast.org/
  The home of Universal Design for learning, this site provides detailed information on new research, curriculum resources, and opportunities for continuing education.

- Children and Adults with Attention Deficit Disorders
  http://www.chadd.org/
  This parent-founded organization's website offers information on attention deficit disorder with and without hyperactivity, *Attention* magazine, membership information, an online community, and other resources.

- Cleft Palate Foundation
  http://www.cleftline.org/
  Connected with the American Cleft Palate–Craniofacial Association, Cleft Palate Foundation provides information for consumers and medical professionals. The focus is on the needs of parents and individuals, including, most critically, a video on feeding the baby with a cleft.

- Council for Exceptional Children
  http://www.cec.sped.org/

This website for educational professionals includes news and information on policy, legislation, professional development, and trends in education. It also has a section for families.

- Education Resource Information Center
http://www.eric.ed.gov/
The world's largest digital library of education literature has many scholarly and research articles on a wide variety of topics, available for free.
- Educator's Reference Desk
http://www.eduref.org/
An educator's portal to ERIC, this site includes a Resource Guide, Lesson Plans, and the AskERIC archives through 2003. It contains a wealth of information for educators.
- Epilepsy Foundation of America
http://www.epilepsyfoundation.org/
This jam-packed site offers information and resources including research, advocacy, living with epilepsy, and e-communities. It has a separate section for parents.
- Family Center of Technology and Disability
http://www.fctd.info/
This is a comprehensive guide to Assistive Technology for beginners and professionals, with a glossary, links, online discussion board, guides for families, and many other resources.
- Family Voices
http://www.familyvoices.org/
This website of a national organization of families and friends of children with special health needs offers statistics, position papers, information, links to other organizations, and listings of regional coordinators and national offices.
- Frank Porter Graham Child Development Center
http://www.fpg.unc.edu/
This website of a nationally recognized research center for the study of children at risk for developmental delays offers information on its projects and publications and has a What's New section.
- The Fred Rogers Company
http://www.fredrogers.org/
The Fred Rogers Company offers free resources to help

parents help children to cope with difficult issues such as disabilities, death, and hospitalization.

- Great Schools
  http://www.greatschools.org/
  The Learning Disabilities section has the subsections Learning Disabilities and ADHD, Autism and Other Disorders, Family Support, Health and Development, Legal Rights and Advocacy, and Assistive Technology. The ability to browse by grade, information on financial issues, and a blog round out the site.

- International Federation for Hydrocephalus and Spina Bifida
  http://www.ifglobal.org/
  The website represents 38 national organizations for people living with hydrocephalus and spina bifida. It offers an information section, newsletter, links to national organizations with information in Spanish, French, Russian, Japanese, and 21 other languages.

- International Rett Syndrome Association
  http://rettsyndrome.org/
  This organization's website provides comprehensive coverage of Rett syndrome and its research, information for families, and news, events, and online communities.

- Learning Disabilities Association
  http://www.ldanatl.org/
  This national organization's website offers several resources for families, including a comprehensive collection of articles organized by audience.

- MedlinePlus
  http://www.nlm.nih.gov/medlineplus/
  MedlinePlus is a comprehensive consumer health website that offers information in a variety of formats, such as print and video, and a variety of reading levels, in both English and Spanish. It is easy to navigate by topic, bodily system, type of information, format of information, or just plain keyword searching.

- Muscular Dystrophy Association
  http://www.mda.org/
  This comprehensive and authoritative website provides basic medical information, research summaries, coping strategies, an online magazine, and a parenting section for

parents of children with MD and parents with MD. The controversial telethon is a part of this site.

- My Child without Limits
http://www.mychildwithoutlimits.org/
United Cerebral Palsy's site is devoted to children birth to age five. It provides an overview of most developmental disabilities, epilepsy, and hearing and vision loss. It includes educational, financial, Assistive Technology, and medical information and a support community for parents and caregivers.

- National Alliance on Mental Illness
http://www.nami.org/
This national advocacy organization provides basic information on various disorders and medications as well as real and virtual peer-to-peer support. It is easy to navigate in both Spanish and English.

- National Assistive Technology Technical Assistance Project (NATTAP)
http://resnaprojects.org/nattap/
This is a portal to the state Assistive Technology centers and lending programs. It also includes information on transition, training, and public awareness and features the full text of IDEA–I and the Assistive Technology Act of 1998.

- National Dissemination Center for Children with Disabilities
http://www.nichcy.org/Pages/Home.aspx
This is the official federal Department of Education's website for special education services. Families, Early Intervention providers, schools and administrators, and state agencies all have their own sections. The site includes fact sheets and publications on specific disabilities, information on grants, a newsletter, and publications.

- National Down Syndrome Society
http://esp.ndss.org/
This informative site has sections for medical information, education, stories, and self-advocacy. It is easily navigated and includes personal stories.

- National Early Childhood Technical Assistance Center (NECTAC)
http://www.nectac.org/default.asp

This website offers an overview of the early childhood special education system as well as a current list of Part C and Part B section 619 state coordinators. Primarily for early childhood education professionals, this site of the National Early Childhood Technical Assistance System is the main support for IDEA Part C programs and Part B section 619.

- National Lekotek Center
  http://www.lekotek.org/
  Devoted to the inclusion of children with special needs through play, Lekotek provides information about appropriate toys and some computer programs. The site has links to Lekotek toy lending libraries, training opportunities, and some information about the importance of play.
- National Organization for Rare Disorders (NORD)
  http://www.rarediseases.org/
  This website includes the Rare Disease Database, a newsletter, and information on some clinical trials and Rare Disease Day US events. Free information is limited unless accessing through a subscribing agency.
- National Rehabilitation Information Center
  http://www.naric.com/
  This library and information center is funded by the National Institute on Disability and Rehabilitation Research. It collects and disseminates the results of federally funded research projects. It has separate sections for the public and for researchers.
- National Spinal Cord Injury Association
  http://www.spinalcord.org/
  Featuring articles, information, links, and support groups for persons living with spinal cord injuries, this website has active online discussion groups on various topics.
- National Tourette Syndrome Association
  http://www.tsa-usa.org/
  This website offers descriptions of organizations, facts about Tourette syndrome, medical, educational, and policy information, support for living with Tourette syndrome, and current research summaries and opportunities. It includes some videos.

- Reading Rockets

  http://www.readingrockets.org/

  Covering all aspects of learning to read, Reading Rockets focuses on the struggling reader and has sections for parents, teachers, principals, and librarians. Basic information on learning disabilities, recommended books, and author interviews can all be found here. Research summaries, resources, blogs, and games round out the site.

- Sibling Support Project

  http://www.siblingsupport.org/

  This one of a kind, dynamic location for all things relating to siblings of all ages is affiliated with Don Meyer and the Kindering Center. It is a one-stop shopping experience for brothers and sisters of individuals with disabilities, whether they are 6, 16, or 60. Here, siblings can find lists of books, locations for Sibshops, current research, and ways to support one another. The site map helps kids, teens, other family members, professionals, and seniors focus on their specific concerns.

- TASH

  http://www.tash.org/

  TASH highlights the needs of people with the most profound and involved disabilities, including multiple disabilities. It advocates full inclusion, has a policy and legislative emphasis. It offers links to resources on seminal topics such as community inclusion, employment, housing, and others.

- Through the Looking Glass (TLG)

  http://www.lookingglass.org/

  Addressing the needs of families in which someone—child, parent, or grandparent—has a disability, TLG is a great resource for medical, educational, legal, and other issues. The focus is on parents with disabilities, and the information, publications, and insights are unique.

- Tots-n-Tech Research Institute

  http://tnt.asu.edu/

  This site provides current information and resources for all audiences on Assistive and Adaptive Technology for young children. It includes links to state technology centers.

- United Cerebral Palsy

  http://www.ucp.org/

UCP.org has a wealth of information on cerebral palsy and other related disabilities. Its One Stop Resource Guide, the innovative My Life without Limits project, an interactive discussion on how to achieve full inclusion, and an extensive Assistive Technology section make this a go-to site.

For Children and Teens

- Cleft Palate Foundation for Teens
  http://www.cleftline.org/teens
  This small but significant site has basic information for teens with craniofacial abnormalities to assist them in understanding and taking on medical management of their issues.

- Epilepsy Foundation of America—Teens Take Charge
  http://www.takechargeteens.org/
  Attached to the Epilepsy Foundation's site, this section focuses on teen subjects such as driving, social issues, and peer profiles in teen-friendly formats such as videos, social networking, and gaming. It is equally useful for teens with epilepsy and their peers who want to learn about epilepsy.

- Kids Get Arthritis Too
  http://www.arthritistoday.org/kgat/
  Three separate sections, one for kids, one for tweens, and one for teens, offer comprehensive and age-appropriate information on juvenile arthritis. Self-care, activities, information, and peer support are all part of these great resources.

- Kids Health Organization
  http://kidshealth.org/kid/ and http://kidshealth.org/teen/index.jsp?tracking=T_Home
  This Nemours Foundation site gives children and teens their due. With separate sections for each, various medical, surgical, health, and disability issues are addressed. There are articles on asthma and allergies, learning and emotional problems, birth defects, and genetic issues, among others. The Teen page covers those issues plus sexuality and sexual health. Information is also available in Spanish for children and teens.

- National Alliance on Mental Illness Child and Teen Action Center
  http://www.nami.org/Template.cfm?Section=Child_and _Teen_Support&template=/Security/Login.cfm
  Providing virtual peer-to-peer support for teens with mental illness, this is a unique and valuable resource.
- National Spinal Cord Injury Association
  http://www.spinalcord.org/
  The site features articles, information, links, and support groups for persons living with spinal cord injuries and has a teen discussion group.
- Planet D
  http://www.diabetes.org/living-with-diabetes/parents -and-kids/planet-d/?utm_source=RightHandRail&utm _medium=SitePromotion4&utm_campaign=PlanetD
  This website for children and teens with diabetes includes basic, age-appropriate information, an online community, profiles of individuals with diabetes, and links to camps. It is affiliated with the American Diabetes Association.
- Proyecto Visión
  http://www.proyectovision.net/index.html
  The World Institute on Disability project connects youth with disabilities to educational and employment opportunities. It includes an extensive range of resources on disability issues, issues specific to the Latino community, employment, and government resources in bilingual format.
- Sibling Support Project
  http://www.siblingsupport.org/
  This is a one of a kind, dynamic location for all things relating to siblings of all ages. It is a place where young brothers and sisters of people with disabilities can find out more, share their concerns, and even play. Central to the site are SibKids and SibTeen, areas where siblings can connect to each other.
- Sickle Cell Kids
  http://www.sicklecellkids.org/
  This playful site provides information for elementary school-age children in a cartoon format.
- TSA for Young People
  http://www.tsa-usa.org/People/kids/kids.html
  Part of the Tourette Syndrome Association, TSA for Young

People offers information, publications, and a newsletter by and for children.

For Spanish Speakers

- American Foundation for the Blind
  http://www.familyconnect.org/parentsitehome.asp?lang=esp
  This site offers a wealth of information on low vision and blindness as they affect people of all ages. The Spanish site is not as extensive as the English but is still an important resource.
- Children and Adults with Attention Deficit Disorders
  http://www.help4adhd.org/index.cfm?varLang=es
  This full-service, parallel Spanish-language site offers information about attention deficit disorder with and without hyperactivity, selections from *Attention* magazine, membership information, responses to individual questions, and other resources.
- ¡Colorin Colorado!
  http://www.colorincolorado.org/
  The Spanish companion site to Reading Rockets, this original resource on bilingual education and reading is for teachers and parents. It includes an education glossary, information on supporting children while they are learning to read, and recommended books and authors. Videos, webcasts, and podcasts make the information more universally accessible.
- Epilepsy Foundation of America
  http://new.epilepsyfoundation.org/epilepsia/
  This exceptional site comprehensively covers adults, children, parenting, and research. It has online communities. Mostly independent of the English-language site, it also address issues specific to the Spanish-speaking community, such as common myths.
- Family Center of Technology and Disability
  http://www.fctd.info/show/index_es
  While not as extensive as its English-language equivalent, this site provides basic information on Assistive Technology in Spanish.
- International Federation for Hydrocephalus and Spina Bifida

http://www.ifglobal.org/es

This umbrella organization represents 38 national organizations for people living with hydrocephalus and spina bifida. It offers an information section, newsletter, links to national organizations, and other related links. It is fully available in six European languages, including Spanish.

- Kids Health Organization
  http://kidshealth.org/parent/centers/spanish_center _esp.html
  This Nemours Foundation site provides extensive information for Spanish-speaking parents, both in translations of the English and in original content. It also gives children and teens their due and has extensive original content in Spanish for them. In separate sections, various medical, surgical, health, and disability issues are addressed. It has articles on asthma and allergies, learning and emotional problems, birth defects, and genetic problems, among others. The Teen page covers those issues, plus sexuality and sexual health.

- MedlinePlus
  http://www.nlm.nih.gov/medlineplus/spanish/medlineplus .html
  This comprehensive, U.S. government consumer health website offers information in a variety of formats—print, video, and basic reading level, in both English and Spanish. It is easy to navigate in Spanish by bodily system, type of information, format of information, or just plain keyword searching. Spanish-language information is, for the most part, a translation of the English.

- National Alliance on Mental Illness
  http://www.nami.org/template.cfm?section=NAMI_en _espa%F1ol
  This national advocacy organization provides basic information on various disorders and medications as well as real and virtual peer-to-peer support. It has extensive links to additional resources and is easy to navigate in both English and Spanish.

- National Dissemination Center for Children with Disabilities
  http://www.nichcy.org/spanish/Pages/default.aspx
  Sponsored by the federal Department of Education, this

Spanish site focuses on special education services and families. It includes fact sheets and publications on specific disabilities.

- National Down Syndrome Society
  http://esp.ndss.org/
  This informative site has sections for medical information, education, personal stories, and self-advocacy. It is easily navigated, and the Spanish blog is a real treasure.
- Proyecto Visión
  http://www.proyectovision.net/index.html
  The World Institute on Disability project connects youth with disabilities to educational and employment opportunities. It includes an extensive range of resources on disability issues, issues specific to the Latino community, employment, and government resources. It is fully bilingual.
- Red de alergia y asma: madres de asmáticos
  http://redalergiayasma.org/
  The Spanish arm of Allergies and Asthma Network/Mother of Asthmatics, this site has independent content and access and is updated regularly. It is a comprehensive overview for Spanish-speaking families dealing with allergies and asthma.

Periodicals, Online and Free

The decline in printed periodicals has been partially offset by an increase in online publications. Many of these are available for free, although some do require registration. Some are affiliated with not-for-profits and some with commercial enterprises. Each bears close examination and should be evaluated using the same standards as for print periodicals. The following list includes some that work well in most libraries.

- *Attention Research Update*
  http://www.helpforadd.com/
  Published by David Rabiner, this e-mail newsletter summarizes and links to current research findings. The financial support of Cogmed is clearly stated in a disclaimer.
- *Countdown Magazine*
  http://countdown.jdrf.org/

Published three times a year, this journal of the Juvenile Diabetes Research Foundation covers coping with type 1 diabetes, current research, and technology.

- *DOTS for Braille Literacy*
  http://www.afb.org/Section.asp?SectionID=6&TopicID=19
  The quarterly newsletter of the American Foundation for the Blind addresses Braille literacy for all ages and levels of readers.

- *Pacesetter*
  http://www.pacer.org/newsletters/pacesetter/
  Published three times a year by the PACER Center, one of the leading parent training centers, *Pacesetter* concentrates on high and low Assistive Technology and bullying issues.

- *Parents with Disabilities Online*
  http://www.disabledparents.net/
  This online newsletter is affiliated with a blog that covers all aspects of being a parent with a disability.

- *Special Ed Advocate*
  http://www.wrightslaw.com/subscribe.htm
  Published monthly by Wrightslaw, the *Special Ed Advocate* covers legal and advocacy issues related to education. Particularly helpful are its many tips.

- *Tots-n-Tech E-Newsletter*
  http://tnt.asu.edu/home/news
  Published four times a year by Tots-n-Tech Research Institute in collaboration with Thomas Jefferson University and Arizona State University, this newsletter explains the basics of Assistive Technology as it is developed for young children.

Internet resources are being developed on a daily basis and provide extraordinary opportunities and resources for people with disabilities and their families that were not available a generation ago. Librarians need to be familiar with individual sites, web searching, and evaluation strategies. We also need to teach searching and evaluation skills to our users, allowing them privacy and independence. Providing computer access in libraries is an important service for families affected by a disability. Offering instruction in consumer health searching, linking to key sites from the library's homepage, and providing access to local and national databases helps parents and children access the electronic information they need. Reciprocal links with local agencies can help position the library as an important and integral part of the disability community.

Resources

American Library Association. 2011. *ALA Guide to Medical and Health Science Reference.* Chicago: ALA Editions.

ipl2 Consortium. 2012. ipl2: Information You Can Trust (homepage). Drexel University. http://www.ipl.org/.

References

Kuosmanen, Lauri, T. Jakobsson, J. Hyttinen, M. Koivunen, and M. Välimäki. 2010. "Usability Evaluation of a Web-Based Patient Information System for Individuals with Severe Mental Health Problems." *Journal of Advanced Nursing* 66, no. 12: 2701–2709.

Roberts, Lorraine. 2010. "Health Information on the Internet: The 5 Cs Website Evaluation Tool." *British Journal of Nursing* 19, no. 5: 322–325.

Zhang, Shenglan, Nell Duke, and Laura M. Jiménez. 2011. "The WWWDOT Approach to Improving Students' Critical Examination of Websites." *Reading Teacher* 65, no. 2: 150–158.

Portals to State Resources

Assistive and Adaptive Technology

- Find your state's federal funded technology assistance project through National Assistive Technology Technical Assistance Partnership (NATTAP) at http://resnaprojects .org/scripts/contacts.pl.

Family Resource Centers

- Parent Technical Assistance Center Network: Find your local, federally mandated parent assistance center by using a map at http://www.parentcenternetwork.org/ parentcenterlisting.html.
- Find your local parent assistance center in an alphabetical list at http://www.familyvillage.wisc.edu/education/pti.html.

While there is no national listing of family resource centers that are bilingual and bicultural, many local programs do provide this service. They can be found by searching the previous resource for areas with large communities of your target language and culture. For example, there are several parent agencies in the Los Angeles area that cater to the needs of Spanish-speaking Mexican Americans.

Other State Agencies

- NICHCY (National Dissemination Center for Children with Disabilities): Discover the myriad of governmental agencies in your state concerned with children with disabilities at http://www2.ed.gov/about/contacts/state/index.html?src=ln. Connect with national disability organizations at http://nichcy.org/org-gateway.

Special Education Services

- IDEA-I Part C: EI Services—The NECTAC (National Early Childhood Technical Assistance Center) provides an A–Z list at http://www.nectac.org/contact/ptccoord.asp. You can also use the search function at http://www.nectac.org/search/confinder.asp.
- IDEA-I Part B: Preschool and School Age Special Education Services—The US Department of Education at http://www2.ed.gov/about/contacts/state/index.html?src=ln.

Glossary

AAC (Augmentative and Alternative Communication): Any device or system that helps someone communicate, such as picture exchange communication systems, text-to-speech synthesizers, sign language, texting, and some apps, among others.

ABA (Applied Behavioral Analysis): One evidence-based therapeutic method of working with children with autism to help them learn appropriate behavior that includes an analysis of the problematic behavior and the environment, using a rewards-based system to help the individual change the behavior, offering alternatives to the behavior, and altering environmental factors that contribute to the behavior at issue.

Accessible Instructional Materials: *See* AIM.

activities of daily living: *See* ADL.

ADL (activities of daily living): The therapeutic category used by rehabilitation specialists that encompasses the things we do every day, such as eating, bathing, dressing, and cleaning up; depending on the context, can also mean aids to daily living, referring to specific items such as weighted forks and ergonomic keyboards.

AIM (Accessible Instructional Materials): Learning materials such as books in an accessible format, including Braille, large print, audio, and digital.

alternate formats: Books produced in formats other than hardcover or softcover with standard print, such as Braille, twin vision, audio, e-book, and large print. *See also* AIM.

app: An application or downloadable program for an iOS device.

Applied Behavioral Analysis: *See* ABA.

Assistive or Adaptive Technology: *See* AT.

AT (Assistive or Adaptive Technology): Technology that helps a person with a disability improve or maintain functional abilities. Examples include scissors that can be squeezed, text-to-voice computer software, ventilators, switch-activated toys, and pens with large, padded grips.

audio induction loop: *See* HEARING LOOP.

Augmentative and Alternative Communication: *See* AAC.

behavior management: A variety of systems or plans that help individuals learn appropriate ways to comport themselves and interact socially with others. *See also* ABA and BEHAVIOR MODIFICATION.

behavior modification: A behavior management system of positively or negatively reinforcing or ignoring desired or undesired behavior to help an individual learn appropriate socialization.

behavioral intervention plan: A course of action developed by the IEP team to prevent or deal with behavioral triggers for children with disabilities such as autism or emotional disabilities that affect behavior.

CC (closed-captioning): The text at the bottom of the scene that transcribes the audio in a program.

CDC (Centers for Disease Control and Prevention): Part of the Department of Health and Human Services, the federal agency charged with promoting public health and safety.

Centers for Disease Control and Prevention: *See* CDC.

closed-captioning: *See* CC.

Committee on Preschool Special Education: *See* CPSE.

Committee on Special Education: *See* CSE.

CPSE (Committee on Preschool Special Education): The agency that evaluates and determines eligibility and educational services for children ages three to five years with disabilities.

CSE (Committee on Special Education): The agency that evaluates and determines eligibility and educational services for children ages five to twenty-one years with disabilities.

DD: *See* DEVELOPMENTAL DISABILITIES.

descriptive videos: Videos in which the silent, on-scene action is described to manifest it for people who are blind.

developmental disabilities (DD): Disabilities that arise before the age of 21 years, continue into adulthood, and affect the intellectual, physical, or emotional development of an individual, for example, autism, intellectual disabilities, spina bifida, and cerebral palsy. No longer the preferred term when referring to individuals with intellectual involvement; replaced by "intellectual disabilities." *See also* INTELLECTUAL DISABILITIES.

diagnosis: The identification made by a medical professional, usually a doctor, of a medical disease or condition. *See also* DISABILITY CLASSIFICATION.

***Diagnostic and Statistical Manual of Mental Disorders*:** *See* DSM.

differentiated instruction: Instruction that is tailored to meet the needs of individual students by altering the content, process, product, or learning environment.

disability classification: A classification assigned by educational professionals to children evaluated for special education services in order to determine eligibility for services. *See also* DIAGNOSIS.

DSM-V (*Diagnostic and Statistical Manual of Mental Disorders*, 5th ed.): Published by the American Psychiatric Association, this manual provides diagnostic criteria for psychiatric disorders and is used by psychiatrists, psychologists, and other mental health professionals. DSM codes are required for most insurance payments.

due process: The right of a parent, guardian, or student to appeal the outcome of an Early Intervention or special education evaluation or placement under IDEA–I.

Early Intervention: *See* EI.

EBM: *See* EVIDENCE-BASED MEDICINE.

EI (Early Intervention): The group of educational services that are provided by states to children from birth to age three who have a disability.

EIS (Early Intervening Services): Services provided to students who are deemed at risk for developing a disability in order to prevent the disability from developing; usually provided before the age of eight.

elevator speech: A speech that lasts the length of time it takes to go between floors of an elevator, usually 30 to 45 seconds.

ELL: *See* ENGLISH-LANGUAGE LEARNER.

English-language learner (ELL): Someone whose first language is not English.

evidence-based medicine (EBM): Medicine that uses treatments based on validated, quantitative research.

exceptional family: A family that has one or more members with a disability.

exceptional parenting: Raising a child with a disability.

executive function: Brain function that mediates and controls the other cognitive processes, particularly those involved in decision making.

Family and Medical Leave Act (FMLA): A federal act that requires large employers to allow caregivers of children with disabilities or other family members up to six weeks of paid or unpaid leave to care for their charges.

Family Resource Center: A place where all members of the family, including children, teens, grandparents, and others, can find information on raising and living with children and youth with disabilities.

FAPE (Free Appropriate Public Education): Refers to the basic right of every child with a disability to an accessible education, most recently restated in IDEA-I. Said education must have no fees beyond those a general education student would be expected to pay, use teaching methods and materials that take the student's disability into account, and adhere to the general education curriculum as closely as possible. *See also* IDEA–I.

far senses: The five senses traditionally taught in schools that we are all familiar with, the ones we grew up with: vision, hearing, taste, smell, and touch.

504 Plan: Required by the Rehabilitation Act of 1973, Section 504, which prohibits schools from discriminating against children with medical conditions and disabilities. A 504 Plan lays out the accommodations necessary for such students to go to school and learn.

FM system: A broadcast system with a transmitter and individual receivers used to amplify sound or for simultaneous interpretation.

FMLA: *See* Family and Medical Leave Act.

Free Appropriate Public Education: *See* FAPE.

gatekeeper: A person who, by dint of his or her centrality, mediates access to information or a community.

general education student: A typically developing student who does not receive special education services.

group home: When used in a pediatric context, congregate foster care facilities for children with disabilities.

hard of hearing: A condition in which a person has difficulty hearing in the standard range.

health literacy: The ability of patients or caregivers to understand the medical information given to them in order to make informed decisions, to follow treatment plans, and to navigate the medical and insurance systems.

hearing loop: A type of induction loop, originally developed to detect submarines, these environmental systems work with receptors in hearing aides to improve reception in public forums such as theaters. Also known as *audio induction loop*.

hi-lo material: Reading materials written to interest teens and adults (high interest) but at an elementary school grade level (low reading level).

IDEA–I (Individuals with Disabilities Education Act—Improved): Passed in 2004, a federal act that gives children with disabilities the right to a free, appropriate education in the Least Restrictive Environment. *See also* FAPE and SPECIAL EDUCATION.

IEP (Individualized Educational Program): A legally binding contract outlining the special education services required for students, aged three to twenty-one years, with a disability classification. *See also* IFSP.

IFSP (Individualized Family Service Plan): The educational plan developed for children receiving Early Intervention services. *See also* IEP.

Individualized Educational Program: *See* IEP.

Individualized Family Service Plan: *See* IFSP.

Individualized Service Plan: *See* ISP.

Individuals with Disabilities Education Act—Improved: *See* IDEA-I.

induction loop: *See* HEARING LOOP.

intellectual disabilities: Disabilities that affect an individual's cognition and ability to learn information. Replaces "developmental disabilities" when referring to individuals with cognitive involvement. *See also* DEVELOPMENTAL DISABILITIES.

iOS device: Any of the touch screen–based Apple products, including the iPhone, iPad, and iPod Touch.

ISP (Individualized Service Plan): A plan of services for adults with developmental disabilities.

LD (learning difference or learning disability): A learning disorder that affects an individual's ability to process information but not his or her ability to understand it. The most common types are dyslexia (reading), dysgraphia or dyspraxia (writing), dyscalculia (math), and nonverbal (body language).

LEA: *See* LOCAL EDUCATION AGENCY.

learning difference: *See* LD.

learning disability: *See* LD.

Least Restrictive Environment: *See* LRE.

LEP: *See* LIMITED ENGLISH PROFICIENCY.

limited English proficiency (LEP): A less than fluent competence with English.

LRE (Least Restrictive Environment): Refers to the right of children with disabilities to be educated with their peers without disabilities to the greatest extent possible.

Local Education Agency (LEA): The governmental body responsible for education in a given geographic area, such as a Board of Education, Department of Education, or Board of Cooperative Educational Services (BOCES).

Medicaid: The federal government insurance program for those who cannot afford insurance. It is administered by the states and is almost automatic for those with a disability who receive Supplemental Security Income.

Medicaid waiver services: Services, particularly for individuals with intellectual disabilities, that are not traditionally medical, such as respite care, after school programs, residential habitation, payments for medication that straight Medicaid would have problems paying for, speech therapy, occupational therapy, physical therapy, and many others.

medical model of disability: The view that disability is a medical problem for the individual that needs to be remediated. Counterposed to social model of disability. *See also* SOCIAL MODEL OF DISABILITY.

Multiple Intelligences: Howard Gardner's theory that intelligence is not just limited to language and math but includes eight intelligences— linguistic, mathematical, spatial, musical, kinesethetic, interpersonal, intrapersonal, and natural— that function as different modalities through which people take in, process, and store information.

National Institute of Mental Health: *See* NIMH.

National Institutes of Health: *See* NIH.

natural environment: An environment outside the therapeutic one where typically developing children spend time; also called "natural setting."

near senses: The senses that relate to our own perception of our bodies, including vestibular, or balance; proprioception, or awareness of one's body in space; introception, or feeling our internal processes such as heartbeat or breathing; and tactile, or experience of the immediate environment (e.g., hot or cold, damp or dry).

neurotypicals: People without autism.

NIH (National Institutes of Health): The section of the Department of Health and Human Services responsible for medical research.

NIMH (National Institute of Mental Health): The section of the National Institutes of Health responsible for research into mental health issues.

O&M (orientation and mobility): Refers to the ability of people to travel independently, especially those who are blind.

occupational therapy (OT): Medical or educational therapy that helps someone develop the skills of daily living or work, such as eating or using a pencil; often associated with fine motor activities. Occupational therapists often provide services for people with sensory integration disorder.

open-captioning: The interpretation of an event into American Sign Language.

orientation and mobility: *See* O&M.

para: *See* PARAPROFESSIONAL.

paraprofessional (para): Someone who works individually with a child with a disability in an educational setting but does not have advanced training.

Parent Resource Center (PRC): A one-stop shopping setting for people seeking information, resources, and referral on parenting issues.

Parent Training and Information Center (PTI): A national network of federally financed Parent Resource Centers.

Part C: The third section of IDEA–I, which covers Early Intervention services.

PCA: *See* PERSONAL CARE ATTENDANT.

PECS (Picture Exchange Communication System): A system of pictures or pictograms, with or without text labels, used by people who are nonverbal to communicate by pointing to the pictures or selecting them on a computer or electronic device. The Mayer-Johnson symbol system is the most common one used in the United States.

personal care attendant (PCA): A trained professional who assists someone with medically necessary day-to-day routines, such as meal planning, preparation, and eating; bathing; using the bathroom; and getting around.

Picture Exchange Communication System: *See* PECS.

PRC: *See* PARENT RESOURCE CENTER.

PTI: *See* PARENT TRAINING AND INFORMATION CENTER.

respite care: Supervision of an individual by a trained and certified person so that the regular caregiver can take time off.

Response to Intervention (RTI): A model used to detect the presence of a specific learning disability that relies on the individual's response to educational methods rather than on the discrepancies between IQ and education achievement, with the hope of minimizing later academic problems through earlier intervention.

RTI: *See* RESPONSE TO INTERVENTION.

SCHIP: *See* STATE CHILDREN'S HEALTH INSURANCE PROGRAM.

SE: *See* SPECIAL EDUCATION.

sensory storytime: A storytime that uses methods from occupational therapy to engage children in learning and self-regulating and that engages all of the near (vestibular, proprioception, introception, tactile) and far (vision, hearing, taste, smell, touch) senses. *See also* FAR SENSES; NEAR SENSES.

service coordinator: The person who arranges and manages the medical, rehabilitational, educational, and vocational services an individual receives; previously known as a *social worker*.

service provider: A trained professional who provides therapeutic interventions (e.g., occupational, physical, or speech therapy), training (e.g., travel training), job coaching, or service coordination to individuals with disabilities.

social model of disability: Views the barriers that people with disabilities face as the result of society's refusal to accept and accommodate differences. *See also* MEDICAL MODEL OF DISABILITY.

social stories: Stories that provide accurate information about a novel or stressful situation to familiarize an individual with it and model appropriate behavior; often used to support people with autism.

special education (SE): Refers to the services allowed for under IDEA–I; often mistakenly used as a destination, as in "He goes to special ed." *See also* SPECIAL EDUCATION SERVICES.

special education services: A group of services and therapies provided to children under IDEA–I to allow them to participate in the educational process, including, but not limited to, speech/language therapy, hearing and vision education services, orientation and mobility services, physical therapy, occupational therapy, travel training, counseling, adaptive physical education, and school health services.

SSI (Supplemental Security Income): An entitlement paid to children and adults with disabilities and limited resources. After the age of 18, only the individual's income and resources are taken into account.

State Children's Health Insurance Program (SCHIP): A federally funded, state-administrated health insurance program for children in poverty who are not eligible for Medicaid.

Supplemental Security Income: *See* SSI.

sticky keys: A keyboard feature that allows a user to engage functions in the Windows and MAC computer operating systems that otherwise would require multiple buttons to be pressed at the same time, by allowing the buttons to be pressed in sequence.

transition services: Those services provided to students aged fourteen and older to help them prepare to leave school and enter the adult world; usually refers to those individuals who will continue to need support after leaving school; can include travel training, job coaching, community experience, and budgeting or other daily living skills, among other things.

twin vision books: Books with parallel print and Braille text, often with textured illustrations.

typically developing child or teen: A child or teen who does not have a disability.

Universal Design: A term borrowed from architecture that refers to design that allows for multiple ways of using products by people of all abilities to the benefit of everyone, for example, curb cuts originally designed for people who use wheelchairs but most commonly used by people with strollers, walkers, and rolling suitcases.

Bibliography

Adaptive Environments Center and Barrier Free Environments. 1995. *The Americans with Disabilities Act Checklist for Readily Achievable Barrier Removal*. U.S. Department of Justice. http://www.ada.gov/racheck.pdf.

Akin, Lynn, and Donna MacKinney. 2004. "Autism, Literacy, and Libraries: The 3 Rs = Routine, Repetition, and Redundancy." *Children and Libraries* 2, no. 2: 35–43.

Alessio, Amy, and David G. Fassler. 2005. "How Can We Help? Counseling Connections for Teens through the Library." *VOYA* 28, no. 4: 284–287.

American Academy of Audiology. 2011. "Get More from Hearing Aids or Cochlear Implants with Hearing Loops." American Academy of Audiology. http://www.audiology.org/resources/consumer/Documents/20110225_FactSheet.pdf.

American Association of School Librarians. 2011. "Position Statement on the School Librarian's Role in Reading." American Library Association. http://www.ala.org/aasl/aaslissues/positionstatements/roleinreading.

———. 2012. "Position Statement on the Role of the School Library Program." American Library Association. http://www.ala.org/aasl/aaslissues/positionstatements/roleslp.

American Library Association. 1996. "Library Bill of Rights." American Library Association. http://www.ala.org/ala/issuesadvocacy/intfreedom/librarybill/index.cfm.

———. 2005. *Anglo-American Cataloguing Rules, Second Edition, 2002 Revision: 2005 Update*. Chicago: American Library Association.

———. 2011. *ALA Guide to Medical and Health Science Reference*. Chicago: ALA Editions.

American Psychological Association. 2004. "School Bullying Is Nothing New, but Psychologists Identify New Ways to Prevent It." American Psychological Association. http://www.apa.org/research/action/bullying.aspx.

American Sign Language University. 2011. American Sign Language curriculum resource center. Lifeprint.com. http://lifeprint.com/.

American Speech-Language-Hearing Association. 2012. "Hearing Assistive Technology." American Speech-Language-Hearing Association. http://www.asha.org/public/hearing/treatment/assist_tech.htm.

Apple, Inc. 2012. "Accessibility." Apple, Inc. http://www.apple.com/accessibility/.

Arnold, Renea, and Nell Colburn. 2005. "Don't Delay: Help Parents Find Language Development Resources." *School Library Journal* 51, no. 6: 31.

Association for Library Service to Children. 2009. *Competencies for Librarians Serving Children in Public Libraries.* Chicago: Association for Library Service to Children. http://www.ala.org/ala/mgrps/divs/alsc/edcareeers/alsccorecomps/corecomps.cfm.

Association for Library Service to Children, Children and Technology Committee. 2009. "Going for Games: What Libraries, and Kids, Can Learn about Gaming." *Children and Libraries* 7, no. 1: 48–50.

Association for Library Service to Children, Managing Children's Services Committee. 2008. "Elevator Speeches: What's So Important about Them?" *Children and Libraries* 6, no. 2: 52.

Association for Library Service to Children and Public Library Association. 2011. *Every Child Ready to Read @ your library.* 2nd ed. Developed by Susan B. Neuman and Donna Celano. Chicago: American Library Association. http://www.everychildreadytoread.org/.

Association of Specialized and Cooperative Library Agencies. 2010. "Library Accessibility: What You Need to Know." American Library Association. http://www.ala.org/ascla/asclaprotools/accessibilitytipsheets/.

Attwood, Tony. 2008. *The Complete Guide to Asperger's Syndrome.* New York: Jessica Kingsley Publishers.

Bailey, D., and R. Simeonsson. 1988. "Assessing the Needs of Families with Handicapped Infants." *Journal of Special Education* 2, no. 1: 117–127.

Bane, Rebecca. 2008. "Let's Pretend: Exploring the Value of Play at the Library." *Children and Libraries* 6, no. 2: 21–23.

Banks, Carrie. 2004. "All Kinds of Flowers Grow Here: The Child's Place for Children with Special Needs at the Brooklyn Public Library." *Children and Libraries* 2, no. 1: 5–10.

Barker, Denise. 2011. "On the Outside Looking In: Public Libraries Serving Young People with Disabilities." *Australasian Public Libraries and Information Services* 24, no. 1: 9–16.

Batshaw, Mark L., Louis Pellegrino, and Nancy J. Roizen. 2007. *Children with Disabilities*. 6th ed. Baltimore: Paul H. Brookes.

Bauman, Margaret. 1999. "Bauman Discusses the Neurobiology of Autism." *Advocate* 35, no 2: 15–17.

Bazelton, Emily. 2013. *Sticks and Stones: Defeating the Culture of Bullying and Rediscovering the Power of Character and Empathy*. New York: Random House.

Biblarz, Dora, Stephen Bosch, and Chris Sugnet. 2001. *Guide to Library User Needs Assessment for Integrated Information Resource Management and Collection Development*. Collection Management and Development Series, no. 11. Lanham, MD: Scarecrow Press.

Biech, Elaine. 2009. *ASTD's Ultimate Train the Trainer: A Complete Guide to Training Success*. Chicago: ALA Editions.

Biel, Lindsey, and Nancy Peske. 2005. *Raising a Sensory Smart Child: The Definitive Handbook to Helping Your Child with Sensory Integration Issues*. New York: Penguin Books.

Bird, Elizabeth. 2011. "Planet Apps." *School Library Journal* 57, no. 1: 26–31.

Blake, Barbara Radke, Robert Sidney Martin, and Yunfei Du. 2011. *Successful Community Outreach: A Step-by-Step Guide to Developing and Implementing a Community Outreach Plan*. New York: Neal-Schuman.

Blue, Elfreda V., and Darra Pace. 2011. "UD and UDL: Paving the Way toward Inclusion and Independence in the School Library." *Knowledge Quest* 39, no. 3: 48–55.

Bodrova, Elena, and Deborah Leong. 2003. "Building Language and Literacy through Play." *Scholastic Early Childhood Today*. http://www.scholastic.com/teachers/article/building-language-literacy-through-play.

Boiesen, Heidi Cortner. 2011. *Outstanding Books for Young People with Disabilities 2011*. Sandvika, Norway: International Board on Books for Young People.

Bondy, Anthony, and Lori Frost. 2011. *A Picture's Worth: PECS and Other Visual Communication Strategies in Autism*. 2nd ed. Bethesda, MD: Woodbine House.

Brady, Lois Jean. 2011. *APPS for Autism: An Essential Guide to over 200 Effective Apps for Improving Communication, Behavior, Social Skills, and More.* Arlington, TX: Future Horizons.

Brown, Amy. 2009. "Don't Stop the Music!" *Children and Libraries* 7, no. 2: 36–41.

Brown, Ann, and Molly Meyers. 2008. "Bringing in the Boys: Using the Theory of Multiple Intelligences to Plan Programs That Appeal to Boys." *Children and Libraries* 6, no. 1: 4–9.

Brown, Peter. 2009. *The Curious Garden.* New York: Little, Brown.

Brown, Stuart. 2009. *Play: How It Shapes the Brain, Opens the Imagination, and Invigorates the Soul.* New York: Avery.

Burchfield, David. 1996. "Teaching ALL Children: Four Developmentally Appropriate Curricular and Instruction Strategies in Primary Grade Classrooms." *Young Children* 52, no. 1: 4–10.

Carp, Jesse. 2011. *Graphic Novels in Your School Library.* Illustrated by Rush Kress. Chicago: ALA Editions.

Casey, Theresa. 2005. *Inclusive Play: Practical Strategies for Children from Birth to Eight.* 2nd ed. Washington, DC: Sage.

CAST: Universal Design for Learning. 2011. "About UDL: What Is Universal Design for Learning?" CAST: Universal Design for Learning. http://www.cast.org/udl/index.html.

Cerny, Rosanne, Penny Markey, and Amanda Williams. 2006. *Outstanding Library Service to Children: Putting the Core Competencies to Work.* Chicago: ALA Editions.

Children's Museum of Houston. 2010. "Para los Niños." Children's Museum of Houston. http://www.cmhouston.org/losninos/.

Cohen, B. P., and L. S. Simkin. 1994. *Library-Based Parent Resource Centers: A Guide to Implementing Programs.* Albany: New York State Developmental Disabilities Planning Council and New York Library Association.

Coleman, Mary J. Sullivan, and Laura Kineger. 2009. *Play and Learn: A Preschool Curriculum for Children of All Abilities.* Roseville, MN: Ablenet.

Copeland, Clayton A. 2011. "School Libraries of the 21st Century: Using Resources and Assistive Technologies to Support Students' Differences and Abilities." *Knowledge Quest* 39, no. 3: 64–69.

Council for Exceptional Children. 2010. "A Primer on the IDEA 2004 Regulations." Council for Exceptional Children. http://www.cec.sped.org/Policy-and-Advocacy/Current-Sped-Gifted-Issues/Copy-of-IDEA/A-Primer-on-the-IDEA-2004-RegulationsIDEA.

Cousins, Lucy. 2009. *Maisy Goes to the Hospital*. Somerville, MA: Candlewick Press.

Craig, Angela, and Chantell L. McDowell. 2013. *Serving At-Risk Teens: Proven Strategies and Programs for Bridging the Gap*. Chicago: Neal-Schuman.

Cummings, Edward O. 2011. "Assistive and Adaptive Technology Resources." *Knowledge Quest* 39, no. 3: 70–73.

D'Amato, Ellen, and Roland K. Yoshida. 1991. "Parental Needs: An Educational Life Cycle Perspective." *Journal of Early Intervention* 15, no. 3: 246–254.

Dewey, Barbara I., and Loretta Parham. 2006. *Achieving Diversity: A How-To-Do-It Manual for Librarians*. New York: Neal-Schuman.

Diamant-Cohen, Betsy. 2010. *Children's Services: Partnerships for Success*. Chicago: ALA Editions.

D'Orazio, Antonette K. 2007. "Small Steps, Big Results." *Children and Libraries* 5, no. 3: 21–23.

Dudden, Rosalind Farnam. 2008. *Using Benchmarking, Needs Assessment, Quality Improvement, Outcome Measurement, and Library Standards: A How-To-Do-It Manual*. New York: Neal-Schuman.

Dunn, Diane Weaver. 2006. "Middle School Helps Parents with Resource Center." Education World. http://www.educationworld.com/a_admin/admin/admin147.shtml.

Durani, Yamani. 2011. "Preparing Your Child for Surgery." KidsHealth from Nemours. http://kidshealth.org/parent/system/surgery/hosp_surgery.html#.

Dykema. 2008. "The Americans with Disabilities Act—New Amendments Take Effect January 1, 2009." Dykema. http://www.dykema.com/labor/news/empissues1208.pdf.

Early Childhood Quality Review Initiative for Public Libraries. 1995. Centereach, NY: Middle County Public Library.

Ehlert, Lois. 1996. *A Sembrar el Sope de Verduras/Growing Vegetable Soup*. Translated by Alma Flor Ada. New York: Houghton Mifflin.

———. 2009. *Growing Vegetable Soup*. Charlotte, NC: Paw Prints.

Elkind, David. 2007. *The Power of Play: How Spontaneous, Imaginative Activities Lead to Happier, Healthier Children*. Jackson, TN: Da Capo Press.

Fadiman, Anne. 1997. *The Spirit Catches You and You Fall Down: A Hmong Child, Her American Doctors, and the Collision of Two Cultures*. New York: Farrar, Straus and Giroux.

Feinberg, Sandra, and Kathleen Deerr. 1995. *Running a Parent/Child Workshop: A How-To-Do-It Manual for Librarians*. New York: Neal-Schuman.

Feinberg, Sandra, and Sari Feldman. 1996. *Serving Children and Families through Partnerships*. New York: Neal-Schuman.

Feinberg, Sandra, and James R. Keller. 2010. "Designing Space for Children and Teens." *American Libraries* 41, no. 4: 34–47. http://americanlibrariesmagazine.org/features/03142010/designing-space-children-and-teens.

Fish, Tom, Paula Rabidoux, and Jillian Ober. 2009. *The Next Chapter Book Club: A Model Community Literacy Program for People with Intellectual Disabilities*. Bethesda, MD: Woodbine House.

Florian, Douglas. 1994. *Vegetable Garden*. New York: Harcourt Children's Books.

Foos, Donald D., and Nancy C. Pack. 1992. *How Libraries Must Comply with the Americans with Disabilities Act (ADA)*. Phoenix, AZ: Orynx Press.

Francis, Alison. 2009. "Thursdays with MacGyver: The Benefits of a Library Therapy Dog." *Children and Libraries* 7, no. 2: 50–52.

Franklin, Renee E. 2011. "Before the Bell Rings: The Importance of Preparing Pre-service School Librarians to Serve Students with Special Needs." *Knowledge Quest* 39, no. 3: 58–63.

Gallagher, Peggy A., Thomas H. Powell, and Cheryl A. Rhodes. 2006. *Brothers and Sisters: A Special Part of Exceptional Families*. 3rd ed. Baltimore: Paul H. Brookes.

Gannotti, Mary E., W. Penn Handwerker, Nora Ellen Groce, and Cynthia Cruz. 2001. "Sociocultural Influences on Disability Status in Puerto Rican Children." *Physical Therapy* 81, no. 9: 1512–1523.

Gardner, Howard. 2004. *Frames of Mind: The Theory of Multiple Intelligences*. New York: Basic Books.

———. 2006. *Multiple Intelligences: New Horizons*. New York: Basic Books.

Ghoting, Saroj Nadkarni, and Pamela Martinez-Díaz. 2006. *Early Literacy Storytimes @ your library: Partnering with Caregivers for Success*. Chicago: American Library Association.

Glozier, Kyle. 1997. "What Every Kid Should Have: A Birthday Every Day." *Mouth Magazine*, November/December: 16.

Gray, Carol. 2010. *The New Social Story Book, Revised and Expanded 10th Anniversary Edition: Over 150 Social Stories That Teach Everyday Social Skills to Children with Autism or Asperger's Syndrome, and Their Peers*. Arlington, TX: Future Horizon.

Gray, Carol, and Abbie Leigh White. 2002. *My Social Stories Book*. Illustrated by Sean McAndrew. Philadelphia: Jessica Kingsley.

Greenspan, Stanley. 2013. "Floortime: What It Really Is and What It Isn't." Interdisciplinary Council on Developmental and Learning Disorders. Accessed February 13. http://www.icdl.com/dirFloortime/documents/WhatFloortimeisandisnot.pdf.

Greenspan, Stanley, and Serena Wieder. 2009. *Engaging Autism: Using the Floortime Approach to Help Children Relate, Communicate, and Think.* Jackson, TN: Da Capo Press.

Greenspan, Stanley I., Serena Wieder, with Robin Simons. 1998. *The Child with Special Needs: Encouraging Intellectual and Emotional Growth.* Jackson, TN: Da Capo Press.

Grover, Sharon, and Lizette D. Hannegan. 2011. *Listening to Learn: Audiobooks Supporting Literacy.* Chicago: ALA Editions.

Hobbs, Tim, Lori Burch, John Sanki, and Cheryl Astolfi. 2001. "Friendship on the Inclusive Electronic Playground." *Teaching Exceptional Children* 33, no. 6: 46–51.

Holmes, Paula. 2007. "A Parent's View: How Libraries Can Open the Door to the 20 Percent." *Children and Libraries* 5, no. 3: 24.

Holt, Cynthia, and Wanda Hole. 2003. "Training Rewards and Challenges of Serving Library Users with Disabilities." *Public Libraries* 42, no. 1: 34–37.

Holt, Leslie Edmonds, and Glen E. Holt. 2010. *Public Library Service for the Poor: Doing All We Can.* Chicago: ALA Editions.

Horning, Kathleen T. 2010. "Can Children's Books Save the World? Advocates for Diversity in Children's Books and Libraries: 2010 May Hill Arbuthnot Honor Lecture." *Children and Libraries* 8, no. 3: 8–17.

Hyttinen, Jari, Tiina Jakobsson, Marita Koivunen, Lauri Kuosmanen, and Maritta Valimaki. 2010. "Usability Evaluation of a Web-Based Patient Information System for Individuals with Severe Mental Health Problems." *Journal of Advanced Nursing* 66, no. 12: 2701–2709.

Institute of Education Sciences. 2011. "Children and Youth with Disabilities." National Center for Education Statistics. http://nces.ed.gov/programs/coe/indicator_cwd.asp.

ipl2 Consortium. 2012. ipl2: Information You Can Trust (homepage). Drexel University. http://www.ipl.org/.

Jendron, Janet. 2012. "AT and Learning Disabilities." South Carolina Assistive Technology Program. Last updated October 9. http://www.sc.edu/scatp/ld.htm.

Kars, Marge, Lynda M. Baker, and Feleta L. Wilson, eds. 2008. *The Medical Library Association Guide to Health Literacy.* New York: Neal-Schuman.

Kepler, Ann. 2011. *The ALA Book of Library Grant Money.* 8th ed. Chicago: ALA Editions.

Keswick, Kitty. 2011. "'D' Is for Dragon . . ." *Knowledge Quest* 39, no. 3: 74–75.

Kind, Viki. 2010. *The Caregiver's Path to Compassionate Decision Making: Making Choices for Those Who Can't.* Austin, TX: Greenleaf Book Group.

Kluth, Paula, and Kelly Chandler-Olcott. 2008. *A Land We Can Share: Teaching Literacy to Students with Autism.* Baltimore: Paul H. Brooks.

Kordt-Thomas, Chad, and Ilene M. Lee. 2006. "Floortime: Rethinking Play in the Classroom." *YC: Journal of the National Association for the Education of Young Children* 61, no. 3: 86–90.

Kranowitz, Carol Stock. 1998. *The Out-of-Sync Child: Recognizing and Coping with Sensory Integration Dysfunction.* New York: Skylight Press.

———. 2003. *The Out-of-Sync Child Has Fun: Activities for Kids with Sensory Processing Disorder.* New York: The Penguin Group.

Krueger, Karla S., and Greg P. Stefanich. 2011. "The School Librarian as an Agent of Scientific Inquiry for Students with Disabilities." *Knowledge Quest* 39, no. 3: 40–47.

Kumin, Libby. 1998. "Literacy and Language." *Down Syndrome News* 21, no. 10: 132–133.

L'Abate, Luciano. 2009. *Praeger Handbook of Play across the Life Cycle: Fun from Infancy to Old Age.* Santa Barbara, CA: Praeger ABC-CLIO.

Langa, Michelle. 1996. *Notes from 1994 Parent Interviews.* Centereach, NY: Middle County Public Library.

The Libraries of Fanwood and Scotch Plains. 2008. *Libraries and Autism: We're Connected.* EngelEntertainment. DVD. 19 min, 40 sec. http://www.thejointlibrary.org/autism/video.htm.

Lushington, Nolan. 2008. *Libraries Designed for Kids.* New York: Neal-Schuman.

Macaulay, David. 2008. "Thirteen Studios: 2008 May Hill Arbuthnot Honor Lecture." *Children and Libraries* 6, no. 3: 9–15.

MacKellar, Pamela, and Stephanie Gerding. 2010. *Winning Grants: A How-To-Do-It Manual for Librarians with Multimedia Tutorials and Grant Development Tools.* New York: Neal-Schuman.

Mates, Barbara T., and William R. Reed. 2011. *Assistive Technology in the Library.* Chicago: ALA Editions.

Mayer, Brian, and Christopher Harris. 2011. *Libraries Got Game: Aligned Learning through Modern Board Games.* Chicago: ALA Editions.

McGrath, Ben. 2004. "Chew On." *New Yorker*, February 2. http://www
.newyorker.com/archive/2004/02/09/040209ta_talk_mcgrath.

Meyer, Don, and Patricia Vadasy. 2008. *Sibshops: Workshop for Siblings
of Children with Special Needs*. Revised edition. Baltimore: Paul H.
Brookes.

Meyers, Elaine, and Harriet Henderson. 2011. "Overview of Every Child
Ready to Read @ your library®, 1st Edition." American Library
Association. http://www.everychildreadytoread.org/project-history%09/
overview-every-child-ready-read-your-library%C2%AE-1st-edition.

Microsoft. 2012. "Microsoft Accessibility: Technology for Everyone."
Microsoft. http://www.microsoft.com/enable/default.aspx.

———. 2012. "Types of Assistive Technology Products." Microsoft. http://
www.microsoft.com/enable/at/types.aspx.

Mulligan, Elaine. 2011. "The Facts on Charter Schools and Students
with Disabilities." National Dissemination Center for Children with
Disabilities. http://nichcy.org/publications/charters.

Myers, David G. 2004. *Psychology*. 7th ed. Hopeland, MI: Worth
Publishers.

Nalewicki, Jennifer. 2011. "Bold Strokes: New Font Helps Dyslexics Read."
Scientific American 42, no. 6. http://www.scientificamerican.com/
article.cfm?id=new-font-helps-dyslexics-read.

National Library Service for the Blind and Physically Handicapped.
2011. *That All May Read*. National Library Service for the Blind and
Physically Handicapped, Library of Congress. http://www.loc.gov/
nls/.

Oberg, Charles. 2003. "The Impact of Childhood Poverty on Health and
Development." *Healthy Generations* 4, no. 1: 2–3. http://www.epi
.umn.edu/mch/resources/hg/hg_childpoverty.pdf.

O'Cummings, Edward O. 2011. "Assistive and Adaptive Technology
Resources." *Knowledge Quest* 39, no. 3: 70–73.

Osborn, Robin, ed. 2004. *From Outreach to Equity: Innovative Models of
Library Policy and Practice*. Chicago: ALA Editions.

PACER Center. 2009. "Least Restrictive Environment (LRE): A
Simplified Guide to Key Legal Requirements." PACER Center
Action Information Sheets. http://www.pacer.org/parent/php/
php-c7.pdf.

———. 2011. *There's an APP for That: iPOD/iPAD 101*. Minneapolis,
MN: PACER Center. http://www.pacer.org/webinars/stc/iPod_iPad
_Resources_Handout050511.pdf.

PACER Center and National Center of Accessible Instructional Materials
at CAST. 2011. *Accessible Instructional Materials (AIM): A Technical*

Guide for Families and Advocates. Minneapolis, MN: PACER Center. http://www.pacer.org/stc/pubs/STC-22.pdf.

PACER Center and Tots-n-Tech. 2011. *EZ AT 2: Simple Assistive Technology Ideas for Children Ages Birth to 3.* Minneapolis, MN: PACER Center. http://www.pacer.org/stc/pubs/EZ-AT-book-2011 -final.pdf.

Parker, Victoria. 2011. *Going to the Hospital.* Chicago: Heinemann Library.

Parrott, Kiera. 2011. "Steal This Storytime: Spectrum Edition." *Library Voice* (blog), February 28. http://libraryvoice.org/2011/02/28/steal -this-storytime-spectrum-storytime-edition/.

Payne, Ruby K., Philip DeVol, and Terie Dreussi Smith. 2005. *Bridges Out of Poverty: Strategies for Professionals and Communities.* Revised ed. Highlands, TX: aha! Process Books.

Perkins School for the Blind. 2011. "The Best Computer Games for Blind Kids." Perkins School for the Blind. http://www.wonderbaby.org/ articles/best-accessible-computer-games-blind-kids.

Porter, Ann, and Sisira Edirippulige. 2007. "Parents of Deaf Children Seeking Hearing Loss-Related Information on the Internet: The Australian Experience." *Journal of Deaf Studies and Deaf Education* 12, no. 2: 518–529.

Powers, Laurie E., George H. S. Singer, and Jo-Ann Sowers. 1996. *On the Road to Autonomy: Promoting Self-Competence in Children and Youth with Disabilities.* Baltimore: Paul H. Brookes.

Prendergast, Tess. 2011. "Beyond Storytime: Children's Librarians Collaborating in Communities." *Children and Libraries* 9, no. 1: 20–26, 40.

Pugliese, Madalaine, and Current Students from the Simmons College Assistive Technology Graduate Program. 2011. "APPsolute Fit: Selecting the Right Mobile Device Apps." *Closing the Gap,* October/ November. http://www.closingthegap.com/media/solutions/ articles/2011/10/1872/1872.pdf.

Roberts, Lorraine. 2010. "Health Information on the Internet: The 5 Cs Website Evaluation Tool." *British Journal of Nursing* 19, no. 5: 322– 325.

Rogovin, Anne. 1990. *Let Me Do It!* Revised ed. Nashville: Abingdon Press.

Rubin, Rhea Joyce. 2001. *Planning for Library Services to People with Disabilities.* ASCLA Changing Horizon Series No. 5. Chicago: Association of Specialized and Cooperative Library Agencies.

Rupp, Rebecca. 2009. "What's the Big Idea? Science and Math at the Library for Preschoolers and Kindergarteners." *Children and Libraries* 7, no. 3: 27–31.

Scheeren, William O. 2010. *Technology for the School Librarian: Theory and Practice*. Santa Barbara, CA: Libraries Unlimited.

Schiller, Pam, and Pat Phipps. 2006. *Starting with Stories: Engaging Multiple Intelligences through Children's Books*. Illustrated by Kathy Ferrell and Debi Johnson. Beltsville, MD: Gryphon House.

Schleien, Stuart J., M. Tipton Ray, and Frederick P. Green. 1997. *Community Recreation and People with Disabilities: Strategies for Inclusion*. 2nd ed. Baltimore: Paul H. Brookes.

Schuchs-Gopaul, Elizabeth L. 2011. "Twelve Things Every JAG Should Know: Legal Issues Facing Military Families with Special Needs Children: A Primer and Introduction." *The Reporter* 38, no. 1: 20–26. http://www.wrightslaw.com/blog/?p=5891.

Schwartz, Sue. 2004. *The New Language of Toys: Teaching Communication Skills to Children with Special Needs*. Bethesda, MD: Woodbine House.

Seeger, Pete. 1967. *Abiyoyo and Other Story Songs for Kids*. CD. Rereleased 1992. Smithsonian Folkways Recordings.

Skokie Public Library. 2011. "Come On In! . . . The Library Is a Friendly Place for Children with Special Needs." Skokie (IL) Public Library. http://www.skokie.lib.il.us/s_kids/kd_COI/index.asp.

Smallwood, Carol, ed. 2010. *Librarians as Community Partners: An Outreach Handbook*. Chicago: ALA Editions.

Snow, Kathie. 2000. *Disability Is Natural: Creating New Lives for Children and Their Families!* Woodland Park, CO: Braveheart Press.

———. 2005. *Disability Is Natural: Revolutionary Common Sense for Raising Successful Children with Disabilities*. 2nd ed. Woodland Park, CO: Braveheart Press.

Socol, Ira David. 2010. "The Unhappy Place: What Libraries Can Do to Welcome Kids Who Struggle with Print." *School Library Journal* 56, no. 5. http://www.schoollibraryjournal.com/article/CA6727276.html.

Solomon, Andrew. 2012. *Far from the Tree: Parents, Children, and the Search for Identity*. New York: Schribner.

Sousa, David A. 2007. *How the Special Needs Brain Learns*. 2nd ed. Thousand Oaks, CA: Corwin.

Stanberry, Kristin, and Marshall Raskind. 2012. "Assistive Technology Tools: Reading." Great Schools. http://www.greatschools.org/special -education/assistive-technology/948-reading-tools.gs?page=1.

Stone, Douglas, Bruce Patton, and Sheila Heen. 2010. *Difficult Conversations: How to Discuss What Matters Most*. New York: Penguin Books.

Streisand, Betsy. 2006. "Not Just Child's Play." *U.S. News and World Report,* August 14: 48.

Sullivan, Michael. 2012. "Never a Dull Moment: Body Piercing? Extreme Sports? Teen Pregnancy? Welcome to the Action-Packed World of Hi/Lo Books." *School Library Journal* 58, no. 2: 31–34.

Tech-Ease. 2011. "4All." Tech-Ease: For All Your Classroom Technology Needs. http://etc.usf.edu/techease/4all/.

Tots-n-Tech. 2010. "Using Assistive Technology to Support Socialization." *Tots-n-Tech E-Newsletter*, June. http://tnt.asu.edu/files/June2010.pdf.

Trivette, Carol M., Carl J. Dunst, and Angela G. Deal. 1996. "Resource-Based Early Intervention Practices." In *The Contexts of Early Intervention: Systems and Settings*, edited by S. K. Thurman, J. R. Cornwell, and S. R. Gottwald. Baltimore: Paul H. Brookes.

United Nations Children's Fund. 1990. "The Convention on the Rights of the Child." UNICEF. http://www.unicef.org/crc/files/Survival _Development.pdf.

U.S. Equal Employment Opportunity Commission. 2008. "ADA Amendments Act of 2008: PL 110-325 (S 3406)." U.S. Equal Employment Opportunity Commission. http://www.eeoc.gov/laws/ statutes/adaaa.cfm.

Vandenbard, R. Todd. 2010. "Tending a Wild Garden: Library Web Design for Persons with Disabilities." *Information, Technology and Libraries* 29, no. 1: 23–29.

Visher, Christy A., and Jeremy Travis. 2003. "Transitions from Prison to Community: Understanding Individual Pathways." *Annual Review of Sociology* 29: 83–113. http://www.caction.org/rrt_new/professionals/ articles/VISHER-PRISON%20TO%20COMMUNITY.pdf.

Walling, Linda Lucas, and Marilyn H. Karrenbrock. 1993. *Disabilities, Children, and Libraries: Mainstreaming Services in Public Libraries and School Library Media Centers*. Englewood, CO: Libraries Unlimited.

Welsch, Mary, and Jean Baily. 2010. *Potential and Possibilities: Model for Providing Children with Disabilities Access to Benefits of Play Experiences*. Chicago: National Lekotek Center. http://www.lekotek .org/general-info/resources/lekotek-white-paper.

Wemett, Lisa. 2007. "The Building Bridges Project: Library Services to Youth with Disabilities." *Children and Libraries* 5, no. 3: 15–20.

Western Australia Association of Toy Libraries. 2010. *A Guide to Starting and Running a Toy Library*. Kalamunda, Austrailia: Western

Australia Association of Toy Libraries. http://www.toylibrary.asn.au/ downloads/Manual-setting-up-and-running-a-toy-library.pdf.

Whelan, Debra Lau. 2009. "The Equal Opportunity Disorder: Autism Is on the Rise, and It Can Affect Any Family. Here's What You Need to Know." *School Library Journal* 55, no. 8. http://www .schoollibraryjournal.com/article/CA6673570.html.

Williams, R. Bruce. 2002. *Multiple Intelligences for Differentiated Learning.* Thousand Oaks, CA: Corwin Press.

Winetrip, Michael. 2011. "Lessons in Coping for Children of Deployed." *The New York Times*, December 5: 12, 19.

Winson, Georgia, and Courtney Adams. 2010. "Collaboration at Its Best: Library and Autism Programs Combine to Serve Special Audience." *Children and Libraries* 8, no. 2: 15–17.

Wojahn, Rebecca Hogue. 2006. "Everyone's Invited: Ways to Make Your Library More Welcoming to Children with Special Needs." *School Library Journal* 52, no. 2: 46–48.

Wong, Peggy, and Allen McGinley. 2010. "Rated E for Everyone: Expanding Services to Children with Special Needs." *School Library Journal* 56, no. 12: 22–23.

Wood, Chip. 2007. *Yardsticks: Children in the Classroom Ages 4–14.* 3rd ed. Turners Falls, MA: Northeast Foundation for Children.

Working Together Project. 2008. *Community-Led Libraries Toolkit.* Vancouver: Libraries in Communities. http://www .librariesincommunities.ca/resources/Community-Led _Libraries_Toolkit.pdf.

World Institute on Disability. 2006. "Latinos with Disabilities in the United States: Understanding and Addressing Barriers to Employment." Proyecto Visión. http://www.proyectovision.net/ documents/pvreport.pdf.

Wright, Pamela, and Pete Wright. 2007. "The Child Find Mandate: What Does It Mean to You?" Wrightslaw. Last revised September 26. http:// www.wrightslaw.com/info/child.find.mandate.htm.

Wrightslaw. 2011. "Military and Department of Defense (DOD) Special Education." Wrightslaw. http://www.wrightslaw.com/info/dod.index .htm.

Zhang, Shenglan, Nell Duke, and Laura M. Jiménez. 2011. "The WWWDOT Approach to Improving Students' Critical Examination of Websites." *Reading Teacher* 65, no. 2: 150–158.

About the Authors

Carrie Banks has been the director of Brooklyn Public Library's (BPL) The Child's Place for Children with Special Needs since 1997. She serves on BPL's Children's Steering Committee and on the Universal Access Community of Interest, which is part of the American Library Association's (ALA) Association for Specialized and Cooperative Library Agencies. She has been the Association for Library Service to Children representative to the Association of Specialized and Cooperative Library Agencies (ASCLA) and has chaired committees including the Service to Special Population Children and Their Caregivers committee of ALA's Children's Services Division and the Schneider Family Book Award committee. She has also served on the Odyssey Award for Excellence in Audio Production committee. She helped draft national guidelines for serving people with disabilities in public libraries. Ms. Banks is a member of the Advisory Board of the National Gardening Association and the Programming Committee for Music for Autism. Ms. Banks's articles have appeared in *Children and Libraries*, a journal of ALA, and she is the author of a chapter about The Child's Place for the book *From Outreach to Equity* (ALA Editions, 2004). She has conducted inclusion training for institutions including BPL, the Brooklyn Museum of Art, the Brooklyn Botanic Garden, the New York Aquarium, and America Reads and is a frequent presenter at ALA conferences, most recently in 2011. Before BPL, Ms. Banks worked at New York Public Library. Her extensive background in services for children with special needs has included working with children who have dyslexia, a history of abuse, pediatric psychiatric diagnoses, and craniofacial differences. In 2000, she received New York University's Samuel and May Rudin Award for Community Services for her work with the disability community. In 2010, she received the Sloan Public Service Award, and, in 2012, she was named a *Library Journal* Mover and Shaker. Ms. Banks received her MLS from Queens College in 1990 and her BS in developmental psychology from Oberlin College in 1982. She is proficient in French and American Sign Language, and she is currently studying Spanish.

Barbara Jordan served as assistant director for Grants and Special Projects and head of Parenting and Clearinghouse Services at Middle Country Public Library (Centereach, NY) during her long tenure at the library. She developed a comprehensive multimedia resource center for parents and professionals and coordinated the Community Resource Database of Long Island, an online directory of health and human services for the Long Island region. Jordan administered the Partners for Inclusion Project at Middle Country, a project aimed at improving opportunities for the inclusion of children with disabilities in community settings. Jordan is co-author of *Audiovisual Resources for Family Programming* (New York: Neal-Schuman, 1994); *A Family Child Care Provider's Guide to New York's Early Intervention Program* (Albany, NY: New York State Department of Health, 1996); *Partners for Inclusion: Welcoming Infants and Toddlers with Disabilities and Their Families into Community Activities: A Replication Guide* (Hauppauge, NY: Suffolk County Department of Health, 1997); and *The Family-Centered Library Handbook* (Feinberg et al., New York: Neal-Schuman, 2007). Jordan has a degree in sociology from Adelphi University and an MLS from Queens College. Now retired, she has two grown sons and lives in Coram, New York, with her husband.

Sandra Feinberg has devoted the past 40 years to public library service and, since 1991, has served as the director of the Middle Country Public Library, the largest and busiest public library on Long Island (NY). An advocate for improving the quality of life for families, she firmly believes in the ability of public libraries to be family- and community-centered institutions. Under her leadership, what began as a local library program for babies, toddlers, and parents has become a national model and change agent for libraries wanting to serve families in a dynamic and collaborative community environment. In 1979, Feinberg created the Parent/Child Workshop, a unique program that welcomes parents and children as young as one year into the library and integrates community resource professionals within the delivery of library services. This program has gone on to be replicated nationally as part of Family Place Libraries.™ In addition to Family Place, Sandy spearheaded the development of the Community Resource Database (CRD) of Long Island (now 2-1-1-Long Island), which includes over 10,000 health and human services on Long Island; the Suffolk Coalition for Parents and Children, a network of more than 17,000 family service professionals, and the Children's Librarians Association of Suffolk County. From 1999 to 2004, she led Middle

Country Public Library through the 40,000-square-foot expansion of two facilities, which included the development of special spaces for young children and teens. Feinberg has received numerous awards—among them, the 2007 Public Library Association Charlie Robinson Award for library directors who are recognized as innovators and risk takers. Under her leadership, Middle Country received the Alfred P. Sloan Award (2005) and the first annual Godfrey Award for Services to Children and Families in Public Libraries (2002). Feinberg graduated with a bachelor of arts degree from Western Michigan University, received a master's degree in library science from the University of Michigan, and earned a degree in professional studies from the State University of New York, Stony Brook. She is the author of numerous articles and six books, is an adjunct professor at the Palmer School of Library and Information Science, Long Island University, and currently serves as chair of the Early Years Institute.

Kathleen Deerr has been working with children and families in public libraries for the past three decades. For the past 10 years she has served as the national Family Places Libraries™ coordinator. During that time, the number of libraries in the Family Places network has tripled. Recognizing early on that children's most important role models are parents and caregivers, Deerr has developed many innovative, interdisciplinary programs that focus on parent-child interactions and has administered programs such as the Partners for Inclusion Project, Reach Out and Read, the Parent Child Home Program, and the national Family Places Libraries™ initiative. She has served as guest lecturer at the Palmer School of Library and Information Science and is the co-author of three Neal-Schuman books: *Running a Parent/Child Workshop, Including Families of Children with Special Needs*, and *The Family-Centered Library Handbook*. A lifelong advocate for children, Deerr has presented workshops and lectures at the state and national levels on the role of the public library in serving, supporting, and designing welcoming, early-learning spaces for young children and families, as well as lectures on the administration and management of Children's and Parents' Services in public libraries. She strongly believes that libraries are a binding thread in the fabric of their communities and play a crucial role in the development of healthy children and families.

Michelle A. Langa, MPA, CSA, is an educator with more than 25 years' experience in the field of special education. In the past, Langa held several administrative positions as the director of different agencies serving children with specials need, the director of special education for a large school district, and the director of a multisite preschool and child care center. As a consultant, Langa has developed three training curricula (one with Feinberg and Jordan) for New York State's Early Intervention program, one of which was developed in collaboration with *Mister Rogers' Neighborhood*. She has also published a number of online articles for LRPNET and Parenthoodweb.com as well as articles for clinical journals. She lives in Durham, New Hampshire.

Index